Spanish Around the House

The Quick Guide to Communicating with Your Spanish-Speaking Employees

José M. Díaz and María F. Nadel

McGraw·Hill

New York   Chicago   ~~San~~   ~~~~   ~~~~ drid   Mexico City
Milan   New Delhi   ~~San Juan~~   ~~Seoul~~   ~~Singapore~~   ~~Sydney~~   Toronto

Library of Congress Cataloging-in-Publication Data

Díaz, José M.
    Spanish around the house : the quick guide to communicating with your Spanish-speaking employees / José Díaz, María Nadel.
       p.   cm.
    ISBN 0-07-144437-8
    1. Spanish language—Conversation and phrase book (for domestics)   I. Nadel, María F.   II. Title.

PC4120.S45 D53   2005
468.3'42—dc22   2004061625

2 3 4 5 6 7 8 9 0   FGR/FGR   0 9 8 7 6

ISBN 0-07-144437-8

Interior design by Jeanette Wojtyla

McGraw-Hill books are available at special quantity discounts to use as premiums and sales promotions, or for use in corporate training programs. For more information, please write to the Director of Special Sales, Professional Publishing, McGraw-Hill, Two Penn Plaza, New York, NY 10121-2298. Or contact your local bookstore.

This book is printed on acid-free paper.

Spanish Around the House

Contents

4 In the Kitchen
En la cocina **45**

Introduction

Spanish Around the House is a comprehensive, easy-to-follow book that offers the essential tools for communicating with Spanish-speaking personnel and/or employees. The authors have selected some occupations in which you will most likely encounter Spanish speakers and have created a book that will help you communicate with these workers and deal with different aspects of their employment. Any attempt you make to communicate in Spanish will help you to establish a good working relationship with these workers by demonstrating respect and appreciation of their culture. At the same time, it will be a satisfactory experience for you to use this book as a point of departure to increase your knowledge of the Spanish language. As your ability to understand the workers improves, you can also use your knowledge to help them improve their knowledge of English.

The Spanish used in this book is standard Spanish that can be understood by any native speaker of the language. It would be impossible to cover all the regionalisms found in the Spanish-speaking countries, but once you become familiar with the vocabulary that appears in this book, you will be able to add to the basics and learn new expressions from the Spanish speakers you encounter. The phonetic pronunciation for the Spanish terms are included.

The book is divided into fourteen chapters. Each chapter includes lists of useful vocabulary that are grouped thematically when possible.

How to Use This Book

You can use this book with very little (or no) preparation. There is nothing in particular you need to know in order to use any given chapter. You can choose a topic that interests you, or you can begin with Chapter 1 and go on from there. And, of course, you can do one or the other depending on your needs at any given time.

As we were trying to come up with some guidelines for using this book, we realized that how you use it depends on the reason you are using it and what is going on at any given moment in the life of your family or business. This will greatly affect where you begin and what chapters you concentrate on. If, for example, you have household help, you might start with Chapters 3 and 4. If your children have a Spanish-speaking caretaker, you might begin with Chapter 12. Are there Spanish-speaking employees at your place of business or in the places where you participate in social activities? In that case, you might turn your attention to Chapters 1 and 13.

Vocabulary

Building a large store of words is important for spoken language. This book is full of everyday words, phrases, and expressions and provides an opportunity to learn words and sentences without worrying about grammar. Each chapter includes lists of useful vocabulary related to the theme of the chapter. We have attempted to use the most generic word, but it would be virtually impossible to cover all the regionalisms found in Spanish-speaking countries. Generally, we have chosen a word that is commonly used in America. As you read through a section, it is not necessary to learn all the words presented, but obviously the more vocabulary you commit to memory, the more confident and fluent your Spanish will be. Some things that will help you are:

1. You may want to create your own personalized vocabulary by writing down the words you find most useful and practicing them out loud regularly. If you decide to create personalized lists, it is a good idea to keep separate lists for nouns, adjectives, and verbs. These lists could be further separated into:

Nouns: feminine/masculine
Verbs: ending in -*ar*, -*er*, or -*ir*

Doing this will not only help you to remember the words, it will help you to use them.

2. You should make it a point to practice and expand what you are learning with the Spanish speakers you encounter. They will also be a valuable source of regionalisms from their country of origin.

3. The English-Spanish/Spanish-English dictionary in Appendix C of this book focuses on the Spanish used at home or in home-related activities. Use it for quick reference to answer the questions: "How do you say that in Spanish?" or "How do you say that in English?" (*¿Cómo se dice en español?* [**koh**-moh seh **dee**-seh ehn ehs-pah-**nyohl**] *¿Cómo se dice en inglés?* [**koh**-moh seh **dee**-seh ehn een-**glehs**]). Note that the thematic vocabulary lists in individual chapters of this book are more detailed and specific than the dictionary vocabulary presented in Appendix C.

Grammar

This is not a grammar book, but throughout the book comments about Spanish grammar and notes refer you to the grammar presentations in Appendix B, "Grammar Essentials." Studying these sections will allow you to deepen your knowledge of a given grammar point.

It is not necessary to become confident with all the topics discussed in Appendix B before turning back to the main text. It is up to you to decide how thoroughly you want to cover a given topic.

If, however, you are interested in learning more about Spanish grammar, you can use Appendix B for a more thorough study. Going through this appendix in detail will allow you to learn the basics without turning to another textbook.

When using the grammar section, make sure to read the examples carefully. Not only do they illustrate the grammar point, they also show you the differences between English and Spanish, which very often do not allow word-for-word translation of sentences.

Pronunciation

In addition to knowing the sounds of the letters in Spanish, you need some knowledge of stress and intonation in order to acquire authentic pronunciation. These aspects are covered in Appendix A, "The Sounds of Spanish." This appendix is geared to beginners and will help you move toward authentic pronunciation.

To further ease communication, we have included the phonetic pronunciation of every Spanish word and phrase used in the book. The stressed syllable appears in bold-face type.

Don't forget that your best source for pronunciation is the Spanish speaker with whom you are communicating. Don't hesitate to ask him or her to pronounce any word or phrase you need. Spanish speakers are always willing to help those who try to communicate with them in Spanish. Listen and imitate the sounds they make.

It also helps to listen to Spanish being spoken every chance you get. Spanish-speaking television newscasters are excellent models, and since you may already be familiar with the topic, you may understand some of the language. You may want to record sections of a program (sports, weather, soap operas, etc.), and listen to them repeatedly.

You can also record your speech and then listen to yourself as a way to check your pronunciation.

Practice

In conclusion, the only way to learn a language is to use it. Take every opportunity you are given to practice, practice, and practice some more. If you wait until you can say something perfectly, you will never speak Spanish. Take chances! You will not only learn to communicate in Spanish, you will also establish new relationships, cement old ones, and learn more about the world around us, here in the United States and Canada and to the south.

Spanish Around the House

Job Application and Interview
Solicitud de empleo y entrevista

(soh-lee-see-**tood** deh ehm-**pleh**-oh ee ehn-treh-**bees**-tah)

Interviewing Prospective Employees
Para entrevistar a un futuro empleado

(**pah**-rah ehn-treh-bees-**tahr** ah oon foo-**too**-roh ehm-pleh-**ah**-doh)

The best way to get to know a prospective employee may be through a job application. The application form that begins on page 3 can be used as a point of departure to establish a conversation and to find out if the applicant truly meets your expectations for an employee. It also makes a good record of information that you may need to access in the future. The information requested on the form appears in both Spanish and English. Although while designing this form the authors tried to be as comprehensive as possible, there are always special situations that may require further questions. The design and organization of this book will help you to find easily those words and expressions you may need to get to know your prospective employee further.

Please note that some of the questions that follow ask information about the applicant that may be sensitive. It is up to you to find the right moment to ask them. Although it may be sensitive in nature, this information may still be important for you to know.

Keep in mind that the laws of the United States do not allow you to ask certain specific questions such as marital status, age, etc., of the applicant. You'll need to become familiar with those laws. Useful sources are available at your local public library.

On the application form that begins on page 3, the word *apellidos* (last names) appears in the plural. That is because in Spanish-speaking countries most people use two last names: their father's last name first and then their mother's maiden name. Married women usually retain their maiden name and then add *de* followed by their husband's last name (i.e., *de García*, etc.). This is, of course, changing with the times. But you may still meet many women who follow the traditional custom.

Interview Questions
Preguntas para la entrevista
(preh-**goon**-tahs **pah**-rah lah ehn-treh-**bees**-tah)

The questions below appear in the same order as the information requested on the application form; that way you can ask them out loud as you go through the application. Some of the questions may repeat those on the form, but you can use them as a point of departure to start a conversation going or if you are not able to, or decide not to, use an application form. Don't forget to take notes.

Personal Information
Información personal
(een-fohr-mah-**syohn** pehr-soh-**nahl)**

What is your name?
¿Cómo se llama usted?[1]
(**koh**-moh seh **yah**-mah oos-**tehd**)

What are your last names?
¿Cuáles son sus apellidos?
(**kwah**-lehs sohn soos ah-peh-**yee**-dohs)

---

1. Notice that in Spanish the upside-down question mark introduces a question. A regular question mark ends the question.

EMPLOYMENT APPLICATION
SOLICITUD DE EMPLEO

Personal Information
Información personal

Name: _____ Last names: _____

Nombre: _____ *Apellidos:* _____

Address: _____

Dirección: _____

Telephone: ( ) _____

Teléfono: ( ) _____

Country of birth: _____

País de nacimiento: _____

Social Security number: _____

Número de seguro social: _____

Car: Yes   No

Coche: Sí   No

Have you studied in a high school?   Yes   No

¿Ha estudiado en una escuela secundaria?   Sí   No

If you have studied, up to what grade did you finish? _____

Si ha estudiado, ¿qué grado terminó? _____

Work Experience
Experiencia de empleo

1. Dates: _____

   Fechas: _____

Place: _____

Lugar: _____

Supervisor: _____

Supervisor(a): _____

Description of responsibilities: _____

Descripción de sus responsabilidades: _____

_____

2. Dates: _____

   Fechas: _____

   Place: _____

   Lugar: _____

   Supervisor: _____

   Supervisor(a): _____

   Description of responsibilities: _____

   Descripción de sus responsabilidades: _____

   _____

3. Dates: _____

   Fechas: _____

   Place: _____

   Lugar: _____

   Supervisor: _____

   Supervisor(a): _____

   Description of responsibilities: _____

   Descripción de sus responsabilidades: _____

   _____

Time Available

Horas disponibles

Days available: _____

Días disponibles: _____

Monday   From _____ Until _____

Lunes   *Desde* _____ *Hasta* _____

Tuesday   From _____ Until _____
Martes   *Desde* _____ *Hasta* _____

Wednesday   From _____ Until _____
Miércoles   *Desde* _____ *Hasta* _____

Thursday   From _____ Until _____
Jueves   *Desde* _____ *Hasta* _____

Friday   From _____ Until _____
Viernes   *Desde* _____ *Hasta* _____

Saturday   From _____ Until _____
Sábado   *Desde* _____ *Hasta* _____

Sunday   From _____ Until _____
Domingo   *Desde* _____ *Hasta* _____

Personal References
Referencias personales

Name: _____
Nombre: _____
Address: _____
Dirección: _____
Telephone: _____
Teléfono: _____

Name: _____
Nombre: _____
Address: _____
Dirección: _____
Telephone: _____
Teléfono: _____

Work References
Referencias de empleo

Name: _____

Nombre: _____

Address: _____

Dirección: _____

Telephone: _____

Teléfono: _____

Name: _____

Nombre: _____

Address: _____

Dirección: _____

Telephone: _____

Teléfono: _____

In Case of Emergency, Notify:
En caso de emergencia, notifique a:

Name: _____

Nombre: _____

Telephone: _____

Teléfono: _____

Cell phone number: _____

Número de celular: _____

Signature: _____   Date: _____

Firma: _____   *Fecha:* _____

What is your address?
¿Cuál es su dirección?
(kwahl ehs soo dee-rehk-**syon**)

What is your phone number?
¿Cuál es su número de teléfono?
(kwahl ehs soo **noo**-meh-roh deh teh-**leh**-foh-noh)

What is your Social Security number?
¿Cuál es el número de su seguro social?
(kwahl ehs ehl **noo**-meh-roh deh soo seh-**goo**-roh soh-**syahl**)

What is your date of birth?
¿Cuál es la fecha de su nacimiento?
(kwahl ehs lah **feh**-chah deh soo nah-see-**myehn**-toh)

What country are you from?
¿De qué país es usted?
(deh keh pah-**ees** ehs oos-**tehd**)

Do you have a car?
¿Tiene usted coche/carro?
(**tyeh**-neh oos-**tehd koh**-cheh/**kah**-rroh)

Have you studied in a high school?
¿Ha estudiado en una escuela secundaria?
(ah ehs-too-**dyah**-doh ehn **oo**-nah ehs-**kweh**-lah seh-koon-**dah**-ryah)

What grade did you finish?
¿Qué grado terminó?
(keh **grah**-doh tehr-mee-**noh**)

Do you know how to write in English?
¿Sabe escribir en inglés?
(**sah**-beh ehs-kree-**beer** ehn een-**glehs**)

Do you have experience in this type of work?
¿Tiene experiencia en este tipo de trabajo?
(**tyeh**-neh ehs-peh-**ryehn**-syah ehn **ehs**-teh **tee**-poh deh trah-**bah**-hoh)

Where did you work before?
¿Dónde trabajó antes?
(**dohn**-deh trah-bah-**hoh ahn**-tehs)

What dates did you work there?
¿Qué fechas trabajó allí?
(keh **feh**-chahs trah-bah-**hoh** ah-**yee**)

Who was your supervisor?
¿Quién fue su supervisor/supervisora?
(kyehn fweh soo soo-pehr-bee-**sohr**/soo-pehr-bee-**soh**-rah)

What responsibilities did you have?
¿Qué responsabilidades tenía?
(keh rrehs-pohn-sah-bee-lee-**dah**-dehs teh-**nee**-ah)

Why did you resign?
¿Por qué renunció?
(pohr keh rreh-noon-**syoh**)

Do you have any questions?
¿Tiene alguna pregunta?
(**tyeh**-neh ahl-**goo**-nah preh-**goon**-tah)

Schedule
El horario
(ehl oh-**rah**-ryoh)

When are you available?
¿Cuándo está disponible?
(**kwahn**-doh ehs-**tah** dees-poh-**nee**-bleh)

At what time can you arrive?
¿A qué hora puede llegar?
(ah keh **oh**-rah **pweh**-deh yeh-**gahr**)

Until what time can you stay?
¿Hasta qué hora puede quedarse?
(**ahs**-tah keh **oh**-rah **pweh**-deh keh-**dahr**-seh)

Can you stay overnight sometimes/every day/during the week?
¿Puede quedarse a dormir algunas veces/todos los días/durante la semana?
(**pweh**-deh keh-**dahr**-seh ah dohr-**meer** ahl-**goo**-nahs **beh**-sehs/**toh**-dohs lohs **dee**-ahs/doo-**rahn**-teh lah seh-**mah**-nah)

Can you stay late in an emergency?
¿Puede quedarse tarde en una emergencia?
(**pweh**-deh keh-**dahr**-seh **tahr**-deh ehn **oo**-nah eh-mehr-**hehn**-syah)

How many hours can you work?
¿Cuántas horas puede trabajar?
(**kwahn**-tahs **oh**-rahs **pweh**-deh trah-bah-**hahr**)

How many days can you work?
¿Cuántos días puede trabajar?
(**kwahn**-tohs **dee**-ahs **pweh**-deh trah-bah-**hahr**)

When can you start to work?
¿Cuándo puede empezar a trabajar?
(**kwahn**-doh **pweh**-deh ehm-peh-**sahr** ah trah-bah-**hahr**)

Do you work someplace else now?
¿Trabaja en otro lugar ahora?
(trah-**bah**-hah ehn **oh**-troh loo-**gahr** ah-**oh**-rah)

Can you work on Saturdays/Sundays?
¿Puede trabajar los sábados/los domingos?
(**pweh**-deh trah-bah-**hahr** lohs **sah**-bah-dohs/lohs doh-**meen**-gohs)

Experience
La experiencia
(lah ehks-peh-**ryehn**-syah)

How did you find out about the job?
¿Cómo se enteró del trabajo?
(**koh**-moh seh ehn-teh-**roh** dehl trah-**bah**-hoh)

Have you done this type of work before?
¿Ha hecho este tipo de trabajo antes?
(ah **eh**-choh **ehs**-teh **tee**-poh deh trah-**bah**-hoh **ahn**-tehs)

Where did you work before?
¿Dónde trabajó antes?
(**dohn**-deh trah-bah-**hoh ahn**-tehs)

Do you have references?
¿Tiene referencias?
(**tyeh**-neh rreh-feh-**rehn**-syahs)

May I call your references?
¿Podría llamar a sus referencias?
(poh-**dree**-ah yah-**mahr** ah soos rreh-feh-**rehn**-syahs)

Likes and Dislikes
Lo que le gusta o no le gusta
(loh keh leh **goos**-tah oh noh leh **goos**-tah)

Do you smoke?
¿Fuma Ud.?
(**foo**-mah oos-**tehd**)

Is there any job you do not like to do?
¿Hay algún trabajo que no le guste hacer?
(**ah**-ee ahl-**goon** trah-**bah**-hoh keh noh leh **goos**-teh ah-**sehr**)

Do you like to work with children?
¿Le gusta trabajar con niños?
(leh **goos**-tah trah-bah-**hahr** kohn **nee**-nyohs)

Do you like working with older people?
¿Le gusta trabajar con ancianos?
(leh **goos**-tah trah-bah-**hahr** kohn ahn-**syah**-nohs)

Do you like animals?
¿Le gustan los animales?
(leh **goos**-tahn lohs ah-nee-**mah**-lehs)

Do you like working outside?
¿Le gusta trabajar afuera?
(leh **goos**-tah trah-bah-**hahr** ah-**fweh**-rah)

Legal Matters
Cuestiones legales
(kwehs-**tyoh**-nehs leh-**gah**-lehs)

How long have you been in the United States?
¿Cuánto tiempo hace que está en los Estados Unidos?
(**kwahn**-toh **tyehm**-poh **ah**-seh keh ehs-**tah** ehn lohs ehs-**tah**-dohs oo-**nee**-dohs)

Are you a United States citizen?
¿Es ciudadano/cuidadana² de los Estados Unidos?
(ehs syoo-dah-**dah**-noh/syoo-dah-**dah**-nah deh lohs ehs-**tah**-dohs oo-**nee**-dohs)

Are you a legal resident?
¿Es Ud. un residente/una residente legal?
(ehs **oos**-tehd oon rreh-see-**dehn**-teh/**oo**-nah rreh-see-**dehn**-teh **leh**-gahl)

Do you have a permanent residence card?
¿Tiene tarjeta de residencia permanente?
(**tyeh**-neh tahr-**heh**-tah deh rreh-see-**dehn**-syah pehr-mah-**nehn**-teh)

Do you have a work permit?
¿Tiene permiso de trabajo?
(**tyeh**-neh pehr-**mee**-soh deh trah-**bah**-hoh)

Do you have a Social Security card?
¿Tiene tarjeta de seguro social?
(**tyeh**-neh tahr-**heh**-tah deh seh-**goo**-roh soh-**syahl**)

Getting to Work
Para viajar al trabajo
(**pah**-rah byah-**hahr** ahl trah-**bah**-hoh)

How can you get here?
¿Cómo puede llegar aquí?
(**koh**-moh **pweh**-deh yeh-**gahr** ah-**kee**)

2. Note that every Spanish noun is either masculine or feminine. Many nouns form the feminine by changing the final -o of the masculine to -a (see page 177).

Do you have a car?
¿Tiene coche/carro?
(**tyeh**-neh **koh**-cheh/**kah**-rroh)

Do you know how to get here by bus/train?
¿Sabe llegar aquí en autobús/en tren?
(**sah**-beh yeh-**gahr** ah-**kee** ehn ah-oo-toh-**boos**/ehn trehn)

Skills
Habilidades
(ah-bee-lee-**dah**-dehs)

Do you drive a car?
¿Sabe conducir?
(**sah**-beh kohn-doo-**seer**)

Do you have a driver's license?
¿Tiene licencia de conducir?
(**tyeh**-neh lee-**sehn**-syah deh kohn-doo-**seer**)

Do you speak English?
¿Habla inglés?
(**hah**-blah een-**glehs**)

Do you read English?
¿Lee inglés?
(**leh**-eh een-**glehs**)

Do you write English?
¿Escribe inglés?
(ehs-**kree**-beh een-**glehs**)

In Case of Emergency/Illness
En caso de emergencia/enfermedad
(ehn **kah**-soh deh eh-mehr-**hehn**-syah/ehn-fehr-meh-**dahd**)

In case of emergency, whom should I call?
En caso de emergencia, ¿a quién debo llamar?
(ehn **kah**-soh deh eh-mehr-**hehn**-syah ah kyehn **deh**-boh yah-**mahr**)

What is his/her phone number?
¿Cuál es su número de teléfono?
(kwahl ehs soo **noo**-meh-roh deh teh-**leh**-foh-noh)

Do you have medical insurance?
¿Tiene seguro médico?
(**tyeh**-neh seh-**goo**-roh **meh**-dee-koh)

Are you allergic to animals?
¿Es alérgico/alérgica a los animales?
(ehs ah-**lehr**-hee-koh/ah-**lehr**-hee-kah ah lohs ah-nee-**mah**-lehs)

Are you allergic to anything else?
¿Es alérgico/alérgica a otra cosa?
(ehs ah-**lehr**-hee-koh/ah-**lehr**-hee-kah ah **oh**-trah **koh**-sah)

To Finish the Interview
Para terminar la entrevista
(**pah**-rah tehr-mee-**nahr** lah ehn-treh-**bees**-tah)

Could (Would) you . . .
¿Podría...
(poh-**dree**-ah...)

> sign here?
> *firmar aquí?*
> (feer-**mahr** ah-**kee**)

> stay until one/two/three, etc., o'clock?
> *quedarse hasta la una/las dos/las tres, etc.?*
> (keh-**dahr**-seh **ahs**-tah lah **oo**-nah/lahs dohs/lahs trehs, etc.)

> come back tomorrow?
> *volver mañana?*
> (bohl-**behr** mah-**nyah**-nah)

> come the day after tomorrow?
> *venir pasado mañana?*
> (beh-**neer** pah-**sah**-doh mah-**nyah**-nah)

come next week?
venir la semana próxima?
(beh-**neer** lah seh-**mah**-nah **prohk**-see-mah)

start immediately/tomorrow/next week/next month?
empezar inmediatamente/mañana/la semana próxima/el mes próximo?
(ehm-peh-**sahr** een-meh-**dyah**-tah-mehn-teh/mah-**nyah**-nah/lah
seh-**mah**-nah **prohk**-see-mah/ehl mehs **prohk**-see-moh)

I am going to think about it, and I will call you on the phone.
Voy a pensarlo y lo/la llamo por teléfono.
(**boh**-ee ah pehn-**sahr**-loh ee loh/lah **yah**-moh pohr teh-**leh**-foh-noh)

I have to talk to my husband/wife first.
Tengo que hablar con mi esposo/esposa primero.
(**tehn**-goh keh ah-**blahr** kohn mee ehs-**poh**-soh/ehs-**poh**-sah pree-**meh**-roh)

Thank you for coming.
Gracias por venir.
(**grah**-syahs pohr beh-**neer**)

I would like . . .
Quisiera...
(kee-**syeh**-rah...)

to know if you are interested in the job.
saber si le interesa el trabajo.
(sah-**behr** see leh een-teh-**reh**-sah ehl trah-**bah**-hoh)

to call your previous job (your previous boss/supervisor).
llamar a su previo empleo (a su jefe/jefa/supervisor/supervisora) anterior.
(yah-**mahr** ah soo **preh**-byoh ehm-**pleh**-oh [ah soo **heh**-feh/
heh-fah/soo pehr-bee-**sohr**/soo-pehr-bee-**soh**-rah] ahn-teh-**ryohr**)

to verify the references.
verificar las referencias.
(beh-ree-fee-**kahr** lahs rreh-feh-**rehn**-syahs)

to introduce you to my husband/wife/son/daughter/children.
presentarle a mi esposo/esposa/hijo/hija/hijos/hijas.
(preh-sehn-**tahr**-leh ah mee ehs-**poh**-soh/ehs-**poh**-sah/**ee**-hoh/**ee**-hah/**ee**-hohs/**ee**-hahs)

Remember that when referring to your children, if they are all boys you should use *hijos* (**ee**-hohs). If you have both boys and girls, use *hijos* (**ee**-hohs). If they are all girls, use *hijas* (**ee**-hahs).

Greetings and Polite Exchanges
Saludos e *intercambios de cortesía*
(sah-**loo**-dohs eh een-tehr-**kahm**-byohs deh kohr-teh-**see**-ah)

There is a formal and an informal way to address a Spanish-speaking person. Which one you use depends on how well you know the person and/or his/her age. It is always best to address someone you do not know well or who is older than you are by using *usted (Ud.)* (oos-**tehd**). Once you get to know someone well and especially if he or she has requested that you do so, use *tú* (too).

To greet someone, say:

Good morning.	*Buenos días.* (**bweh**-nohs **dee**-ahs)
Good afternoon.	*Buenas tardes.* (**bweh**-nahs **tahr**-dehs)
Good evening./Good night.	*Buenas noches.* (**bweh**-nahs **noh**-chehs)
Hi.	*Hola.* (**oh**-lah)
How are you?	*¿Cómo está usted?* (**koh**-moh ehs-**tah** oos-**tehd**)
	¿Cómo estás tú? (**koh**-moh ehs-**tahs** too)
How is it going?	*¿Cómo le va?* (**koh**-moh leh bah)
I am fine, thanks. And you?	*Estoy bien, gracias. ¿Y Ud.?* (ehs-**toh**-ee byehn **grah**-syahs ee oos-**tehd**)
Very well.	*Muy bien.* (**moo**-ee byehn)
So-so.	*Regular./Así, así.* (rreh-goo-**lahr**/ah-**see** ah-**see**)

To say good-bye to someone, say:

Good-bye.   *Adiós.* (ah-**dyohs**)
See you later.   *Hasta luego.* (**ahs**-tah **lweh**-goh)
See you tomorrow.   *Hasta mañana.* (**ahs**-tah mah-**nyah**-
                              nah)
See you Monday.   *Hasta el lunes.* (**ahs**-tah ehl **loo**-nehs)
See you Tuesday.   *Hasta el martes.* (**ahs**-tah ehl **mahr**-
                              tehs)
See you Wednesday.   *Hasta el miércoles.* (**ahs**-tah ehl **myehr**-
                              koh-lehs)
See you Thursday.   *Hasta el jueves.* (**ahs**-tah ehl **hweh**-
                              behs)
See you Friday.   *Hasta el viernes.* (**ahs**-tah ehl **byehr**-
                              nehs)
See you Saturday.   *Hasta el sábado.* (**ahs**-tah ehl **sah**-bah-
                              doh)
See you Sunday.   *Hasta el domingo.* (**ahs**-tah ehl doh-
                              meen-goh)
Have a nice day.   *¡Que le vaya bien!*[3] (keh leh **bah**-yah
                              byehn)

To introduce someone, say:

This is (person's name).   *Este/Esta es (person's name).* (**ehs**-
                              teh/**ehs**-tah ehs...)
A pleasure.   *Mucho gusto.* (**moo**-choh **goos**-toh)
The pleasure is mine.   *El gusto es mío.* (ehl **goos**-toh ehs **mee**-
                              oh)

To thank someone, say:

Thank you.   *Gracias.* (**grah**-syahs)
Thank you very much.   *Muchas gracias.* (**moo**-chahs **grah**-
                              syahs)
I'm very grateful.   *Muy agradecido/agradecida.* (**moo**-ee
                              ah-grah-deh-**see**-doh/ah-grah-deh-
                              see-dah)

3. Notice that an upside-down exclamation point introduces an exclamation. A regular exclamation point ends the exclamation.

Many thanks!   *¡Mil gracias!* (meel **grah**-syahs)

You are welcome.   *De nada.* (deh **nah**-dah)

To apologize or express regret, use:

I'm sorry.   *Lo siento.* (loh **syehn**-toh)

I'm very sorry.   *Lo siento mucho.* (loh **syehn**-toh **moo**-choh)

Forgive me.   *Perdón.* (pehr-**dohn**)

Excuse me.   *Con su permiso.* (kohn soo pehr-**mee**-soh)

To express surprise, say:

Really?   *¿De veras?* (deh **beh**-rahs)

You don't say!   *¡No me diga!* (noh meh **dee**-gah)

What a surprise!   *¡Qué sorpresa!* (keh sohr-**preh**-sah)

How strange!   *¡Qué raro!/¡Qué extraño!* (keh **rrah**-roh/keh ehs-**trah**-nyoh)

To express agreement/disagreement, say:

OK.   *Bueno./Vale.* (**bweh**-noh/**bah**-leh)

I agree.   *De acuerdo.* (deh ah-**kwehr**-doh)

It's true.   *Es cierto./Es verdad.* (ehs **syehr**-toh/ehs **behr**-dahd)

You're right.   *Tiene razón.* (**tyeh**-neh rrah-**sohn**)

Of course!   *¡Cómo no!/¡Claro que sí!* (**koh**-moh noh/**klah**-roh keh see)

Of course not!   *¡Claro que no!* (**klah**-roh keh noh)

You're wrong.   *No tiene razón.* (noh **tyeh**-neh rrah-**sohn**)

To express approval/encouragement, say:

Great!   *¡Qué bueno!/¡Estupendo!* (keh **bweh**-noh/ehs-too-**pehn**-doh)

Fantastic!   *¡Fantástico!/¡Fenomenal!* (fahn-**tahs**-tee-koh/feh-noh-meh-**nahl**)

What a great idea!   *¡Qué buena idea!* (keh **bweh**-nah ee-**deh**-ah)

Perfect!	*¡Perfecto!* (pehr-**fehk**-toh)
Very good!	*¡Muy bien!* (**moo**-ee byehn)

To express disapproval, say:

How horrible/terrible!	*¡Qué horror!/¡Qué horrible (terrible)!*(keh oh-**rrohr**/keh oh-**rree**-bleh [teh-**rree**-bleh])
What a disaster!	*¡Qué desastre!* (keh deh-**sahs**-treh)

To express happiness, say:

I am (very) happy.	*Estoy (muy) contento/contenta.* (ehs-**toh**-ee [**moo**-ee] kohn-**tehn**-toh/kohn-**tehn**-tah)
What happiness!	*¡Qué alegría!/¡Qué felicidad!* (keh ah-leh-**gree**-ah/keh feh-lee-see-**dahd**)

To express sadness, say:

I am (very) sad.	*Estoy (muy) triste.* (ehs-**toh**-ee [**moo**-ee] **trees**-teh)
How sad!/What sadness!	*¡Qué triste!/¡Qué tristeza!* (keh **trees**-teh/keh trees-**teh**-sah)
What a shame/a pity!	*¡Qué lástima!/¡Qué pena!* (keh **lahs**-tee-mah/keh **peh**-nah)

To express embarrassment, say:

I'm (very) embarrassed.	*Estoy (muy) avergonzado/avergonzada.* (ehs-**toh**-ee [**moo**-ee] ah-behr-gohn-**sah**-doh/ah-behr-gohn-**sah**-dah)
What a shame/an embarrassment!	*¡Qué vergüenza!* (keh behr-**gwehn**-sah)

To ask, socially, about someone's family, say:

Are you married?	*¿Es usted casado/casada?* (ehs oos-**tehd** kah-**sah**-doh/kah-**sah**-dah)
Are you single?	*¿Es Ud. soltero/soltera?* (ehs oos-**tehd** sohl-**teh**-roh/sohl-**teh**-rah)

Do you have any children?

¿Tiene Ud. hijos/hijas? (**tyeh**-neh **oos**-tehd **ee**-hohs/**ee**-hahs)

How old are they?

¿Cuántos años tienen? (**kwahn**-tohs **ah**-nyohs **tyeh**-nehn)

The Family
La familia
(lah fah-**mee**-lyah)

The family is very important in Hispanic culture. In any gathering you will find members of a family spanning several generations. Even relatives who in other cultures may not be considered close members of the family, are treated as close family by Hispanics. This includes any relative, by blood or by marriage, no matter how far removed.

Relatives
Los parientes
(lohs pah-**ryehn**-tehs)

aunt	*la tía* (lah **tee**-ah)
boyfriend	*el novio* (ehl **noh**-byoh)
brother	*el hermano* (ehl ehr-**mah**-noh)
brother-in-law	*el cuñado* (ehl koo-**nyah**-doh)
cousin	*el primo/la prima* (ehl **pree**-moh/lah **pree**-mah)
daughter	*la hija* (lah **ee**-hah)
daughter-in-law	*la nuera* (lah **nweh**-rah)
father	*el padre* (ehl **pah**-dreh)
father-in-law	*el suegro* (ehl **sweh**-groh)

girlfriend	*la novia* (lah **noh**-byah)
goddaughter	*la ahijada* (lah ah-ee-**hah**-dah)
godfather	*el padrino* (ehl pah-**dree**-noh)
godmother	*la madrina* (lah mah-**dree**-nah)
godson	*el ahijado* (ehl ah-ee-**hah**-doh)
granddaughter	*la nieta* (lah **nyeh**-tah)
grandfather	*el abuelo* (ehl ah-**bweh**-loh)
grandmother	*la abuela* (lah ah-**bweh**-lah)
grandson	*el nieto* (ehl **nyeh**-toh)
great-granddaughter	*la bisnieta* (lah bees-**nyeh**-tah)
great-grandfather	*el bisabuelo* (ehl bee-sah-**bweh**-loh)
great-grandmother	*la bisabuela* (lah bee-sah-**bweh**-lah)
great-grandson	*el bisnieto* (ehl bees-**nyeh**-toh)
husband	*el esposo* (ehl ehs-**poh**-soh)
mother	*la madre* (lah **mah**-dreh)
mother-in-law	*la suegra* (lah **sweh**-grah)
nephew	*el sobrino* (ehl soh-**bree**-noh)
niece	*la sobrina* (lah soh-**bree**-nah)
relative	*el pariente/la parienta* (ehl pah-**ryehn**-teh/lah par-**ryehn**-tah)
sister	*la hermana* (lah ehr-**mah**-nah)
sister-in-law	*la cuñada* (lah koo-**nyah**-dah)
son	*el hijo* (ehl **ee**-hoh)
son-in-law	*el yerno* (ehl **yehr**-noh)
stepbrother	*el hermanastro* (ehl ehr-mah-**nahs**-troh)
stepdaughter	*la hijastra* (lah ee-**hahs**-trah)
stepfather	*el padrastro* (ehl pah-**drahs**-troh)
stepmother	*la madrastra* (lah mah-**drahs**-trah)
stepsister	*la hermanastra* (lah ehr-mah-**nahs**-trah)
stepson	*el hijastro* (ehl ee-**hahs**-troh)
uncle	*el tío* (ehl **tee**-oh)
wife	*la esposa* (lah ehs-**poh**-sah)

Describing a Person Physically
Para describir a una persona físicamente
(**pah**-rah dehs-kree-**beer** ah **oo**-nah pehr-**soh**-na **fee**-see-kah-mehn-teh)

In order to describe what a person looks like you must use the verb *ser* (sehr) (to be):

I am	*soy* (**soh**-ee)
you are (*familiar*)	*eres* (**eh**-rehs)
he/she is; you are (*polite, singular*)	*es* (ehs)
we are	*somos* (**soh**-mohs)
they are; you are (*polite, plural*)	*son* (sohn)

Also remember that the ending of the adjective changes depending on whether the person you are describing is male or female and on whether you are describing one or more than one person. Adjectives ending in *-o* change the *-o* to *-a* to form the feminine. Most other adjectives have the same form for both genders. You may want to review how to make adjectives agree with nouns in Appendix B on pages 178–79. Use the following adjectives to describe someone physically:

athletic	*atlético* (ah-**tleh**-tee-koh)
bald	*calvo* (**kahl**-boh)
blond/fair	*rubio* (**rroo**-byoh)
brunette/dark	*moreno* (moh-**reh**-noh)
fat	*gordo/grueso* (**gohr**-doh/**grweh**-soh)
good-looking	*guapo* (**gwah**-poh)
large	*grande* (**grahn**-dch)
pretty (a woman)	*bonita/hermosa* (boh-**nee**-tah/ehr-**moh**-sah)
redheaded	*pelirrojo* (peh-lee-**rroh**-hoh)
short	*bajo* (**bah**-hoh)
skinny	*flaco* (**flah**-koh)
slender	*esbelto* (ehs-**behl**-toh)
small	*pequeño* (peh-**keh**-nyoh)
strong	*fuerte* (**fwehr**-teh)
tall	*alto* (**ahl**-toh)
thin	*delgado* (dehl-**gah**-doh)
ugly	*feo* (**feh**-oh)

Describing a Person's Personality and Intelligence
Para describir la personalidad y la inteligencia de una persona
(**pah**-rah dehs-kree-**beer** lah pehr-soh-nah-lee-**dahd** ee lah een-teh-lee-**hehn**-syah deh **oo**-nah pehr-**soh**-nah)

Use the following adjectives to describe someone's personality and intelligence. Again, use the verb *ser* (sehr) (to be) and don't forget to make the adjective agree with the noun it describes.

boring	*aburrido* (ah-boo-**rree**-doh)
calm	*tranquilo/quieto* (trahn-**kee**-loh/**kyeh**-toh)
charming	*encantador* (ehn-kahn-tah-**dohr**)
conceited	*vanidoso/engreído* (bah-nee-**doh**-soh/ehn-greh-**ee**-doh)
conservative	*conservador* (kohn-sehr-bah-**dohr**)
courageous	*valiente* (bah-**lyehn**-teh)
crazy	*loco* (**loh**-koh)
dumb	*tonto* (**tohn**-toh)
fun	*divertido* (dee-behr-**tee**-doh)
generous	*generoso* (heh-neh-**roh**-soh)
happy	*alegre* (ah-**leh**-greh)
hard-working	*trabajador* (trah-bah-hah-**dohr**)
healthy	*saludable/sano* (sah-loo-**dah**-bleh/**sah**-noh)
honest/trustworthy	*honrado* (ohn-**rrah**-doh)
independent	*independiente* (een-deh-pehn-**dyehn**-teh)
intelligent	*inteligente/listo* (een-teh-lee-**hehn**-teh/**lees**-toh)
interesting	*interesante* (een-teh-reh-**sahn**-teh)
lazy	*perezoso* (peh-reh-**soh**-soh)
liberal	*liberal* (lee-beh-**rahl**)
nice	*simpático* (seem-**pah**-tee-koh)
optimistic	*optimista* (ohp-tee-**mees**-tah)
pessimistic	*pesimista* (peh-see-**mees**-tah)
pleasant	*agradable* (ah-grah-**dah**-bleh)

polite/courteous	*cortés* (kohr-**tehs**)
responsible	*responsable* (rrehs-pohn-**sah**-bleh)
sad	*triste* (**trees**-teh)
sane	*cuerdo* (**kwer**-doh)
serious	*serio* (**seh**-ryoh)
sincere	*sincero* (seen-**seh**-roh)
slow	*lento* (**lehn**-toh)
spoiled	*malcriado* (mahl-**kryah**-doh)
talkative	*hablador* (ah-blah-**dohr**)
unpleasant/disagreeable	*antipático* (ahn-tee-**pah**-tee-koh)

Describing a Person's Emotions and Feelings
Para describir las emociones y los sentimientos de una persona
(**pah**-rah dehs-kree-**beer** lahs eh-moh-**syoh**-nehs ee lohs sehn-tee-**myehn**-tohs deh **oo**-nah pehr-**soh**-nah)

At times, you and your employees will have to tell each other how you feel or explain why you are acting a certain way. In contrast to the descriptions you learned above, adjectives that describe transitory or temporary feelings and emotions use the verb *estar* (ehs-**tahr**) (to be).

I am	*estoy* (ehs-**toh**-ee)
you are (*familiar*)	*estás* (ehs-**tahs**)
he/she is; you are (*polite, singular*)	*está* (ehs-**tah**)
we are	*estamos* (ehs-**tah**-mohs)
they are; you are (*polite, plural*)	*están* (ehs-**tahn**)

Use the following adjectives to describe someone's emotions, feelings, or the condition they are in at a particular moment in time. Remember to make the adjective agree with the noun it describes.

angry	*enojado* (eh-noh-**hah**-doh)
busy	*ocupado* (oh-koo-**pah**-doh)
confused	*confundido* (kohn-foon-**dee**-doh)
depressed	*deprimido* (deh-pree-**mee**-doh)
exhausted	*agotado* (ah-goh-**tah**-doh)

grateful	*agradecido* (ah-grah-deh-**see**-doh)
happy	*alegre/contento* (ah-**leh**-greh/kohn-**tehn**-toh)
nervous	*nervioso* (nehr-**byoh**-soh)
relaxed	*relajado* (rreh-lah-**hah**-doh)
sad	*triste* (**trees**-teh)
sick	*enfermo* (ehn-**fehr**-moh)
tired	*cansado* (kahn-**sah**-doh)
worried	*preocupado* (preh-oh-koo-**pah**-doh)

Describing a Person's Religion
Para describir la religión de una persona
(**pah**-rah dehs-kree-**beer** lah rreh-lee-**hyohn** deh **oo**-nah pehr-**soh**-nah)

Use the following adjectives to talk about religious affiliation. Use the verb *ser* (sehr) (to be) and remember to make the adjective agree with the noun it describes.

Catholic	*católico* (kah-**toh**-lee-koh)
Christian	*cristiano* (krees-**tyah**-noh)
Jewish	*judío* (hoo-**dee**-oh)
Moslem	*musulmán* (moo-sool-**mahn**)
Protestant	*protestante* (proh-tehs-**tahn**-teh)

Describing a Person's Nationality
Para describir la nacionalidad de una persona
(**pah**-rah dehs-kree-**beer** lah nah-syoh-nah-lee-**dahd** deh **oo**-nah pehr-**soh**-nah)

Asking about your employee's country of origin shows that you are interested in him or her as a person. It is also a way to increase your knowledge about other countries and cultures, which your employee will likely appreciate.

Ask the following question to find out where someone is from:

| Where are you from? | *¿De dónde es Ud.?* (deh **dohn**-deh ehs oos-**tehd**) |

I am from . . .	*Soy de...* (**soh**-ee deh...)

To find out his or her nationality, you may ask:

What is your nationality?	*¿Cuál es su nacionalidad?* (kwahl ehs soo nah-syoh-nah-lee-**dahd**)
I am . . .	*Soy...* (**soh**-ee...)

Notice that to express where someone is from, or a person's nationality, you will always use the verb *ser* (sehr) (to be): *soy, eres, es, somos, son*, (**soh**-ee, **eh**-rehs, ehs, **soh**-mohs, sohn).

Are you from . . . ?	*¿Es Ud. de...?* (ehs oos-**tehd** deh...)
Yes, I am from . . .	*Sí, soy de...* (see, **soh**-ee deh...)
No, I am not from . . . , I am from . . .	*No, no soy de..., soy de...* (noh, noh **soh**-ee deh..., **soh**-ee deh...)

Here is a list of the Spanish-speaking countries and their corresponding nationalities. Note that with the exception of the nationalities for "Costa Rican," "Nicaraguan," and "Spanish," changing the final -*o* to an -*a* forms the feminine form of the nationalities. Adjectives that end in -*e* in the masculine singular have the same ending for both genders. Adjectives of nationality that end in a consonant add an -*a* to the masculine form to express the feminine form. You may want to review how to make an adjective agree with the noun it describes in Appendix B on page 178–79.

Argentina (ahr-hehn-**tee**-nah)	*argentino/argentina* (ahr-hehn-**tee**-noh/ahr-hehn-**tee**-nah)
Bolivia (boh-**lee**-byah)	*boliviano/boliviana* (boh-lee-**byah**-noh/boh-lee-**byah**-nah)
Chile (**chee**-leh)	*chileno/chilena* (chee-**leh**-noh/chee-**leh**-nah)
Colombia (koh-**lohm**-byah)	*colombiano/colombiana* (koh-lohm-**byah**-noh/koh-lohm-**byah**-nah)
Costa Rica (**kohs**-tah **rree**-kah)	*costarricense* (kohs-tah-rree-**sehn**-seh)
Cuba (**koo**-bah)	*cubano/cubana* (koo-**bah**-noh/koo-**bah**-nah)

Ecuador (eh-kwah-**dohr**)

ecuatoriano/ecuatoriana (eh-kwah-toh-**ryah**-noh/eh-kwah-toh-**ryah**-nah)

El Salvador (ehl sahl-bah-**dohr**)

salvadoreño/salvadoreña (sahl-bah-doh-**reh**-nyoh/sahl-bah-doh-**reh**-nyah)

España (ehs-**pah**-nyah)

español/española (ehs-pah-**nyohl**/ehs-pah-**nyoh**-lah)

Guatemala (gwah-teh-**mah**-lah)

guatemalteco/guatemalteca (gwah-teh-mahl-**teh**-koh/gwah-teh-mahl-**teh**-kah)

Honduras (ohn-**doo**-rahs)

hondureño/hondureña (ohn-doo-**reh**-nyoh/ohn-doo-**reh**-nyah)

México (**meh**-hee-koh)

mexicano/mexicana (meh-heh-**kah**-noh/meh-heh-**kah**-nah)

Nicaragua (nee-kah-**rah**-gwah)

nicaragüense (nee-kah-rah-**gwehn**-seh)

Panamá (pah-nah-**mah**)

panameño/panameña (pah-nah-**meh**-nyoh/pah-nah-**meh**-nyah)

Paraguay (pah-rah-**gwah**-ee)

paraguayo/paraguaya (pah-rah-**gwah**-yoh/pah-rah-**gwah**-yah)

Perú (peh-**roo**)

peruano/peruana (peh-**rwah**-noh/peh-**rwah**-nah)

Puerto Rico (**pwehr**-toh **rree**-koh)

puertorriqueño/puertorriqueña (pwehr-toh-rree-**keh**-nyoh/pwehr-toh-rree-**keh**-nyah)

República Dominicana (reh-**poo**-blee-kah doh-mee-nee-**kah**-nah)

dominicano/dominicana (doh-mee-nee-**kah**-noh/doh-mee-nee-**kah**-nah)

Uruguay (oo-roo-**gwah**-ee)

uruguayo/uruguaya (oo-roo-**gwah**-yoh/oo-roo-**gwah**-yah)

Venezuela (beh-neh-**sweh**-lah)

venezolano/venezolana (beh-neh-soh-**lah**-noh/beh-neh-soh-**lah**-nah)

The House
La casa
(lah **kah**-sah)

Parts of the House
Las partes de la casa
(lahs **pahr**-tehs deh lah **kah**-sah)

The following is a general list of the things you may find in a house or apartment. It is followed by lists organized according to the different rooms in the home.

attic	*el desván* (ehl dehs-**bahn**)
backyard	*el patio* (ehl **pah**-tyoh)
balcony	*el balcón* (ehl bahl-**kohn**)
banister	*el pasamanos* (ehl pah-sah-**mah**-nohs)
basement	*el sótano* (ehl **soh**-tah-noh)
bench	*el banco* (ehl **bahn**-koh)
blind	*la persiana* (lah pehr-**syah**-nah)
carpet	*la alfombra* (lah ahl-**fohm**-brah)
ceiling	*el techo* (ehl **teh**-choh)
chain	*la cadena* (lah kah-**deh**-nah)
chimney	*la chimenea* (lah chee-meh-**neh**-ah)
curtain	*la cortina* (lah kohr-**tee**-nah)

deadbolt	*el pestillo* (ehl pehs-**tee**-yoh)
door	*la puerta* (lah **pwehr**-tah)
doorbell	*el timbre* (ehl **teem**-breh)
drawer	*el cajón* (ehl kah-**hohn**)
driveway	*la entrada (para carros)* (lah ehn-**trah**-dah [**pah**-rah **kah**-rrohs])
fence	*la cerca* (lah **sehr**-kah)
fire extinguisher	*el extintor* (ehl ehs-teen-**tohr**)
floor	*el suelo/el piso* (ehl **sweh**-loh/ehl **pee**-soh)
gate	*la verja* (lah **behr**-hah)
guest room	*el cuarto de huéspedes* (ehl **kwahr**-toh deh **wehs**-peh-dehs)
hallway	*el pasillo* (ehl pah-**see**-yoh)
key	*la llave* (lah **yah**-beh)
latch	*el cerrojo* (ehl seh-**rroh**-hoh)
lock	*la cerradura* (lah seh-rrah-**doo**-rah)
mailbox	*el buzón* (ehl boo-**sohn**)
padlock	*el candado* (ehl kahn-**dah**-doh)
pantry	*la despensa* (lah dehs-**pehn**-sah)
playroom	*el cuarto de juego* (ehl **kwahr**-toh deh **hweh**-goh)
porch	*el portal* (ehl pohr-**tahl**)
roof	*el techo* (ehl **teh**-choh)
staircase	*la escalera* (lah ehs-kah-**leh**-rah)
stepladder	*la escalera* (lah ehs-kah-**leh**-rah)
terrace	*la terraza* (lah teh-**rrah**-sah)
wall	*la pared* (lah pah-**rehd**)
window	*la ventana* (lah behn-**tah**-nah)
windowshade	*la persiana* (lah pehr-**syah**-nah)

Electrical Devices
Los aparatos eléctricos
(lohs ah-pah-**rah**-tohs eh-**lehk**-tree-kohs)

You will find many electrical devices in the home. Some of them are listed later according to the room where you can find them. But the following can be found in almost any room of the house:

air conditioner	el *aire acondicionado* (ehl **ah**-ee-reh ah-kohn-dee-syoh-**nah**-doh)
alarm	la *alarma* (lah ah-**lahr**-mah)
doorbell	el *timbre* (ehl **teem**-breh)
electrical outlet	el *enchufe* (ehl ehn-**choo**-feh)
fuse box	la *caja de fusibles* (lah **kah**-hah deh foo-**see**-blehs)
heater	el *calentador* (ehl kah-lehn-tah-**dohr**)
lightbulb	la *bombilla* (lah bohm-**bee**-yah)
light switch	el *interruptor* (ehl een-teh-rroop-**tohr**)
meter	el *contador* (ehl kohn-tah-**dohr**)
plug	el *enchufe* (ehl ehn-**choo**-feh)
thermostat	el *termostato* (ehl tehr-mohs-**tah**-toh)

In the Living Room
En la sala
(ehn lah **sah**-lah)

armchair	el *sillón*/la *butaca* (ehl see-**yohn**/lah boo-**tah**-kah)
ashtray	el *cenicero* (ehl seh-nee-**seh**-roh)
bookshelf	el *estante* (ehl ehs-**tahn**-teh)
clock	el *reloj* (ehl rreh-**loh**)
coffee table	la *mesita de centro* (lah meh-**see**-tah deh **sehn**-troh)
cushion	el *cojín* (ehl koh-**heen**)
fireplace	la *chimenea* (lah chee-meh-**neh**-ah)
lamp	la *lámpara* (lah **lahm**-pah-rah)

lampshade	*la pantalla* (lah pahn-**tah**-yah)
piano	*el piano* (ehl **pyah**-noh)
picture	*el cuadro* (ehl **kwah**-droh)
radio	*el radio* (ehl **rrah**-dyoh)
rug	*la alfombra* (lah ahl-**fohm**-brah)
sofa	*el sofá* (ehl soh-**fah**)
telephone	*el teléfono* (ehl teh-**leh**-foh-noh)
television set	*el televisor* (ehl teh-leh-bee-**sohr**)
vase	*el florero* (ehl floh-**reh**-roh)

In the Bedroom
En el dormitorio/el cuarto de dormir
(ehn ehl dohr-mee-**toh**-ryoh/ehl **kwahr**-toh deh dohr-**meer**)

Your bedroom is a place where you want to make sure everything is right. A good night's sleep in a familiar and comfortable place is key to one's well-being. Here is a list of words and verbs dealing with the bedroom:

alarm clock	*el reloj despertador* (ehl rreh-**loh** dehs-pehr-tah-**dohr**)
bed	*la cama* (lah **kah**-mah)
bedspread	*la colcha* (lah **kohl**-chah)
blanket	*la frazada* (lah frah-**sah**-dah)
chest of drawers	*la cómoda* (lah **koh**-moh-dah)
closet	*el armario* (ehl ahr-**mah**-ryoh)
dresser	*la cómoda* (lah **koh**-moh-dah)
dressing table	*el tocador* (ehl toh-kah-**dohr**)
linen	*la ropa blanca* (lah **rroh**-pah **blahn**-kah)
mattress	*el colchón* (ehl kohl-**chohn**)
night table	*la mesita de noche* (lah meh-**see**-tah deh **noh**-cheh)
pillow	*la almohada* (lah ahl-moh-**ah**-dah)
pillowcase	*la funda de almohada* (lah **foon**-dah deh ahl-moh-**ah**-dah)
sheet	*la sábana* (lah **sah**-bah-nah)

Verbs

to change the linen	*cambiar la ropa de cama* (kahm-**byahr** lah **rroh**-pah deh **kah**-mah)
to fall asleep	*dormirse (ue)*[1] (dohr-**meer**-seh)
to get up	*levantarse* (leh-bahn-**tahr**-seh)
to go to bed	*acostarse (ue)* (ah-kohs-**tahr**-seh)
to make the bed	*hacer la cama* (ah-**sehr** lah **kah**-mah)
to sleep	*dormir (ue)* (dohr-**meer**)
to wake up	*despertarse (ie)* (dehs-pehr-**tahr**-seh)

Talking About How You Slept
Para hablar sobre cómo durmió
(**pah**-rah ah-**blahr soh**-breh **koh**-moh door-**myoh**)

Here is a way to talk about how you slept last night:

How did you sleep?	*¿Cómo durmió?* (**koh**-moh door-**myoh**)
I slept . . .	*Dormí...* (dohr-**mee**...)
well.	*bien.* (byehn)
badly.	*mal.* (mahl)

In the Bathroom
En el baño
(ehn ehl **bah**-nyoh)

bathtub	*la bañera* (lah bah-**nyeh**-rah)
cold-water tap	*el grifo de agua fría* (ehl **gree**-foh deh **ah**-gwah **free**-ah)
faucet	*el grifo* (ehl **gree**-foh)
hot-water tap	*el grifo de agua caliente* (ehl **gree**-foh deh **ah**-gwah kah-**lyehn**-teh)
medicine chest	*el botiquín* (ehl boh-tee-**keen**)
mirror	*el espejo* (ehl ehs-**peh**-hoh)
rug	*la alfombrilla* (lah ahl-fohm-**bree**-yah)

---

1. To learn how to conjugate these Spanish verbs go to pages 186–88 in Appendix B.

scale	*la pesa* (lah **peh**-sah)
shower	*la ducha* (lah **doo**-chah)
sink	*el lavabo/el lavamanos* (ehl lah-**bah**-boh/ehl lah-bah-**mah**-nohs)
soap dish	*la jabonera* (lah hah-boh-**neh**-rah)
toilet	*el retrete/el inodoro* (ehl rreh-**treh**-teh/ehl ee-noh-**doh**-roh)
toilet paper	*el papel higiénico* (ehl pah-**pehl** ee-**hyeh**-nee-koh)
towel rack	*el toallero* (ehl toh-ah-**yeh**-roh)
water	*el agua* (ehl **ah**-gwah)

Verbs

to bathe	*bañarse*[2] (bah-**nyahr**-seh)
to brush one's hair	*cepillarse el pelo* (seh-pee-**yahr**-seh ehl **peh**-loh)
to brush one's teeth	*cepillarse los dientes* (seh-pee-**yahr**-seh lohs **dyehn**-tehs)
to comb one's hair	*peinarse* (peh-ee-**nahr**-seh)
to dry oneself	*secarse* (seh-**kahr**-seh)
to put make-up on	*maquillarse* (mah-kee-**yahr**-seh)
to shave	*afeitarse* (ah-feh-ee-**tahr**-seh)
to shower	*ducharse* (doo-**chahr**-seh)
to wash	*lavarse* (lah-**bahr**-seh)

In the Home Office
En la oficina en casa
(ehn lah oh-fee-**see**-nah ehn **kah**-sah)

answering machine	*el contestador automático* (ehl kohn-tehs-tah-**dohr** ah-oo-toh-**mah**-tee-koh)
ballpoint pen	*el bolígrafo* (ehl boh-**lee**-grah-foh)
bookcase	*el estante* (ehl ehs-**tahn**-teh)

2. As you see, most verbs dealing with personal grooming are reflexive verbs. If you need to review or learn how reflexive verbs are conjugated, go to pages 187–88 in Appendix B.

calculator	*la calculadora* (lah kahl-koo-lah-**doh**-rah)
computer	*la computadora* (lah kohm-poo-tah-**doh**-rah)
copy machine	*la copiadora* (lah koh-pyah-**doh**-rah)
desk	*el escritorio* (ehl ehs-kree-**toh**-ryoh)
envelope	*el sobre* (ehl **soh**-breh)
eraser	*la goma de borrar* (lah **goh**-mah deh boh-**rrahr**)
file cabinet	*el fichero* (ehl fee-**cheh**-roh)
file	*el archivo* (ehl ahr-**chee**-boh)
ink-jet printer	*la impresora de chorro de tinta* (lah eem-preh-**soh**-rah deh **choh**-rroh deh **teen**-tah)
letter	*la carta* (lah **kahr**-tah)
paper	*el papel* (ehl pah-**pehl**)
paper clip	*el sujetapapeles* (ehl soo-heh-tah-pah-**peh**-lehs)
paperweight	*el pisapapeles* (ehl pee-sah-pah-**peh**-lehs)
pen	*la pluma* (lah **ploo**-mah)
pencil	*el lápiz* (ehl **lah**-pees)
pencil sharpner	*el sacapuntas* (ehl sah-kah-**poon**-tahs)
printer	*la impresora* (lah eem-preh-**soh**-rah)
stamp	*el sello* (ehl **seh**-yoh)
staple	*la grapa* (lah **grah**-pah)
stapler	*la grapadora* (lah grah-pah-**doh**-rah)
wastepaper basket	*la papelera* (lah pah-peh-**leh**-rah)

Verbs

to file	*archivar* (ahr-chee-**bahr**)
to staple	*sujetar con grapas* (soo-heh-**tahr** kohn **grah**-pahs)

Talking on the Telephone
Para hablar por teléfono
(**pah**-rah ah-**blahr** pohr teh-**leh**-foh-noh)

It is likely that your employee will need to answer the telephone and take messages for you. You may also take messages from a friend or family member of your employee. The following are some useful words and expressions for making a call or answering the telephone:

area code	*el código de área* (ehl **koh**-dee-goh deh **ah**-reh-ah)
busy	*ocupado* (oh-koo-**pah**-doh)
call	*la llamada* (lah yah-**mah**-dah)
dial tone	*el tono de marcar* (ehl **toh**-noh deh mahr-**kahr**)
receiver	*el auricular* (ehl ah-oo-ree-koo-**lahr**)
Hello.	*Aló./Bueno./Diga./Dígame.* (ah-**loh**/**bweh**-noh/**dee**-gah/**dee**-gah-meh)
I would like to speak to . . .	*Quisiera hablar con...* (kee-**syeh**-rah ah-**blahr** kohn...)
Is (name) there?	*¿Está (name)?* (ehs-**tah**...)
Are (names) there?	*¿Están (names)?* (ehs-**tahn**...)
Who should I say is calling?	*¿De parte de quién?* (deh **pahr**-teh deh kyehn)
Who is speaking?	*¿Quién habla?* (kyehn **ah**-blah)
It's (name).	*Es (name)./Habla (name).* (ehs.../**ah**-blah...)
Just a moment, please.	*Un momento, por favor.* (oon moh-**mehn**-toh pohr fah-**bohr**)
I'm sorry. (Name) is not here.	*Lo siento. (Name) no está.* (loh **syehn**-toh... noh ehs-**tah**)
I'm sorry. (Names) are not here.	*Lo siento. (Names) no están.* (loh **syehn**-toh... noh chs-**tahn**)
He/She will return at . . .	*Regresa a la(s)...* (rreh-**greh**-sah ah lah[s]...)
Could you call later?	*¿Podría llamar más tarde?* (poh-**dree**-ah yah-**mahr** mahs **tahr**-deh)

What is your phone number?	*¿Cuál es su número de teléfono?* (kwahl ehs soo **noo**-meh-roh deh teh-**leh**-foh-noh)
May I take a message?	*¿Puedo tomar un mensaje?* (**pweh**-doh toh-**mahr** oon mehn-**sah**-heh)
More slowly please.	*Más despacio, por favor.* (**mahs** dehs-**pah**-syoh pohr fah-**bohr**)
You have the wrong number.	*Tiene el número equivocado.* (**tyeh**-neh ehl **noo**-meh-roh eh-kee-boh-**kah**-doh)

Verbs

to call	*llamar* (yah-**mahr**)
to dial	*marcar* (mahr-**kahr**)
to hang up	*colgar (ue)* (kohl-**gahr**)
to pick up	*descolgar (ue)* (dehs-kohl-**gahr**)
to ring	*sonar (ue)* (soh-**nahr**)

Chores and Cleaning the House
Los quehaceres y la limpieza de la casa
(lohs keh-ah-**seh**-rehs ee lah leem-**pyeh**-sah deh lah **kah**-sah)

It's time to clean the house. Although some of the machines, gadgets, or objects used to clean the house may be listed under specific rooms, the following is a general list of what you need to clean the house. There are several ways to ask someone to do something. One way is to use the command form. For more information on giving commands go to Appendix B on pages 198–200. Remember that in all languages using the equivalent of "please" goes a long way.

Please . . .	*Por favor...* (pohr fah-**bohr**...)
clean the kitchen.	*limpie la cocina.* (**leem**-pyeh lah koh-**see**-nah)
dust the furniture.	*sacuda los muebles.* (sah-**koo**-dah lohs **mweh**-blehs)
wash the clothes.	*lave la ropa.* (**lah**-beh lah **rroh**-pah)
wash the dishes.	*friegue los platos.* (**fryeh**-geh lohs **plah**-tohs)

By putting *no* in front of the verb in the command form, you will ask someone not to do something.

A much easier way to ask someone to do something is as follows:

Please . . .	*Haga el favor de...* (**ah**-gah ehl fah-**bohr** deh...)
clean the kitchen.	*limpiar la cocina.* (leem-**pyahr** lah koh-**see**-nah)
dust the furniture.	*sacudir los muebles.* (sah-koo-**deer** lohs **mweh**-blehs)
wash the clothes.	*lavar la ropa.* (lah-**bahr** lah **rroh**-pah)
wash the dishes.	*fregar los platos.* (freh-**gahr** lohs **plah**-tohs)

Some things used for cleaning the house are:

broom	*la escoba* (lah ehs-**koh**-bah)
brush	*el cepillo* (ehl seh-**pee**-yoh)
bucket	*el cubo* (ehl **koo**-boh)
feather duster	*el plumero* (ehl ploo-**meh**-roh)
garbage bag	*la bolsa de la basura* (lah **bohl**-sah deh lah bah-**soo**-rah)
mop	*el trapeador* (ehl trah-peh-ah-**dohr**)
paper towel	*la toalla de papel* (lah toh-**ah**-yah deh pah-**pehl**)
rag	*el trapo* (ehl **trah**-poh)
scouring pad	*el estropajo* (ehl ehs-troh-**pah**-hoh)
sponge	*la esponja* (lah ehs-**pohn**-hah)
towel	*la toalla* (lah toh-**ah**-yah)
trashcan	*el basurero* (ehl bah-soo-**reh**-roh)
vacuum cleaner	*la aspiradora* (lah ahs-pee-rah-**doh**-rah)

Verbs

to carry	*llevar* (yeh-**bahr**)
to clean	*limpiar* (leem-**pyahr**)
to close	*cerrar (ie)* (seh-**rrahr**)
to disinfect	*desinfectar* (deh-seen-fehk-**tahr**)
to dust	*sacudir el polvo* (sah-koo-**deer** ehl **pohl**-boh)

to lift	*levantar* (leh-bahn-**tahr**)
to mop	*trapear* (trah-peh-**ahr**)
to move	*mover (ue)* (moh-**behr**)
to open	*abrir* (ah-**breer**)
to pick up	*recoger* (rreh-koh-**hehr**)
to put away	*guardar* (gwahr-**dahr**)
to scrub (the floor)	*fregar (ie) (el suelo)* (freh-**gahr** [ehl **sweh**-loh])
to sweep	*barrer* (bah-**rrehr**)
to throw away	*tirar* (tee-**rahr**)
to turn off	*apagar* (ah-pah-**gahr**)
to turn on	*encender (ie)* (ehn-sehn-**dehr**)
to vacuum	*pasar la aspiradora* (pah-**sahr** lah ahs-pee-rah-**doh**-rah)
to wash	*lavar* (lah-**bahr**)
to wash dishes	*fregar (ie) (la vajilla)* (freh-**gahr** [lah bah-**hee**-yah])
to wet	*mojar* (moh-**hahr**)

Many household cleaning products are generally known by their brand names. For example, it is often easier to make yourself understood if you say, "Brillo," "Windex," etc. than by using the generic name in Spanish. So, when in doubt, try using the brand name, and you'll have a pretty good chance of being understood.

In the Laundry Room/Laundromat
En la lavandería
(ehn lah lah-bahn-deh-**ree**-ah)

Whether you do your laundry at home or at a laundromat, any instructions you give to an employee will likely include some of the following:

It's necessary to . . . the clothes.	*Hay que... la ropa.* (**ah**-ee keh... lah **rroh**-pah)
dry	*secar* (seh-**kahr**)
fold	*doblar* (doh-**blahr**)
iron	*planchar* (plahn-**chahr**)

put away	*guardar* (gwahr-**dahr**)
rinse	*enjuagar* (ehn-hwah-**gahr**)
soak	*remojar* (rreh-moh-**hahr**)
wash	*lavar* (lah-**bahr**)
wring	*exprimir* (ehs-pree-**meer**)
You have to . . .	*Tiene que...* (**tyeh**-neh keh...)
choose the temperature.	*escoger la temperatura.* (ehs-koh-**hehr** lah tehm-peh-rah-**too**-rah)
choose the wash time.	*escoger el tiempo del lavado.* (ehs-koh-**hehr** ehl **tyehm**-poh dehl lah-**bah**-doh)
remove a spot.	*quitar una mancha.* (kee-**tahr** oo-nah **mahn**-chah)
separate the colors from the white.	*separar la ropa de color de la blanca.* (seh-pah-**rahr** lah **rroh**-pah deh koh-**lohr** deh lah **blahn**-kah)
sew on a button.	*coser un botón.* (koh-**sehr** oon boh-**tohn**)
wash by hand.	*lavar a mano.* (lah-**bahr** ah **mah**-noh)
wash in cold/warm/hot water.	*lavar con agua fría/tibia/caliente.* (lah-**bahr** kohn **ah**-gwah **free**-ah/**tee**-byah/kah-**lyehn**-teh)
The load is . . .	*La carga es...* (lah **kahr**-gah ehs...)
delicate.	*delicada.* (deh-lee-**kah**-dah)
heavy.	*pesada.* (peh-**sah**-dah)
light.	*ligera.* (lee-**heh**-rah)
medium.	*mediana.* (meh-**dyah**-nah)
The machine is . . .	*La máquina está...* (lah **mah**-kee-nah chs-**tah**...)
empty.	*vacía.* (bah-**see**-ah)
full.	*llena.* (**yeh**-nah)
off.	*apagada.* (ah-pah-**gah**-dah)
on.	*encendida.* (ehn-sehn-**dee**-dah)
open.	*abierta.* (ah-**byehr**-tah)

It's . . .	*Está...* (ehs-**tah**...)
clean.	*limpio.* (**leem**-pyoh)
dirty.	*sucio.* (**soo**-syoh)
dry.	*seco.* (**seh**-koh)
faded.	*descolorido.* (dehs-koh-loh-**ree**-doh)
ruined.	*arruinado.* (ah-rrwee-**nah**-doh)
stained.	*manchado.* (mahn-**chah**-doh)
torn.	*rasgado.* (rrahs-**gah**-doh)
wet.	*mojado.* (moh-**hah**-doh)
worn.	*gastado.* (gahs-**tah**-doh)

If the noun you are describing is feminine in gender, the adjectives mentioned above will end in *-a*.

Different loads of laundry require different products. It is important to be clear when you tell the person who is doing the laundry what to use.

You have to use . . .	*Tiene que usar...* (**tyeh**-neh keh oo-**sahr**...)
bleach.	*el blanqueador.* (ehl blahn-keh-ah-**dohr**)
detergent.	*el detergente.* (ehl deh-tehr-**hehn**-teh)
fabric softener.	*el suavizante.* (ehl swah-bee-**sahn**-teh)
spot remover.	*el quitamanchas.* (ehl kee-tah-**mahn**-chahs)
starch.	*el almidón.* (ehl ahl-mee-**dohn**)

Other laundry necessities:

clothes hanger	*la percha* (lah **pehr**-chah)
clothesline	*la tendedera* (lah tehn-deh-**deh**-rah)
clothespins	*las pinzas* (lahs **peen**-sahs)
dryer	*la secadora* (lah seh-kah-**doh**-rah)
iron	*la plancha* (lah **plahn**-chah)
ironing board	*la tabla de planchar* (lah **tah**-blah deh plahn-**chahr**)

laundry basket   *el cesto de la ropa sucia* (ehl **sehs**-toh
                         deh lah **rroh**-pah **soo**-syah)

washing machine   *la lavadora* (lah lah-bah-**doh**-rah)

If the laundry is done at a laundromat (*la lavandería*) (lah lah-bahn-deh-**ree**-ah), the following will also be helpful to your employee:

You have to put X coins in   *Tiene que poner X monedas en*
the machine.   *la máquina.* (**tyeh**-neh keh poh-**nehr**...
                                 moh-**neh**-dahs ehn lah **mah**-kee-nah)

Don't leave the clothes   *No deje la ropa sin atender.* (noh **deh**-
unattended.   heh lah **rroh**-pah seen ah-tehn-**dehr**)

At the Dry Cleaners
En la tintorería
(ehn lah teen-toh-reh-**ree**-ah)

Some clothing carries the label "dry clean" (*lavar en seco*) (lah-**bahr** ehn **seh**-koh). It is important to point out to your employee which articles need to be taken to the dry cleaners.

Some words you may need are:

dry cleaner   *el tintorero/la tintorera* (ehl teen-toh-
                         reh-roh/lah teen-toh-**reh**-rah)

to dry-clean   *lavar en seco* (lah-**bahr** ehn **seh**-koh)

Mending Clothes
Para remendar la ropa
(**pah**-rah rreh-mehn-**dahr** lah **rroh**-pah)

needle   *la aguja* (lah ah-**goo**-hah)
pin   *el alfiler* (ehl ahl-fee-**lehr**)
scissors   *las tijeras* (lahs tee-**heh**-rahs)
sewing machine   *la máquina de coser* (lah **mah**-kee-nah
                         deh koh-**sehr**)
thread   *el hilo* (ehl **ee**-loh)

For a complete list of clothing and vocabulary dealing with clothing, go to Chapter 10.

In an Apartment Building
En un edificio de apartamentos
(ehn oon eh-dee-**fee**-syoh deh ah-pahr-tah-**mehn**-tohs)

If you happen to live in an apartment building, here is some vocabulary you may want to learn:

apartment	el apartamento (ehl ah-pahr-tah-**mehn**-toh)
elevator	el ascensor (ehl ahs-sehn-**sohr**)
entrance	la entrada (lah ehn-**trah**-dah)
exit	la salida (lah sah-**lee**-dah)
floor/story	el piso (ehl **pee**-soh)
neighborhood	el barrio (ehl **bah**-rryoh)
parking lot	el estacionamiento (ehl ehs-tah-syoh-nah-**myehn**-toh)
rent	el alquiler (ehl ahl-kee-**lehr**)
sidewalk	la acera (lah ah-**seh**-rah)

Some apartment buildings have their own employees for maintenance and management. Some of these people are:

doorman	el portero (ehl pohr-**teh**-roh)
janitor	el conserje (ehl kohn-**sehr**-heh)
superintendent/porter	el conserje (ehl kohn-**sehr**-heh)

Here's some vocabulary to use with your doorman or janitor:

bag/sack	la bolsa (lah **bohl**-sah)
door	la puerta (lah **pwehr**-tah)
mail	la correspondencia (lah koh-rrehs-pohn-**dehn**-syah)
package	el paquete (ehl pah-**keh**-teh)
tip	la propina (lah proh-**pee**-nah)

Verbs

to announce	*anunciar* (ah-noon-**syahr**)
to call	*llamar* (yah-**mahr**)
to carry	*llevar* (yeh-**bahr**)
to close	*cerrar (ie)* (seh-**rrahr**)
to help	*ayudar* (ah-yoo-**dahr**)
to move (residence)	*mudarse* (moo-**dahr**-seh)
to open	*abrir* (ah-**breer**)
to pick up	*recoger* (rreh-koh-**hehr**)
to rent an apartment	*alquilar un apartamento* (ahl-kee-**lahr** oon ah-pahr-tah-**mehn**-toh)
to take out the garbage	*sacar la basura* (sah-**kahr** lah bah-**soo**-rah)

In the Kitchen
En la cocina
(ehn lah koh-**see**-nah)

In many households the family spends a lot of time in the kitchen. It is a place where adults as well as children socialize and feel close to each other while cooking and eating. Before you get down to serious cooking, you'll need some practical vocabulary.

Electrical Appliances in the Kitchen
Los aparatos eléctricos en la cocina
(lohs ah-pah-**rah**-tohs eh-**lehk**-tree-kohs ehn lah koh-**see**-nah)

These appliances will make your tasks easier:

coffee mill	*el molinillo de café* (ehl moh-lee-**nee**-yoh deh kah-**feh**)
dishwasher	*el lavaplatos* (ehl lah-bah-**plah**-tohs)
gas stove	*la cocina* (lah koh-**see**-nah)
grill	*la parrilla* (lah pah-**rree**-yah)
kitchen range	*la estufa/la cocina* (lah ehs-**too**-fah/lah koh-**see**-nah)

45

microwave oven	*el horno a microondas* (ehl **ohr**-noh ah mee-kroh-**ohn**-dahs)
mixer	*la batidora* (lah bah-tee-**doh**-rah)
oven	*el horno* (ehl **ohr**-noh)
range	*el fogón* (ehl foh-**gohn**)
refrigerator	*el refrigerador/la nevera* (ehl rreh-free-heh-rah-**dohr**/lah neh-**beh**-rah)
stove	*la cocina* (lah koh-**see**-nah)
toaster	*la tostadora* (lah tohs-tah-**doh**-rah)

Containers and Utensils
Los envases y los utensilios
(lohs ehn-**bah**-sehs ee lohs oo-tehn-**see**-lyohs)

Here are the different containers, gadgets, and utensils you may need:

aluminium foil	*el papel de aluminio* (ehl pah-**pehl** deh ah-loo-**mee**-nyoh)
apron	*el delantal* (ehl deh-lahn-**tahl**)
basket	*la cesta* (lah **sehs**-tah)
bowl	*el tazón* (ehl tah-**sohn**)
bucket	*el cubo* (ehl **koo**-boh)
can opener	*el abrelatas* (ehl ah-breh-**lah**-tahs)
coffee filter	*el filtro de café* (ehl **feel**-troh deh kah-**feh**)
coffee pot	*la cafetera* (lah kah-feh-**teh**-rah)
colander	*el colador* (ehl koh-lah-**dohr**)
cupboard	*el armario/la alacena* (ehl ahr-**mah**-ryoh/lah ah-lah-**seh**-nah)
cutting board	*la tabla para cortar* (lah **tah**-blah **pah**-rah kohr-**tahr**)
drainboard	*el escurridero* (ehl ehs-koo-rree-**deh**-roh)
frying pan	*la sartén* (lah sahr-**tehn**)
funnel	*el embudo* (ehl ehm-**boo**-doh)
garbage can	*el cubo de basura* (ehl **koo**-boh deh bah-**soo**-rah)

glove	*el guante* (ehl **gwahn**-teh)
jar	*el tarro/el frasco* (ehl **tah**-rroh/ehl **frahs**-koh)
kettle	*la olla para hervir agua* (lah **oh**-yah **pah**-rah ehr-**beer ah**-gwah)
ladle	*el cucharón* (ehl koo-chah-**rohn**)
lid	*la tapa* (lah **tah**-pah)
matches	*los fósforos* (lohs **fohs**-foh-rohs)
pan	*la cazuela/la olla* (lah kah-**sweh**-lah/lah **oh**-yah)
pot	*la cacerola* (lah kah-seh-**roh**-lah)
pressure-cooker	*la olla de presión* (lah **oh**-yah deh preh-**syohn**)
sink (kitchen)	*el fregadero* (ehl freh-gah-**deh**-roh)
skillet	*la sartén* (lah sahr-**tehn**)
strainer	*el colador* (ehl koh-lah-**dohr**)
towel (kitchen)	*la toalla de cocina* (lah toh-**ah**-yah deh koh-**see**-nah)
whisk	*el batidor* (ehl bah-tee-**dohr**)

Meals
Las comidas
(lahs koh-**mee**-dahs)

appetizer	*el entremés* (ehl ehn-treh-**mehs**)
breakfast	*el desayuno* (ehl deh-sah-**yoo**-noh)
dessert	*el postre* (ehl **pohs**-treh)
dinner	*la cena* (lah **seh**-nah)
lunch	*el almuerzo* (ehl ahl-**mwehr**-soh)
snack	*la merienda* (lah meh-**ryehn**-dah)

Verbs

to dine (have dinner)	*cenar* (seh-**nahr**)
to eat breakfast	*desayunar* (deh-sah-yoo-**nahr**)
to eat lunch	*almorzar (ue)* (ahl-mohr-**sahr**)

to fast   *ayunar* (ah-yoo-**nahr**)
to have a snack   *merendar (ie)* (meh-rehn-**dahr**)

Breakfast
El desayuno
(ehl deh-sah-**yoo**-noh)

Since breakfast foods are usually rather specific to that meal, we have listed them separately. Of course, different people have different ideas of what breakfast should be.

Talking About Breakfast
Para hablar sobre el desayuno
(**pah**-rah ah-**blahr soh**-breh ehl deh-sah-**yoo**-noh)

What do you want for breakfast? *¿Qué quieres en el desayuno?* (keh
                                 kyeh-rehs ehn ehl deh-sah-**yoo**-noh)
For breakfast I want . . .   *En el desayuno yo quiero...* (ehn ehl
                                 deh-sah-**yoo**-noh yoh **kyeh**-roh...)

Typical Breakfast Foods
La comida típica del desayuno
(lah koh-**mee**-dah **tee**-pee-kah dehl deh-sah-**yoo**-noh)

bacon   *el tocino* (ehl toh-**see**-noh)
butter   *la mantequilla* (lah mahn-teh-**kee**-yah)
cereal   *el cereal* (ehl seh-reh-**ahl**)
cheese   *el queso* (ehl **keh**-soh)
coffee   *el café* (ehl kah-**feh**)
cookie   *la galleta* (lah gah-**yeh**-tah)
cottage cheese   *el requesón* (ehl rreh-keh-**sohn**)
cracker   *la galleta salada* (lah gah-**yeh**-tah sah-
                                 lah-dah)
cream cheese   *el queso crema* (ehl **keh**-soh **kreh**-mah)
cream   *la crema* (lah **kreh**-mah)
egg   *el huevo* (ehl **weh**-boh)

egg white	*la clara* (lah **klah**-rah)
egg yolk	*la yema* (lah **yeh**-mah)
ham	*el jamón* (ehl hah-**mohn**)
hard-boiled egg	*el huevo duro* (ehl **weh**-boh **doo**-roh)
juice	*el jugo*[1] (ehl **hoo**-goh)
margarine	*la margarina* (lah mahr-gah-**ree**-nah)
milk	*la leche* (lah **leh**-cheh)
oatmeal	*la avena* (lah ah-**beh**-nah)
omelette	*la tortilla*[2] (lah tohr-**tee**-yah)
roll	*el panecillo* (ehl pah-neh-**see**-yoh)
sausage	*la salchicha* (lah sahl-**chee**-chah)
scrambled egg	*el huevo revuelto* (ehl **weh**-boh rreh-**bwehl**-toh)
skim milk	*la leche desnatada* (lah **leh**-cheh dehs-nah-**tah**-dah)
tea	*el té* (ehl teh)
toast	*el pan tostado* (ehl pahn tohs-**tah**-doh)
yogurt	*el yogurt* (ehl yoh-**goor**)

Meats
Las carnes
(lahs **kahr**-nehs)

beef	*la carne de vaca* (lah **kahr**-neh deh **bah**-kah)
chop	*la chuleta* (lah choo-**leh**-tah)
deer	*el ciervo* (ehl **syehr**-boh)
ground beef	*la carne molida* (lah **kahr**-neh moh-**lee**-dah)
lamb	*el cordero* (ehl kohr-**deh**-roh)
meatball	*la albóndiga* (lah ahl-**bohn**-dee-gah)

1. To refer to a particular kind of juice, use *el jugo de...* (ehl **hoo**-goh deh...) + the name of the fruit. A list of fruits appears later in this chapter.
2. Note that the word *tortilla* has different meanings in different countries. In Mexican cuisine, a *tortilla* is a flat pancake made of corn or flour. In the rest of the Spanish-speaking world, a *tortilla* means "omelette." To make the distinction you may want to say "egg omelette" (*la tortilla de huevos*) (lah tohr-**tee**-yah deh **weh**-bohs).

pork	*la carne de cerdo* (lah **kahr**-neh deh **sehr**-doh)
rabbit	*el conejo* (ehl koh-**neh**-hoh)
steak	*el bistec* (ehl bees-**tehk**)
veal	*la ternera* (lah tehr-**neh**-rah)

Poultry
Las aves de corral
(lahs **ah**-behs deh koh-**rrahl**)

chicken	*el pollo* (ehl **poh**-yoh)
duck	*el pato* (ehl **pah**-toh)
hen	*la gallina* (lah gah-**yee**-nah)
turkey	*el pavo* (ehl **pah**-boh)

Shellfish
Los mariscos
(lohs mah-**rees**-kohs)

clam	*la almeja* (lah ahl-**meh**-hah)
crab	*el cangrejo* (ehl kahn-**greh**-hoh)
fish	*el pescado* (ehl pehs-**kah**-doh)
lobster	*la langosta* (lah lahn-**gohs**-tah)
mussel	*el mejillón* (ehl meh-hee-**yohn**)
oyster	*la ostra* (lah **ohs**-trah)
scallop	*la viera* (lah **byeh**-rah)
shrimp	*el camarón* (ehl kah-mah-**rohn**)
squid	*el calamar* (ehl kah-lah-**mahr**)

Fish
Los pescados
(lohs pehs-**kah**-dohs)

anchovy	*la anchoa* (lah ahn-**choh**-ah)
bass	*la perca* (lah **pehr**-kah)

cod	*el bacalao* (ehl bah-kah-**lah**-oh)
flounder	*el lenguado* (ehl lehn-**gwah**-doh)
salmon	*el salmón* (ehl sahl-**mohn**)
sardine	*la sardina* (lah sahr-**dee**-nah)
sole	*el lenguado* (ehl lehn-**gwah**-doh)
trout	*la trucha* (lah **troo**-chah)
tuna	*el atún* (ehl ah-**toon**)

Fruits
Las frutas
(lahs **froo**-tahs)

apple	*la manzana* (lah mahn-**sah**-nah)
apricot	*el albaricoque/el durazno* (ehl ahl-bah-ree-**koh**-keh/ehl doo-**rahs**-noh)
banana	*el plátano* (ehl **plah**-tah-noh)
blackberry	*la mora* (lah **moh**-rah)
blueberry	*el arándano* (ehl ah-**rahn**-dah-noh)
cantaloupe	*el melón* (ehl meh-**lohn**)
cherry	*la cereza* (lah seh-**reh**-sah)
coconut	*el coco* (ehl **koh**-koh)
date	*el dátil* (ehl **dah**-teel)
fig	*el higo* (ehl **ee**-goh)
grape	*la uva* (lah **oo**-bah)
grapefruit	*la toronja* (lah toh-**rohn**-hah)
lemon	*el limón* (ehl lee-**mohn**)
lime	*la lima* (lah **lee**-mah)
melon	*el melón* (ehl meh-**lohn**)
orange	*la naranja* (lah nah-**rahn**-hah)
peach	*el melocotón* (ehl meh-loh-koh-**tohn**)
pear	*la pera* (lah **peh**-rah)
pineapple	*la piña* (lah **pee**-nyah)
plum	*la ciruela* (lah see-**rweh**-lah)
prune	*la ciruela pasa* (lah see-**rweh**-lah **pah**-sah)
raisin	*la pasa* (lah **pah**-sah)

raspberry	*la frambuesa* (lah frahm-**bweh**-sah)
strawberry	*la fresa* (lah **freh**-sah)
tangerine	*la mandarina* (lah mahn-dah-**ree**-nah)
watermelon	*la sandía* (lah sahn-**dee**-ah)

Vegetables
Los vegetales
(lohs beh-heh-**tah**-lehs)

artichoke	*la alcachofa* (lah ahl-kah-**choh**-fah)
asparagus	*el espárrago* (ehl ehs-**pah**-rrah-goh)
bean	*el frijol* (ehl free-**hohl**)
beet	*la remolacha* (lah rreh-moh-**lah**-chah)
broccoli	*el brécol* (ehl **breh**-kohl)
cabbage	*la col/el repollo* (lah kohl/ehl rreh-**poh**-yoh)
carrot	*la zanahoria* (lah sah-nah-**oh**-ryah)
cauliflower	*la coliflor* (lah koh-lee-**flohr**)
celery	*el apio* (ehl **ah**-pyoh)
chickpea	*el garbanzo* (ehl gahr-**bahn**-soh)
chives	*los cebollinos* (lohs seh-boh-**yee**-nohs)
corn	*el maíz* (ehl mah-**ees**)
cucumber	*el pepino* (ehl peh-**pee**-noh)
eggplant	*la berenjena* (lah beh-rehn-**heh**-nah)
garlic	*el ajo* (ehl **ah**-hoh)
green pea	*el guisante* (ehl gee-**sahn**-teh)
leek	*el puerro* (ehl **pweh**-rroh)
lentil	*la lenteja* (lah lehn-**teh**-hah)
lettuce	*la lechuga* (lah leh-**choo**-gah)
mushroom	*la seta/el hongo* (lah **seh**-tah/ehl **ohn**-goh)
onion	*la cebolla* (lah seh-**boh**-yah)
peanut	*el cacahuete/el maní* (ehl kah-kah-**weh**-teh/ehl mah-**nee**)
pepper	*la pimienta* (lah pee-**myehn**-tah)
pine nut	*el piñón* (ehl pee-**nyohn**)

potato	*la papa/la patata* (lah **pah**-pah/lah pah-**tah**-tah)
pumpkin	*la calabaza* (lah kah-lah-**bah**-sah)
radish	*el rábano* (ehl **rrah**-bah-noh)
spinach	*la espinaca* (lah ehs-pee-**nah**-kah)
squash	*la calabaza* (lah kah-lah-**bah**-sah)
tomato	*el tomate* (ehl toh-**mah**-teh)
walnut	*la nuez* (lah nwehs)
yam	*la batata* (lah bah-**tah**-tah)
zucchini	*el calabacín* (ehl kah-lah-bah-**seen**)

Grains
Los granos
(lohs **grah**-nohs)

barley	*la cebada* (lah seh-**bah**-dah)
cornmeal	*la harina de maíz* (lah ah-**ree**-nah deh mah-**ees**)
oats	*la avena* (lah ah-**beh**-nah)
rice	*el arroz* (ehl ah-**rrohs**)

Spices and Ingredients
Las especias y los ingredientes
(lahs ehs-**peh**-syahs ee lohs een-greh-**dyehn**-tehs)

To make sure your food is prepared and seasoned the way you like it, here is a list of spices and ingredients you should learn:

bay leaves	*el laurel* (ehl lah-oo-**rehl**)
breadcrumbs	*el pan rallado* (ehl pahn rrah-**yah**-doh)
broth	*el caldo* (ehl **kahl**-do)
capers	*las alcaparras* (lahs ahl-kah-**pah**-rrahs)
cinnamon	*la canela* (lah kah-**neh**-lah)
clove of garlic	*el diente de ajo* (ehl **dyehn**-teh deh **ah**-hoh)
clove	*el clavo* (ehl **klah**-boh)

flour	*la harina* (lah ah-**ree**-nah)
garlic	*el ajo* (ehl **ah**-hoh)
ginger	*el gengibre* (ehl hehn-**hee**-breh)
mayonnaise	*la mayonesa* (lah mah-yoh-**neh**-sah)
mustard	*la mostaza* (lah mohs-**tah**-sah)
nutmeg	*la nuez moscada* (lah nwehs mohs-**kah**-dah)
oil	*el aceite* (ehl ah-**seh**-ee-teh)
olive oil	*el aceite de oliva* (ehl ah-**seh**-ee-teh deh oh-**lee**-bah)
parsley	*el perejil* (ehl peh-reh-**heel**)
pepper	*la pimienta* (lah pee-**myehn**-tah)
saffron	*el azafrán* (ehl ah-sah-**frahn**)
salt	*la sal* (lah sahl)
sauce	*la salsa* (lah **sahl**-sah)
seasoning	*el condimento* (ehl kohn-dee-**mehn**-toh)
sugar	*el azúcar* (ehl ah-**soo**-kahr)
thyme	*el tomillo* (ehl toh-**mee**-yoh)
vanilla	*la vainilla* (lah bah-ee-**nee**-yah)
vinegar	*el vinagre* (ehl bee-**nah**-greh)
yeast	*la levadura* (lah leh-bah-**doo**-rah)

Drinks
Las bebidas
(lahs beh-**bee**-dahs)

Nonalcoholic Drinks
Las bebidas sin alcohol
(lahs beh-**bee**-dahs seen ahl-**kohl**)

Many nonalcoholic drinks are of course known by their brand names. Here is a list of generic beverages:

cocoa	*el cacao* (ehl kah-**kah**-oh)
coffee	*el café* (ehl kah-**feh**)

juice	*el jugo* (ehl **hoo**-goh)
lemonade	*la limonada* (lah lee-moh-**nah**-dah)
mineral water	*el agua mineral* (ehl **ah**-gwah mee-neh-**rahl**)
punch	*el ponche* (ehl **pohn**-cheh)
soft drink	*el refresco* (ehl rreh-**frehs**-koh)
tea	*el té* (ehl teh)
water	*el agua* (ehl **ah**-gwah)

You may also want to specify how you like your drinks:

cold drink	*la bebida fría* (lah beh-**bee**-dah **free**-ah)
hot drink	*la bebida caliente* (lah beh-**bee**-dah kah-**lyehn**-teh)

Alcoholic Drinks
Las bebidas alcohólicas
(lahs beh-**bee**-dahs ahl-**koh**-lee-kahs)

When requesting an alcoholic drink in Spanish you usually ask for *una copa* (**oo**-nah **koh**-pah) or *un trago* (oon **trah**-goh).

Other terms related to drinks are:

bottle	*la botella* (lah boh-**teh**-yah)
corkscrew	*el sacacorchos* (ehl sah-kah-**kohr**-chohs)
glass (stemmed)	*la copa* (lah **koh**-pah)
glass	*el vaso* (ehl **bah**-soh)
liter	*el litro* (ehl **lee**-troh)
with/without . . .	*con/sin...* (kohn/seen...)
ice	*hielo* (**yeh**-loh)
lemon	*limón* (lee-**mohn**)
olives	*aceitunas* (ah-seh-ee-**too**-nahs)
water	*agua* (**ah**-gwah)

Here are the names of some alcoholic drinks:

beer	*la cerveza* (lah sehr-**beh**-sah)
brandy	*el coñac* (ehl koh-**nyahk**)

champagne	*el champán* (ehl chahm-**pahn**)
cider	*la sidra* (lah **see**-drah)
gin	*la ginebra* (lah hee-**neh**-brah)
light beer	*la cerveza ligera* (lah sehr-**beh**-sah lee-**heh**-rah)
port	*el oporto* (ehl oh-**pohr**-toh)
red wine	*el vino tinto* (ehl **bee**-noh **teen**-toh)
rum	*el ron* (ehl rrohn)
sherry	*el jerez* (ehl heh-**rehs**)
sparkling wine	*el vino espumoso* (ehl **bee**-noh ehs-poo-**moh**-soh)
vermouth	*el vermut* (ehl behr-**moo**)
whisky	*el whisky* (ehl **wees**-kee)
white wine	*el vino blanco* (ehl **bee**-noh **blahn**-koh)

A number of other alcoholic drinks are not listed here because they are known in Spanish by their English names (*el scotch*, *el vodka*, etc.).

Verbs

to drink	*beber* (beh-**behr**)
to mix	*mezclar* (mehs-**klahr**)
to pour	*echar* (eh-**chahr**)
to serve a drink	*servir (i) una copa* (sehr-**beer** **oo**-nah **koh**-pah)

Recipes
Las recetas
(lahs rreh-**seh**-tahs)

If you read a cookbook in Spanish, you'll see that, as in English, the command form of the verb is used to give instructions. Even though the command form is more common, you may also see instructions given in the infinitive. This is a good time to review how to form Spanish commands (Appendix B on pages 198–200). Some of the most common instructions you will need in order to share or to read a recipe in Spanish are on the next pages.

	Infinitive	Command
to add	*añadir* (ah-nyah-**deer**)	*Añada...* (ah-**nyah**-dah...)
to bake	*hornear* (ohr-neh-**ahr**)	*Hornee...* (ohr-neh-eh...)
to beat	*batir* (bah-**teer**)	*Bata...* (**bah**-tah...)
to boil	*hervir (ie)* (ehr-**beer**)	*Hierva...* (**yehr**-bah...)
to brown	*dorar* (doh-**rahr**)	*Dore...* (**doh**-reh...)
to burn	*quemar* (keh-**mahr**)	*Queme...* (**keh**-meh...)
to cook	*cocinar* (koh-see-**nahr**)	*Cocine...* (koh-**see**-neh...)
to cover	*tapar* (tah-**pahr**)	*Tape...* (**tah**-peh...)
to cut	*cortar* (kohr-**tahr**)	*Corte...* (**kohr**-teh...)
to defrost	*descongelar* (dehs-kohn-heh-**lahr**)	*Descongele...* (dehs-kohn-**heh**-leh...)
to fry	*freír (i)* (freh-**eer**)	*Fría...* (**free**-ah...)
to grill	*asar a la parrilla* (ah-**sahr** ah lah pah-**rree**-yah)	*Ase a la parrilla...* (ah-seh ah lah pah-**rree**-yah...)
to heat	*calentar (ie)* (kah-lehn-**tahr**)	*Caliente...* (kah-**lyehn**-teh...)
to insert	*meter* (meh-**tehr**)	*Meta...* (**meh**-tah...)
to measure	*medir (i)* (meh-**deer**)	*Mida...* (**mee**-dah...)
to mix	*mezclar* (mehs-**klahr**)	*Mezcle...* (**mehs**-kleh...)
to peel	*pelar* (peh-**lahr**)	*Pele...* (**peh**-leh...)
to prepare	*preparar* (preh-pah-**rahr**)	*Prepare...* (preh-**pah**-reh...)
to remove	*quitar* (kee-**tahr**)	*Quite...* (**kee**-teh...)
to roast	*asar* (ah-**sahr**)	*Ase...* (**ah**-seh...)
to season	*sazonar* (sah-soh-**nahr**)	*Sazone...* (sah-**soh**-neh...)
to serve	*servir (i)* (sehr-**beer**)	*Sirva...* (**seer**-bah...)
to simmer	*hervir (ie) a fuego lento* (ehr-**beer** ah **fweh**-goh **lehn**-toh)	*Hierva a fuego lento.* (**yehr**-bah ah **fweh**-goh **lehn**-toh)
to spill	*derramar* (deh-rrah-**mahr**)	*Derrame...* (deh-**rrah**-meh...)
to sprinkle	*rociar* (rroh-**syahr**)	*Rocíe...* (rroh-**see**-eh...)
to stir	*revolver (ue)* (rreh-bohl-**behr**)	*Revuelva...* (rreh-**bwehl**-bah...)
to take out	*sacar* (sah-**kahr**)	*Saque...* (**sah**-keh...)
to uncover	*destapar* (dehs-tah-**pahr**)	*Destape...* (dehs-**tah**-peh...)

Measuring Quantities
Para medir cantidades
(**pah**-rah meh-**deer** kahn-tee-**dah**-dehs)

Knowing how to express quantities is crucial to any cooking project.

a bottle	*una botella* (**oo**-nah boh-**teh**-yah)
a bunch	*un atado/un manojo* (oon ah-**tah**-doh/oon mah-**noh**-hoh)
a cup	*una taza* (**oo**-nah **tah**-sah)
a dozen	*una docena* (**oo**-nah doh-**seh**-nah)
a gallon	*un galón* (oon gah-**lohn**)
a gram	*un gramo* (oon **grah**-moh)
a kilogram	*un kilogramo* (oon kee-loh-**grah**-moh)
a liter	*un litro* (oon **lee**-troh)
a pair	*un par* (oon pahr)
a piece	*un pedazo* (oon peh-**dah**-soh)
a pinch	*una pizca* (**oo**-nah **pees**-kah)
a pint	*una pinta* (**oo**-nah **peen**-tah)
a pound	*una libra* (**oo**-nah **lee**-brah)
a quart (of)	*un cuarto (de)* (oon **kwahr**-toh [deh])
a tablespoonful	*una cucharada* (**oo**-nah koo-chah-**rah**-dah)
a teaspoonful	*una cucharadita* (**oo**-nah koo-chah-rah-**dee**-tah)
an ounce	*una onza* (**oo**-nah **ohn**-sah)
half (of)	*la mitad (de)* (lah mee-**tahd** [deh])
measuring cup	*la taza de medir* (lah **tah**-sah deh meh-**deer**)
measuring spoon	*la cuchara de medir* (lah koo-**chah**-rah deh meh-**deer**)

To express "a half," "a fourth," etc., consult Chapter 14 on pages 157–58.

In the Dining Room
En el comedor
(ehn ehl koh-meh-**dohr**)

bowl	*el tazón/el sopero* (ehl tah-**sohn**/ehl soh-**peh**-roh)
cabinet	*la vitrina* (lah bee-**tree**-nah)
chair	*la silla* (lah **see**-yah)
cup	*la taza* (lah **tah**-sah)
fork	*el tenedor* (ehl teh-neh-**dohr**)
glass	*el vaso* (ehl **bah**-soh)
knife	*el cuchillo* (ehl koo-**chee**-yoh)
leftovers	*las sobras* (lahs **soh**-brahs)
napkin	*la servilleta* (lah sehr-bee-**yeh**-tah)
peppermill	*el molinillo de pimienta* (ehl moh-lee-**nee**-yoh deh pee-**myehn**-tah)
plate	*el plato* (ehl **plah**-toh)
platter	*la fuente* (lah **fwehn**-teh)
salt shaker	*el salero* (ehl sah-**leh**-roh)
saucer	*el platillo* (ehl plah-**tee**-yoh)
set of dishes	*la vajilla* (lah bah-**hee**-yah)
silverware	*la vajilla de plata* (lah bah-**hee**-yah deh **plah**-tah)
spoon	*la cuchara* (lah koo-**chah**-rah)
table	*la mesa* (lah **meh**-sah)
tablecloth	*el mantel* (ehl mahn-**tehl**)
tablespoon	*la cuchara* (lah koo-**chah**-rah)
teaspoon	*la cucharita* (lah koo-chah-**ree**-tah)
tray	*la bandeja* (lah bahn-**deh**-hah)
wine glass	*la copa* (lah **koh**-pah)

Verbs

to chew	*masticar* (mahs-tee-**kahr**)
to clear the table	*quitar la mesa* (kee-**tahr** lah **meh**-sah)
to savor	*saborear* (sah-boh-reh-**ahr**)
to set the table	*poner la mesa* (poh-**nehr** lah **meh**-sah)
to try/taste	*probar (ue)* (proh-**bahr**)

To Express Your Opinion About Food
Para expresar su opinión sobre la comida
(**pah**-rah ehs-preh-**sahr** soo oh-pee-**nyohn soh**-breh lah koh-**mee**-dah)

The following adjectives can be used with the verb *estar* (ehs-**tahr**) (meaning "to be") to express your opinion about food. Again, you may want to review the agreement of adjective endings in Appendix B on pages 178–79 as well as the various uses of the verbs *ser* (sehr) and *estar* (ehs-**tahr**), each meaning "to be," on pages 188–90.

burned	*quemado* (keh-**mah**-doh)
delicious	*delicioso/rico* (deh-lee-**syoh**-soh/**rree**-koh)
dry	*seco* (**seh**-koh)
fresh	*fresco* (**frehs**-koh)
hard/tough	*duro* (**doo**-roh)
juicy	*jugoso* (hoo-**goh**-soh)
lukewarm	*tibio* (**tee**-byoh)
raw	*crudo* (**kroo**-doh)
rotten	*podrido* (poh-**dree**-doh)
salty	*salado* (sah-**lah**-doh)
spicy	*picante* (pee-**kahn**-teh)
spoiled	*podrido* (poh-**dree**-doh)
sweet	*dulce* (**dool**-seh)
tasty	*sabroso* (sah-**broh**-soh)
tender	*tierno* (**tyehr**-noh)

Read the following sentences:

It is bitter.	*Está amargo.* (ehs-**tah** ah-**mahr**-goh)
It is sweet.	*Está dulce.* (ehs-**tah dool**-seh)

Now, if you were to replace *está* (ehs-**tah**) with *es* (ehs), you will be saying something quite different.

When you use *está* (ehs-**tah**), you are saying that the item in front of you is bitter or sweet, at this moment. If you use *ser* (sehr) you are describing an inherent characteristic of the item.

For example:

Sugar is sweet.	*El azúcar es dulce.* (ehl ah-**soo**-kahr ehs **dool**-seh)
The coffee is sweet.	*El café está dulce.* (ehl kah-**feh** ehs-**tah** **dool**-seh)

In the latter case, *está* (ehs-**tah**) refers to that particular cup of coffee, not to "coffee in general."

Use the following question to ask someone how he or she likes the food prepared. The answer to the question will express that person's wishes.

How do you like your food?	*¿Cómo te gusta la comida?* (**koh**-moh teh **goos**-tah lah koh-**mee**-dah)

You can substitute *la comida* (lah koh-**mee**-dah) in the example above with the name of any single food item.

How do you like the meat?	*¿Cómo te gusta la carne?* (**koh**-moh teh **goos**-tah lah **kahr**-neh)
I like it breaded.	*Me gusta empanada.* (meh **goos**-tah ehm-pah-**nah**-dah)

Now, what if the food you are asking about is in the plural form?

How do you like the carrots?	*¿Cómo te gustan las zanahorias?* (**koh**-moh teh **goos**-tahn lahs sah-nah-**oh**-ryahs)
I like them boiled.	*Me gustan hervidas.* (meh **goos**-tahn ehr-**bee**-dahs)

Again, when talking about foods or other items in the plural, the only thing you have to change is *gusta* (**goos**-tah) to *gustan* (**goos**-tahn).

Here are some other ways to have your food prepared. Note that we show these adjectives only in the masculine form. If you are describing feminine or plural nouns you will need to change the adjective endings. Consult Appendix B on pages 178–79 for the agreement of adjectives.

baked	*asado al horno* (ah-**sah**-doh ahl **ohr**-noh)
boiled	*hervido* (ehr-**bee**-doh)

breaded	*empanado* (ehm-pah-**nah**-doh)
fat-free	*sin grasa* (seen **grah**-sah)
fried	*frito* (**free**-toh)
golden brown	*dorado* (doh-**rah**-doh)
grilled	*a la parrilla* (ah lah pah-**rree**-yah)
kosher	*autorizado por la ley judía* (ah-oo-toh-ree-**sah**-doh pohr lah **leh**-ee hoo-**dee**-ah)
organic	*orgánico* (ohr-**gah**-nee-koh)
roasted	*asado* (ah-**sah**-doh)
stewed	*guisado* (gee-**sah**-doh)
stuffed	*relleno* (rreh-**yeh**-noh)
sugar-free	*sin azúcar* (seen ah-**soo**-kahr)
toasted	*tostado* (tohs-**tah**-doh)
vegetarian	*vegetariano* (beh-heh-tah-**ryah**-noh)
well-done	*bien cocinado* (byehn koh-see-**nah**-doh)
well-seasoned	*bien sazonado* (byehn sah-soh-**nah**-doh)

You can study the verb *gustar* (to like) in greater detail in Appendix B on pages 191–92.

In the Garden and on the Patio
En el jardín y en el patio
(ehn ehl hahr-**deen** ee ehn ehl **pah**-tyoh)

Flowers and Plants
Las flores y las plantas
(lahs **floh**-rehs ee lahs **plahn**-tahs)

azalea	*la azalea* (lah ah-sah-**leh**-ah)
carnation	*el clavel* (ehl klah-**behl**)
chrysanthemum	*el crisantemo* (ehl kree-sahn-**teh**-moh)
crocus	*el azafrán* (ehl ah-sah-**frahn**)
daffodil	*el narciso* (ehl nahr-**see**-soh)
dahlia	*la dalia* (lah **dah**-lyah)
daisy	*la margarita* (lah mahr-gah-**ree**-tah)
dandelion	*el diente de león* (ehl **dyehn**-teh deh leh-**ohn**)
fern	*el helecho* (ehl eh-**leh**-choh)
geranium	*el geranio* (ehl heh-**rah**-nyoh)
gladiolus	*el gladiolo* (ehl glah-**dyoh**-loh)
heather	*el brezo* (ehl **breh**-soh)
honeysuckle	*la madreselva* (lah mah-dreh-**sehl**-bah)
hyacinth	*el jacinto* (ehl hah-**seen**-toh)
hydrangea	*la hortensia* (lah ohr-**tehn**-syah)
iris	*el lirio* (ehl **lee**-ryoh)

ivy	*la hiedra* (lah **yeh**-drah)
jasmine	*el jazmín* (ehl hahs-**meen**)
lavender	*el espliego* (ehl ehs-**plyeh**-goh)
lilac	*la lila* (lah **lee**-lah)
lily	*el lirio* (ehl **lee**-ryoh)
magnolia	*la magnolia* (lah mahg-**noh**-lyah)
marigold	*la maravilla* (lah mah-rah-**bee**-yah)
narcissus	*el narciso* (ehl nahr-**see**-soh)
oleander	*la adelfa* (lah ah-**dehl**-fah)
orchid	*la orquídea* (lah ohr-**kee**-deh-ah)
pansy	*el pensamiento* (ehl pehn-sah-**myehn**-toh)
peony	*la peonía* (lah peh-oh-**nee**-ah)
poppy	*la amapola* (lah ah-mah-**poh**-lah)
rhododendron	*el rododendro* (ehl rroh-doh-**dehn**-droh)
rose	*la rosa* (lah **rroh**-sah)
sunflower	*el girasol* (ehl hee-rah-**sohl**)
tulip	*el tulipán* (ehl too-lee-**pahn**)
violet	*la violeta* (lah byoh-**leh**-tah)

Trees
Los árboles
(lohs **ahr**-boh-lehs)

acacia	*la acacia* (lah ah-**kah**-syah)
birch	*el abedul* (ehl ah-beh-**dool**)
cedar	*el cedro* (ehl **seh**-droh)
cypress	*el ciprés* (ehl see-**prehs**)
ebony	*el ébano* (ehl **eh**-bah-noh)
elm	*el olmo* (ehl **ohl**-moh)
eucalyptus	*el eucalipto* (ehl eh-oo-kah-**leep**-toh)
fir	*el pino noruego* (ehl **pee**-noh noh-**rweh**-goh)
hemlock	*el abeto del Canadá* (ehl ah-**beh**-toh dehl kah-nah-**dah**)
mahogany	*la caoba* (lah kah-**oh**-bah)
maple	*el arce* (ehl **ahr**-seh)

oak	*el roble/la encina* (ehl **rroh**-bleh/lah ehn-**see**-nah)
palm	*la palmera* (lah pahl-**meh**-rah)
pine	*el pino* (ehl **pee**-noh)
poplar	*el álamo/el chopo* (ehl **ah**-lah-moh/ehl **choh**-poh)
redwood	*la secoya* (lah seh-**koh**-yah)
spruce	*el abeto* (ehl ah-**beh**-toh)
willow	*el sauce* (ehl **sah**-oo-seh)
weeping willow	*el sauce llorón* (ehl sah-**oo**-seh yoh-**rohn**)

Taking Care of the Garden
El cuidado del jardín
(ehl kwee-**dah**-doh dehl hahr-**deen**)

Taking care of the garden—especially the flowers—makes your home a welcoming place. The following lists will be helpful whether you have a big garden around your house or a flower box on your windowsill.

annuals	*las anuales* (lahs ah-**nwah**-lehs)
bouquet	*el ramo* (ehl **rrah**-moh)
bud	*el capullo* (ehl kah-**poo**-yoh)
bulb	*el bulbo* (ehl **bool**-boh)
bunch	*el manojo* (ehl mah-**noh**-hoh)
clipping	*el recorte* (ehl rreh-**kohr**-teh)
flower bed	*el cantero* (ehl kahn-**teh**-roh)
flowerpot	*la maceta/el tiesto* (lah mah-**seh**-tah/ehl **tyehs**-toh)
grass	*la hierba* (lah **yehr**-bah)
hanging basket	*la canasta colgada* (lah kah-**nahs**-tah kohl-**gah**-dah)
perennials	*las perennes* (lahs peh-**rehn**-nehs)
plant	*la planta* (lah **plahn**-tah)
pot	*la maceta* (lah mah-**seh**-tah)
root	*la raíz* (lah rrah-**ees**)
scissors	*las tijeras* (lahs tee-**heh**-rahs)
seed	*la semilla* (lah seh-**mee**-yah)

soil	*la tierra* (lah **tyeh**-rrah)
vase	*el florero* (ehl floh-**reh**-roh)
watering can	*la regadera* (lah rreh-gah-**deh**-rah)
weed	*la hierba* (lah **yehr**-bah)

The following list will prove very useful when you need to describe the state of your flowers and plants. Use the verb *estar* (ehs-**tahr**) and don't forget to change the ending of the adjective depending on what you are describing.

alive	*vivo* (**bee**-boh)
dead	*muerto* (**mwehr**-toh)
dry	*seco* (**seh**-koh)
wet	*mojado* (moh-**hah**-doh)
withered	*marchito* (mahr-**chee**-toh)

For example:

The flowers are withered.	*Las flores están marchitas.* (lahs floh-**rehs** ehs-**tahn** mahr-**chee**-tahs)

Now we'll move on to the rest of the yard. Let's begin with the trees and the terms related to taking care of them.

bark	*la corteza* (lah kohr-**teh**-sah)
branch	*la rama* (lah **rrah**-mah)
bush	*el arbusto* (ehl ahr-**boos**-toh)
leaf	*la hoja* (lah **oh**-hah)
shrub	*el arbusto* (ehl ahr-**boos**-toh)

To talk with your Spanish-speaking gardener, you'll need a more expanded vocabulary that deals with tools and garden materials. The following list will help:

blower/leaf blower	*la sopladora* (lah soh-plah-**doh**-rah)
broom	*la escoba* (lah ehs-**koh**-bah)
compost	*el abono* (ehl ah-**boh**-noh)
container	*el recipiente* (ehl rreh-see-**pyehn**-teh)
dump	*el basurero* (ehl bah-soo-**reh**-roh)
fertilizer	*el abono* (ehl ah-**boh**-noh)
garbage	*la basura* (lah bah-**soo**-rah)

gas chainsaw	*el serrucho de gas* (ehl seh-**rroo**-choh deh gahs)
glove	*el guante* (ehl **gwahn**-teh)
greenhouse	*el invernadero* (ehl een-behr-nah-**deh**-roh)
hole	*el hoyo* (ehl **oh**-yoh)
hose	*la manguera* (lah mahn-**geh**-rah)
lawnmower	*el cortacésped* (ehl kohr-tah-**sehs**-pehd)
pick (tool)	*el pico* (ehl **pee**-koh)
pitchfork	*la horca* (lah **ohr**-kah)
pruner	*la podadera* (lah poh-dah-**deh**-rah)
push broom	*el cepillo* (ehl seh-**pee**-yoh)
rake	*el rastrillo* (ehl rrahs-**tree**-yoh)
rock	*la roca* (lah **rroh**-kah)
rototiller	*el rototiller* (ehl rroh-toh-**tee**-lehr)
shovel	*la pala* (lah **pah**-lah)
stone	*la piedra* (lah **pyeh**-drah)
trash can	*el basurero* (ehl bah-soo-**reh**-roh)
wheelbarrow	*la carretilla* (lah kah-rreh-**tee**-yah)

A garden becomes even more welcoming with a few amenities.

bench	*el banco* (ehl **bahn**-koh)
folding chair	*la silla plegable* (lah **see**-yah pleh-**gah**-bleh)
fountain	*la fuente* (lah **fwehn**-teh)
hammock	*la hamaca* (lah ah-**mah**-kah)
pond	*la charca/el estanque* (lah **chahr**-kah/ehl ehs-**tahn**-keh)
shade	*la sombra* (lah **sohm**-brah)
sun hat	*el sombrero* (ehl sohm-**breh**-roh)
swimming pool	*la piscina* (lah pee-**see**-nah)
swing	*el columpio* (ehl koh-**loom**-pyoh)
table	*la mesa* (lah **meh**-sah)
umbrella	*la sombrilla* (lah sohm-**bree**-yah)

Verbs

to add	*añadir* (ah-nyah-**deer**)
to blow	*soplar* (soh-**plahr**)
to bring	*traer* (trah-**ehr**)
to brush	*cepillar* (seh-pee-**yahr**)

to clean	*limpiar* (leem-**pyahr**)
to cut	*cortar* (kohr-**tahr**)
to dig	*excavar* (ehs-kah-**bahr**)
to grow (cultivate)	*cultivar* (kool-tee-**bahr**)
to grow (in size)	*crecer* (kreh-**sehr**)
to load	*cargar* (kahr-**gahr**)
to measure	*medir (i)* (meh-**deer**)
to mix	*mezclar* (mehs-**klahr**)
to move	*mover (ue)* (moh-**behr**)
to plant	*plantar/sembrar (ie)* (plahn-**tahr**/sehm-**brahr**)
to prepare	*preparar* (preh-pah-**rahr**)
to prune	*podar* (poh-**dahr**)
to pull out	*arrancar* (ah-rrahn-**kahr**)
to rake	*rastrillar* (rrahs-tree-**yahr**)
to spray	*rociar* (rroh-**syahr**)
to sweep	*barrer* (bah-**rrehr**)
to take out	*sacar* (sah-**kahr**)
to unload	*descargar* (dehs-kahr-**gahr**)
to water	*regar (ie)* (rreh-**gahr**)

Taking Care of the Pool
El cuidado de la piscina
(ehl kwee-**dah**-doh deh lah pee-**see**-nah)

Let's not forget the swimming pool (*la piscina* [lah pee-**see**-nah]) and the fact that it requires special attention. It must be cleaned regularly and must always meet your town's ordinances.

bleach	*la lejía* (lah leh-**hee**-ah)
brush	*el cepillo* (ehl seh-**pee**-yoh)
chlorine	*el cloro* (ehl **kloh**-roh)
cover	*la cubierta* (lah koo-**byehr**-tah)
crack	*la grieta* (lah **gryeh**-tah)
diving board	*el trampolín* (ehl trahm-poh-**leen**)
drain	*el desagüe* (ehl deh-**sah**-gweh)
fence	*la cerca* (lah **sehr**-kah)
filter	*el filtro* (ehl **feel**-troh)

heater	*el calentador* (ehl kah-lehn-tah-**dohr**)
ladder	*la escalera* (lah ehs-kah-**leh**-rah)
net	*la red* (lah rrehd)
pump	*la bomba* (lah **bohm**-bah)
thermometer	*el termómetro* (ehl tehr-**moh**-meh-troh)
tile	*el azulejo* (ehl ah-soo-**leh**-hoh)
vacuum	*la aspiradora* (lah ahs-pee-rah-**doh**-rah)

Pets
Los animales domésticos
(lohs ah-nee-**mah**-lehs doh-**mehs**-tee-kohs)

Pets are often an important part of the household. They add joy to a family's leisure time, but they also require a lot of care, attention, and love. Here are some useful words and expressions for dealing with pets:

bird	*el pájaro* (ehl **pah**-hah-roh)
cat	*el gato* (ehl **gah**-toh)
dog	*el perro* (ehl **peh**-rroh)
fish	*el pez/los peces* (ehl pehs/lohs **peh**-sehs)
frog	*la rana* (lah **rrah**-nah)
goldfish	*el pez dorado* (ehl pehs doh-**rah**-doh)
guinea pig	*el cuy* (ehl kwee)
hamster	*el hámster* (ehl **ahms**-tehr)
parrot	*la cotorra* (lah koh-**toh**-rrah)
puppy	*el perrito* (ehl peh-**rree**-toh)
rabbit	*el conejo* (ehl koh-**neh**-hoh)
turtle	*la tortuga* (lah tohr-**too**-gah)

Parts of an Animal's Body
Las partes del cuerpo de un animal
(lahs **pahr**-tehs dehl **kwehr**-poh deh oon ah-nee-**mahl**)

beak	*el pico* (ehl **pee**-koh)
claws	*las garras* (lahs **gah**-rrahs)
fangs	*los colmillos* (lohs kohl-**mee**-yohs)

feathers	*las plumas* (lahs **ploo**-mahs)
fur	*la piel* (lah pyehl)
legs	*las patas* (lahs **pah**-tahs)
paws	*las patas* (lahs **pah**-tahs)
tail	*la cola* (lah **koh**-lah)
teeth	*los dientes* (lohs **dyehn**-tehs)
wings	*las alas* (lahs **ah**-lahs)

To talk about what your animals like to do, use the following:

He/She/It likes . . .	*Le gusta...* (leh **goos**-tah...)
to bark.	*ladrar.* (lah-**drahr**)
to bite.	*morder (ue).* (mohr-**dehr**)
to climb.	*trepar.* (treh-**pahr**)
to do tricks.	*hacer trucos.* (ah-**sehr troo**-kohs)
to hide.	*esconderse.* (ehs-kohn-**dehr**-seh)
to run around.	*corretear.* (koh-rreh-teh-**ahr**)
to scratch.	*rascarse.* (rrahs-**kahr**-seh)
to scratch (the furniture).	*arañar (los muebles).* (ah-rah-**nyahr** [lohs **mweh**-blehs])
to sing.	*cantar.* (kahn-**tahr**)
to sleep.	*dormir (ue).* (dohr-**meer**)

Caring for Pets
El cuidado de los animales domésticos
(ehl kwee-**dah**-doh deh lohs ah-nee-**mah**-lehs doh-**mehs**-tee-kohs)

They live in a(n) . . .	*Viven en una...* (**bee**-behn ehn una...)
aquarium.	*pecera.* (peh-**seh**-rah)
box.	*caja.* (**kah**-hah)
cage.	*jaula.* (**ha**-oo-lah)
doghouse.	*casa de perro.* (**kah**-sah deh **peh**-rroh)
fishbowl.	*pecera.* (peh-**seh**-rah)
They live in . . .	*Viven en...* (**bee**-behn ehn...)
the apartment.	*el apartamento.* (ehl ah-pahr-tah-**mehn**-toh)
the house.	*la casa.* (lah **kah**-sah)

the yard.	*el patio.* (ehl **pah**-tyoh)
the stable.	*el establo.* (ehl ehs-**tah**-bloh)
They eat . . .	*Comen...* (**koh**-mehn...)
birdseed.	*semillas.* (seh-**mee**-yahs)
cat food.	*comida para gatos.* (koh-**mee**-dah **pah**-rah **gah**-tohs)
dog food.	*comida para perros.* (koh-**mee**-dah **pah**-rah **peh**-rrohs)
fish food.	*comida para peces.* (koh-**mee**-dah **pah**-rah **peh**-sehs)

Verbs

to bathe	*bañar* (bah-**nyahr**)
to brush	*cepillar* (seh-pee-**yahr**)
to feed	*dar de comer* (dahr deh koh-**mehr**)
to give water	*dar de beber* (dahr deh beh-**behr**)
to take care of	*cuidar de* (kwee-**dahr** deh)
to walk	*sacar a pasear* (sah-**kahr** ah pah-seh-**ahr**)

Some other words and expressions that will come in handy in caring for pets are:

His/Her name is . . .	*Se llama...* (seh **yah**-mah...)
He/She belongs to . . .	*Es de...* (ehs deh...)
He/She is X years old.	*Tiene X años.* (**tyeh**-neh... **ah**-nyohs)
He/She is . . .	*Es...* (ehs...)
friendly.	*amistoso.* (ah-mees-**toh**-soh)
healthy.	*saludable.* (sah-loo-**dah**-bleh)
male/female.	*macho/hembra.* (**mah**-choh/**ehm**-brah)
He/She is . . .	*Está...* (ehs-**tah**...)
sick.	*enfermo.* (ehn-**fehr**-moh)
spoiled.	*malcriado.* (mahl-**kryah**-doh)
trained.	*entrenado.* (ehn-treh-**nah**-doh)
He/She needs a . . .	*Necesita...* (neh-seh-**see**-tah...)
collar.	*un collar.* (oon koh-**yahr**)
leash.	*una correa.* (**oo**-nah koh-**rreh**-ah)
shot.	*una inyección/una vacuna.* (**oo**-nah een-yehk-**syohn**/**oo**-nah bah-**koo**-nah)

He/She needs to go to the . . .	*Necesita ir al...* (neh-seh-**see**-tah eer ahl...)
park.	*parque.* (**pahr**-keh)
veterinarian.	*veterinario.* (beh-teh-ree-**nah**-ryoh)

Farm Animals
Los animales en la finca
(lohs ah-nee-**mah**-lehs ehn lah **feen**-kah)

Farm animals are sometimes treated almost like pets. Here is a list of typical farm animals:

cow	*la vaca* (lah **bah**-kah)
donkey	*el burro* (ehl **boo**-rroh)
duck	*el pato* (ehl **pah**-toh)
goat	*la cabra* (lah **kah**-brah)
hen	*la gallina* (lah gah-**yee**-nah)
horse	*el caballo* (ehl kah-**bah**-yoh)
lamb	*la oveja* (lah oh-**beh**-hah)
mare	*la yegua* (lah **yeh**-gwah)
pig	*el cerdo* (ehl **sehr**-doh)
rooster	*el gallo* (ehl **gah**-yoh)

Fixing the House
Para reparar la casa
(**pah**-rah rreh-pah-**rahr** lah **kah**-sah)

Trades
Los oficios
(lohs oh-**fee**-syohs)

For home maintenence and repair you will deal with a number of different tradespeople. First, let's begin with a list of the occupations that involve fixing or working in and around the house:

bricklayer	*el/la albañil* (ehl/lah ahl-bah-**nyeel**)
carpenter	*el carpintero/la carpintera* (ehl kahr-peen-**teh**-roh/lah kahr-peen-**teh**-rah)
chimney sweep	*el deshollinador/la deshollinadora* (ehl dehs-oh-yee-nah-**dohr**/lah dehs-oh-yee-nah-**doh**-rah)
contractor	*el/la contratista* (ehl/lah kohn-trah-**tees**-tah)
electrician	*el/la electricista* (ehl/lah eh-lehk-tree-**sees**-tah)

exterminator	*el fumigador/la fumigadora* (ehl foo-mee-gah-**dohr**/lah foo-mee-gah-**doh**-rah)
gardener	*el jardinero/la jardinera* (ehl hahr-dee-**neh**-roh/lah hahr-dee-**neh**-rah)
helper	*el/la ayudante* (ehl/lah ah-yoo-**dahn**-teh)
laborer	*el obrero/la obrera* (ehl oh-**breh**-roh/lah oh-**breh**-rah)
locksmith	*el cerrajero/la cerrajera* (ehl seh-rrah-**heh**-roh/lah seh-rrah-**heh**-rah)
painter	*el pintor/la pintora* (ehl peen-**tohr**/lah peen-**toh**-rah)
plumber	*el plomero/la plomera* (ehl ploh-**meh**-roh/lah ploh-**meh**-rah)

In Spanish you may find that some occupations do not have a particular title. So, it may be easier at times to ask for the person who fixes the roof, *la persona que arregla el techo* (lah pehr-**soh**-nah keh ah-**rreh**-glah ehl **teh**-choh), etc.

Explaining Problems
Para explicar los problemas
(**pah**-rah ehs-plee-**kahr** lohs proh-**bleh**-mahs)

Things do not always go the way we expect. All too often, gadgets and appliances in the house break down or do not work properly. It is important to be able to explain the problems as clearly as possible. These phrases should help you to do so:

I have a problem with . . .	*Tengo un problema con...* (**tehn**-goh oon proh-**bleh**-mah kohn...)
It is not working.	*No funciona.* (noh foon-**syoh**-nah)
It is broken.	*Está roto./Se rompió.* (ehs-**tah rroh**-toh/seh rrohm-**pyoh**)
It cracked.	*Se quebró.* (seh keh-**broh**)
It split (up/into two).	*Se partió.* (seh pahr-**tyoh**)

It is loose.	*Está flojo.* (ehs-**tah floh**-hoh)
It is clogged.	*Está atascado.* (ehs-**tah** ah-tahs-**kah**-doh)
Can you come immediately?	*¿Puede venir inmediatamente?* (**pweh**-deh beh-**neer** een-meh-**dyah**-tah-mehn-teh)
My address is . . .	*Mi dirección es...* (mee dee-rehk-**syohn** ehs...)

To describe where a problem exists, you need to learn the following expressions:

Where is the problem?	*¿Dónde está el problema?* (**dohn**-deh ehs-**tah** ehl proh-**bleh**-mah)
The problem seems to be in the/on the . . .	*El problema parece estar en...* (ehl proh-**bleh**-mah pah-**reh**-seh ehs-**tahr** ehn...)
back/bottom.	*el fondo.* (ehl **fohn**-doh)
corner (inside).	*el rincón.* (ehl rreen-**kohn**)
corner (outside).	*la esquina.* (lah ehs-**kee**-nah)
edge.	*el borde.* (ehl **bohr**-deh)
end.	*la punta.* (lah **poon**-tah)
front.	*el frente.* (ehl **frehn**-teh)
middle.	*el medio.* (ehl **meh**-dyoh)
surface.	*la superficie.* (lah soo-pehr-**fee**-syeh)

Here are some of the household devices that may need to be repaired from time to time:

fan	*el ventilador* (ehl behn-tee-lah-**dohr**)
garage door	*la puerta del garage* (lah **pwehr**-tah dehl gah-**rah**-heh)
heater	*el calentador* (ehl kah-lehn-tah-**dohr**)
security system	*el sistema de seguridad* (ehl sees-**teh**-mah deh seh-goo-ree-**dahd**)

Take some time to review the vocabulary in Chapter 3, "The House." This will help you express yourself when you explain what needs to be repaired.

Finalizing the Contract
Para finalizar el contrato
(**pah**-rah fee-nah-lee-**sahr** ehl kohn-**trah**-toh)

Some questions you may ask when finalizing a contract involve the price
and the estimated time it will take to finish the job. As you know, these are
some of the most important aspects that need to be discussed before work
begins.

Can you give me an estimate in writing?	*¿Puede darme un presupuesto por escrito?* (**pweh**-deh **dahr**-meh oon preh-soo-**pwehs**-toh pohr ehs-**kree**-toh)
How much is it going to cost me?	*¿Cuánto me va a costar?* (**kwahn**-toh meh bah ah kohs-**tahr**)
Do I have to sign a contract?	*¿Tengo que firmar un contrato?* (**tehn**-goh keh feer-**mahr** oon kohn-**trah**-toh)
It is too expensive.	*Es demasiado caro.* (ehs deh-mah-**syah**-doh **kah**-roh)
Can we negotiate the price?	*¿Podemos negociar el precio?* (poh-**deh**-mohs neh-goh-**syahr** ehl **preh**-syoh)
I need to discuss it with my husband/wife.	*Necesito discutirlo con mi esposo/esposa.* (neh-seh-**see**-toh dees-koo-**teer**-loh kohn mee ehs-**poh**-soh/ehs-**poh**-sah)
When can you start?	*¿Cuándo puede empezar?* (**kwahn**-doh **pweh**-deh ehm-peh-**sahr**)
How long is it going to take to finish the job?	*¿Cuánto tiempo va a tardar en terminar el trabajo?* (**kwahn**-toh **tyehm**-poh bah ah tahr-**dahr** ehn tehr-mee-**nahr** ehl trah-**bah**-hoh)
Can you finish the work by . . . ?	*¿Puede terminar el trabajo para el...?* (**pweh**-deh tehr-mee-**nahr** ehl trah-**bah**-hoh **pah**-rah ehl...)
Do you have insurance?	*¿Tiene Ud. seguro?* (**tyeh**-neh oos-**tehd** seh-**goo**-roh)

Can I pay you cash/with a check/with a credit card?	*¿Puedo pagarle en efectivo/con un cheque/con una tarjeta de crédito?* (**pweh**-doh pah-**gahr**-leh ehn eh-fehk-**tee**-boh/kohn oon **cheh**-keh/kohn **oo**-nah tahr-**heh**-tah deh **kreh**-dee-toh)
Do you guarantee your work?	*¿Garantiza Ud. el trabajo?* (gah-rahn-**tee**-sah oos-**tehd** ehl trah-**bah**-hoh)
For how long do you guarantee the job?	*¿Por cuánto tiempo garantiza el trabajo?* (pohr **kwahn**-toh **tyehm**-poh gah-rahn-**tee**-sah ehl trah-**bah**-hoh)

The home owner is never finished when it comes to fixing up the house. Wear and tear, the elements, the age of the house, or simply a desire to redecorate can keep a home owner quite busy. At the beginning of this chapter we listed the names of some of the trades related to home repair. The following section provides more detailed vocabulary related to the most common trades. Although we have labeled the lists, you will find that this vocabulary often overlaps categories.

Remember: when you deal with any contractor, make sure you always check references!

The Electrician
El/la electricista
(ehl/lah eh-lehk-tree-**sees**-tah)

clamp	*la abrazadera* (lah ah-brah-sah-**deh**-rah)
electric cord	*el cordón eléctrico* (ehl kohr-**dohn** eh-**lehk**-tree-koh)
fuse box	*la caja de fusibles* (lah **kah**-hah deh foo-**see**-blehs)
meter	*el contador* (ehl kohn-tah-**dohr**)
tape	*la cinta adhesiva/la cinta de pegar* (lah **seen**-tah ahd-eh-**see**-bah/lah **seen**-tah deh peh-**gahr**)
wire	*el alambre* (ehl ah-**lahm**-breh)

Verbs

to fix	*arreglar* (ah-rreh-**glahr**)
to plug	*enchufar* (ehn-choo-**fahr**)
to turn off	*apagar* (ah-pah-**gahr**)
to turn on	*encender (ie)* (ehn-sehn-**dehr**)
to unplug	*desenchufar* (deh-sehn-choo-**fahr**)

The Plumber
El plomero/la plomera
(ehl ploh-**meh**-roh/lah ploh-**meh**-rah)

faucet	*la llave/el grifo* (lah **yah**-beh/ehl **gree**-foh)
pipe	*el tubo* (ehl **too**-boh)
pipeline	*la tubería* (lah too-beh-**ree**-ah)
shower head	*la alcachofa de ducha* (lah ahl-kah-**choh**-fah deh **doo**-chah)
wrench	*la llave inglesa* (lah **yah**-beh een-**gleh**-sah)

Verbs

to clog up	*atascar* (ah-tahs-**kahr**)
to unclog	*desatascar* (dehs-ah-tahs-**kahr**)

The Painter
El pintor/la pintora
(ehl peen-**tohr**/lah peen-**toh**-rah)

brush	*el cepillo* (ehl seh-**pee**-yoh)
can	*la lata* (lah **lah**-tah)
chisel	*el cincel* (ehl seen-**sehl**)
color	*el color* (ehl koh-**lohr**)
crack	*la grieta* (lah **gryeh**-tah)
hole	*el hoyo* (ehl **oh**-yoh)

ladder	*la escalera* (lah ehs-kah-**leh**-rah)
paintbrush	*la brocha* (lah **broh**-chah)
paint	*la pintura* (lah peen-**too**-rah)
sandpaper	*el papel de lija* (ehl pah-**pehl** deh **lee**-hah)
scraper	*el raspador* (ehl rrahs-pah-**dohr**)
wall	*la pared* (lah pah-**rehd**)
wallpaper	*el papel de empapelar* (ehl pah-**pehl** deh ehm-pah-peh-**lahr**)

Verbs

to lacquer	*pintar con laca* (peen-**tahr** kohn **lah**-kah)
to plaster	*enyesar* (ehn-yeh-**sahr**)
to plaster over a hole	*llenar/tapar un hoyo* (yeh-**nahr**/tah-**pahr** oon **oh**-yoh)
to sand	*lijar* (lee-**hahr**)
to wallpaper	*empapelar* (ehm-pah-peh-**lahr**)

The Carpenter
El carpintero/la carpintera
(ehl kahr-peen-**teh**-roh/lah kahr-peen-**teh**-rah)

block	*el bloque* (ehl **bloh**-keh)
brace	*la abrazadera* (lah ah-brah-sah-**deh**-rah)
drill	*el taladro* (ehl tah-**lah**-droh)
duct	*el conducto* (ehl kohn-**dook**-toh)
foundation	*la fundación/el cimiento* (lah foon-dah-**syohn**/ehl see-**myehn**-toh)
frame	*la armadura* (lah ahr-mah-**doo**-rah)
glue	*la cola/la goma* (lah **koh**-lah/lah **goh**-mah)
gutter	*el canal* (ehl kah-**nahl**)
hammer	*el martillo* (ehl mahr-**tee**-yoh)
hinge	*la bisagra* (lah bee-**sah**-grah)

insulation	*el aislamiento térmico* (ehl ah-ees-lah-**myehn**-toh **tehr**-mee-koh)
joint	*la unión* (lah oo-**nyohn**)
level	*el nivel* (ehl nee-**behl**)
measuring tape	*la cinta métrica/la cinta de medir* (lah **seen**-tah **meh**-tree-kah/lah **seen**-tah deh meh-**deer**)
nail	*el clavo* (ehl **klah**-boh)
nut	*la tuerca* (lah **twehr**-kah)
plan	*el plano* (ehl **plah**-noh)
plane	*el cepillo/la garlopa* (ehl seh-**pee**-yoh/lah gahr-**loh**-pah)
pliers	*los alicates* (lohs ah-lee-**kah**-tehs)
rafter	*la viga* (lah **bee**-gah)
railing	*la baranda* (lah bah-**rahn**-dah)
saw	*el cerrucho* (ehl seh-**rroo**-choh)
scaffold	*el andamio* (ehl ahn-**dah**-myoh)
screw	*el tornillo* (ehl tohr-**nee**-yoh)
screwdriver	*el destornillador* (ehl dehs-tohr-nee-yah-**dohr**)
shingles	*las tablillas* (lahs tah-**blee**-yahs)
stud	*el poste* (ehl **pohs**-teh)
toolbox	*la caja de herramientas* (lah **kah**-hah deh eh-rrah-**myehn**-tahs)
trim	*la moldadura* (lah mohl-dah-**doo**-rah)
trowel	*la paleta/la llana* (lah pah-**leh**-tah/lah **yah**-nah)

Verbs

to measure	*medir (i)* (meh-**deer**)
to mix	*mezclar* (mehs-**klahr**)
to pour	*echar* (ch-**chahr**)
to staple	*sujetar con grapas* (soo-heh-**tahr** kohn **grah**-pahs)

Construction Materials
Los materiales de construcción
(lohs mah-teh-**ryah**-lehs deh kohns-trook-**syohn**)

asphalt	*el asfalto* (ehl ahs-**fahl**-toh)
brass	*el latón* (ehl lah-**tohn**)
brick	*el ladrillo* (ehl lah-**dree**-yoh)
bronze	*el bronce* (ehl **brohn**-seh)
cement	*el cemento* (ehl seh-**mehn**-toh)
clay	*la arcilla* (lah ahr-**see**-yah)
concrete	*el hormigón/el concreto* (ehl ohr-mee-**gohn**/ehl kohn-**kreh**-toh)
copper	*el cobre* (ehl **koh**-breh)
flagstone	*la losa* (lah **loh**-sah)
glass	*el vidrio* (ehl **bee**-dryoh)
gravel	*la grava* (lah **grah**-bah)
iron	*el hierro* (ehl **yeh**-rroh)
linoleum	*el linóleo* (ehl lee-**noh**-leh-oh)
lumber	*la madera* (lah mah-**deh**-rah)
marble	*el mármol* (ehl **mahr**-mohl)
mortar	*el mortero* (ehl mohr-**teh**-roh)
plaster	*el yeso* (ehl **yeh**-soh)
plastic	*el plástico* (ehl **plahs**-tee-koh)
plywood	*la madera contrachapada* (lah mah-**deh**-rah kohn-trah-chah-**pah**-dah)
putty	*la masilla* (lah mah-**see**-yah)
rubber	*la goma* (lah **goh**-mah)
sand	*la arena* (lah ah-**reh**-nah)
slab	*la losa* (lah **loh**-sah)
steel	*el acero* (ehl ah-**seh**-roh)
stone	*la piedra* (lah **pyeh**-drah)
stucco	*el estuco* (ehl ehs-**too**-koh)
tar	*la brea/el chapapote* (lah **breh**-ah/ehl chah-pah-**poh**-teh)
tile (roof)	*la teja* (lah **teh**-hah)
tile (wall)	*el azulejo* (ehl ah-soo-**leh**-hoh)

tile (floor)	*la baldosa* (lah bahl-**doh**-sah)
wood	*la madera* (lah mah-**deh**-rah)

Measurements, Size, and Weight
Las medidas, el tamaño, y el peso
(lahs meh-**dee**-dahs, ehl tah-**mah**-nyoh, ee ehl **peh**-soh)

What size is it?	*¿De qué tamaño es?* (deh keh tah-**mah**-nyoh ehs)
How much does it measure?	*¿Cuánto mide?* (**kwahn**-toh **mee**-deh)
It measures . . .	*Mide...* (**mee**-deh...)
a centimeter.	*un centímetro.* (oon sehn-**tee**-meh-troh)
a foot.	*un pie.* (oon pyeh)
an inch.	*una pulgada.* (**oo**-nah pool-**gah**-dah)
a meter.	*un metro.* (oon **meh**-troh)
a ton.	*una tonelada.* (**oo**-nah toh-neh-**lah**-dah)
a yard.	*una yarda.* (**oo**-nah **yahr**-dah)
What is . . . ?	*¿Cuál es... ?* (kwahl ehs...)
the height	*la altura* (lah ahl-**too**-rah)
the length	*el largo* (ehl **lahr**-goh)
the weight	*el peso* (ehl **peh**-soh)
the width	*el ancho* (ehl **ahn**-choh)
It is . . .	*Es...* (ehs...)
a cubic foot.	*un pie cúbico.* (oon pyeh **koo**-bee-koh)
a square foot.	*un pie cuadrado.* (oon pyeh kwah-**drah**-doh)

Verbs

to measure	*medir (i)* (meh-**deer**)
to weigh	*pesar* (peh-**sahr**)

To learn how to express "half," "a fourth," etc., see "Fractions" in Chapter 14 on pages 157–58.

Places Around Town
Los lugares en el pueblo

(lohs loo-**gah**-rehs ehn ehl **pweh**-bloh)

By becoming familiar with the places and sites around town your family uses regularly your employees will be better able to help you. It is also important for them to learn how to get around town. Once they learn to get from one place to another, they will be able to help with errands and other activities outside the home.

Around the Neighborhood
Por el barrio
(pohr ehl **bah**-rryoh)

beauty salon	*el salón de belleza* (ehl sah-**lohn** deh beh-**yeh**-sah)
church	*la iglesia* (lah ee-**gleh**-syah)
clinic	*la clínica* (lah **klee**-nee-kah)
clothing store	*la tienda de ropa* (lah **tyehn**-dah deh **rroh**-pah)
college	*la universidad* (lah oo-nee-behr-see-**dahd**)

83

community center	*el centro social* (ehl **sehn**-troh soh-**syahl**)
courthouse	*la corte* (lah **kohr**-teh)
dentist's office	*la consulta del dentista* (lah kohn-**sool**-tah dehl dehn-**tees**-tah)
department store	*el almacén* (ehl ahl-mah-**sehn**)
doctor's office	*la consulta del médico* (lah kohn-**sool**-tah dehl **meh**-dee-koh)
downtown	*el centro* (ehl **sehn**-troh)
drugstore	*la farmacia* (lah fahr-**mah**-syah)
fire station	*la estación de bomberos* (lah ehs-tah-**syohn** deh bohm-**beh**-rohs)
florist	*la florería* (lah floh-reh-**ree**-ah)
grocery store	*la tienda de comida* (lah **tyehn**-dah de koh-**mee**-dah)
gas station	*la gasolinera* (lah gah-soh-lee-**neh**-rah)
hospital	*el hospital* (ehl ohs-pee-**tahl**)
jail	*la cárcel* (lah **kahr**-sehl)
library	*la biblioteca* (lah bee-blyoh-**teh**-kah)
mall	*el centro comercial* (ehl **sehn**-troh koh-mehr-**syahl**)
mosque	*la mezquita* (lah mehs-**kee**-tah)
movie theater	*el cine* (ehl **see**-neh)
museum	*el museo* (ehl moo-**seh**-oh)
office	*la oficina* (lah oh-fee-**see**-nah)
park	*el parque* (ehl **pahr**-keh)
police station	*el cuartel de policía* (ehl kwahr-**tehl** deh poh-lee-**see**-ah)
post office	*el correo* (ehl koh-**rreh**-oh)
restaurant	*el restaurante* (ehl rrehs-tah-oo-**rahn**-teh)
school	*la escuela* (lah ehs-**kweh**-lah)
synagogue	*la sinagoga* (lah see-nah-**goh**-gah)
temple	*el templo* (ehl **tehm**-ploh)
theater	*el teatro* (ehl teh-**ah**-troh)
university	*la universidad* (lah oo-nee-behr-see-**dahd**)

video store	*la tienda de vídeos* (lah **tyehn**-dah deh **bee**-deh-ohs)
zoo	*el zoológico* (ehl soh-**loh**-hee-koh)

In addition to the places and sites listed above, a typical neighborhood also has the following features:

avenue	*la avenida* (lah ah-beh-**nee**-dah)
block	*la cuadra* (lah **kwah**-drah)
boulevard	*el paseo* (ehl pah-**seh**-oh)
bridge	*el puente* (ehl **pwehn**-teh)
building	*el edificio* (ehl eh-dee-**fee**-syoh)
bus stop	*la parada de autobuses* (lah pah-**rah**-dah deh ah-oo-toh-**boo**-sehs)
corner	*la esquina* (lah ehs-**kee**-nah)
fence	*la cerca* (lah **sehr**-kah)
fountain	*la fuente* (lah **fwehn**-teh)
intersection	*la bocacalle* (lah boh-kah-**kah**-yeh)
mailbox	*el buzón* (ehl boo-**sohn)**
newsstand	*el quiosco* (ehl **kyohs**-koh)
one-way street	*la calle de dirección única* (lah **kah**-yeh deh dee-rehk-**syohn oo**-nee-kah)
parking lot	*el estacionamiento* (ehl ehs-tah-syoh-nah-**myehn**-toh)
parking meter	*el parquímetro* (ehl pahr-**kee**-meh-troh)
pedestrian crossing	*el paso de peatones* (ehl **pah**-soh deh peh-ah-**toh**-nehs)
sidewalk	*la acera* (lah ah-**seh**-rah)
sign	*el letrero* (ehl leh-**treh**-roh)
skyscraper	*el rascacielos* (ehl rrahs-kah-**syeh**-lohs)
square	*la plaza* (lah **plah**-sah)
square block	*la manzana* (la mahn-**sah**-nah)
street	*la calle* (lah **kah**-yeh)
subway station	*la estación de metro* (lah ehs-tah-**syohn** deh **meh**-troh)
taxi stand	*la parada de taxis* (lah pah-**rah**-dah deh **tahk**-sees)

traffic	*el tránsito* (ehl **trahn**-see-toh)
train station	*la estación de trenes* (lah ehs-tah-**syohn** deh **treh**-nehs)
tunnel	*el túnel* (ehl **too**-nehl)

Traffic Signs
Las señales de tráfico
(lahs seh-**nyah**-lehs deh **trah**-fee-koh)

railroad crossing	*el cruce de ferrocarril* (ehl **kroo**-seh deh feh-rroh-kah-**rreel**)
right of way sign	*la señal de preferencia* (lah seh-**nyahl** deh preh-feh-**rehn**-syah)
stop sign	*la señal de parar* (lah seh-**nyahl** deh pah-**rahr**)
traffic light	*el semáforo* (ehl seh-**mah**-foh-roh)
Do not enter!	*¡Dirección prohibida!* (dee-rehk-**syohn** proh-ee-**bee**-dah)
School crossing!	*¡Cruce escolar!* (**kroo**-seh ehs-koh-**lahr**)
Stop!	*¡Pare!* (**pah**-reh)
Yield!	*¡Ceda!* (**seh**-dah)

Getting Around Town
Para ir de un lugar a otro
(**pah**-rah eer deh oon loo-**gahr** ah **oh**-troh)

Sometimes you or your employee may need to ask for directions or for more information on how to get to a place.

I am lost.	*Estoy perdido/perdida.* (ehs-**toh**-ee pehr-**dee**-doh/pehr-**dee**-dah)
Would you tell me where . . . is?	*¿Podría decirme dónde está...?* (poh-**dree**-ah deh-**seer**-meh **dohn**-deh ehs-**tah**...)

It is . . .   Está... (ehs-**tah**...)

    at the intersection of . . .   en el cruce de... (ehn ehl **kroo**-seh deh...)

    behind . . .   detrás de... (deh-**trahs** deh...)

    down the street.   calle abajo. (**kah**-yeh ah-**bah**-hoh)

    downstairs.   abajo. (ah-**bah**-hoh)

    facing . . .   frente a... (**frehn**-teh ah...)

    far away.   lejos. (**leh**-hohs)

    in front of . . .   enfrente de... (ehn-**frehn**-teh deh...)

    inside.   adentro. (ah-**dehn**-troh)

    nearby.   cerca. (**sehr**-kah)

    next to . . .   al lado de... (ahl **lah**-doh deh...)

    on the corner.   en la esquina. (ehn lah ehs-**kee**-nah)

    on the next block.   en la próxima cuadra. (ehn lah **prohk**-see-mah **kwah**-drah)

    on the first (second/third . . .) floor.   en el primer (segundo/tercer...) piso. (ehn ehl pree-**mehr** [seh-**goon**-doh/tehr-**sehr**...] pee-soh)

    outside.   afuera. (ah-**fweh**-rah)

    over there.   allí. (ah-**yee**)

    to the east.   al este. (ahl **ehs**-teh)

    to the north.   al norte. (ahl **nohr**-teh)

    to the south.   al sur. (ahl soor)

    to the west.   al oeste. (ahl oh-**ehs**-teh)

    up the street.   calle arriba. (**kah**-yeh ah-**rree**-bah)

    upstairs.   arriba. (ah-**rree**-bah)

    X minutes away.   a X minutos. (ah... mee-**noo**-tohs)

    X blocks away.   a X cuadras. (ah... **kwah**-drahs)

On foot you have to . . .   A pie Ud. tiene que... (ah pyeh oos-**tehd tyeh**-neh keh...)

    continue straight ahead.   seguir derecho. (seh-**geer** deh-**reh**-choh)

    cross . . .   cruzar... (kroo-**sahr**...)

take the first (second/ third . . .) street.	*tomar la primera (segunda/tercera...) calle.* (toh-**mahr** lah pree-**meh**-rah [seh-**goon**-dah/tehr-**seh**-rah...] **kah**-yeh)
turn left.	*doblar a la izquierda.* (doh-**blahr** ah lah ees-**kyehr**-dah)
turn right.	*doblar a la derecha.* (doh-**blahr** ah lah deh-**reh**-chah)
You should take . . .	*Ud. debe tomar...* (oos-**tehd deh**-beh toh-**mahr**...)
a bus.	*un autobús.* (oon ah-oo-toh-**boos**)
a cab.	*un taxi.* (oon **tahk**-see)
a subway.	*un metro.* (oon **meh**-troh)
You should get off at . . .	*Ud. debe bajarse en...* (oos-**tehd deh**-beh bah-**hahr**-seh ehn...)

At the Bank
En el banco
(ehn ehl **bahn**-koh)

At times, one of your employees may need to run a personal errand at the bank, or you may need to discuss finances in general. Here is a list of vocabulary terms you may use:

account	*la cuenta* (lah **kwehn**-tah)
ATM	*el cajero automático* (ehl kah-**heh**-roh ah-oo-toh-**mah**-tee-koh)
bill	*el billete* (ehl bee-**yeh**-teh)
cash	*el dinero en efectivo* (ehl dee-**neh**-roh ehn eh-fek-**tee**-boh)
change (loose coins)	*el suelto/el cambio* (ehl **swehl**-toh/ehl **kahm**-byoh)
check	*el cheque* (ehl **cheh**-keh)
checking account	*la cuenta corriente* (lah **kwehn**-tah koh-**rryehn**-teh)
coin(s)	*la(s) moneda(s)* (lah[s] moh-**neh**-dah[s])

credit card	*la tarjeta de crédito* (lah tahr-**heh**-tah deh **kreh**-dee-toh)
loan	*el préstamo* (ehl **prehs**-tah-moh)
money	*el dinero* (ehl dee-**neh**-roh)
savings account	*la cuenta de ahorros* (lah **kwehn**-tah deh ah-**oh**-rrohs)
teller	*el cajero/la cajera* (ehl kah-**heh**-roh/lah kah-**heh**-rah)
traveler's check	*el cheque de viajero* (ehl **cheh**-keh deh byah-**heh**-roh)
window	*la ventanilla* (lah behn-tah-**nee**-yah)

Verbs

to borrow	*pedir (i) prestado* (peh-**deer** prehs-**tah**-doh)
to cash	*cobrar/cambiar* (koh-**brahr**/kahm-**byahr**)
to deposit	*depositar/hacer un depósito* (deh-poh-see-**tahr**/ah-**sehr** oon deh-**poh**-see-toh)
to exchange	*cambiar* (kahm-**byahr**)
to save	*ahorrar* (ah-oh-**rrahr**)
to withdraw	*sacar* (sah-**kahr**)

At the Post Office
En la oficina de correos
(ehn lah oh-fee-**see**-nah deh koh-**rreh**-ohs)

Do you need some errands done at the post office? Here is a list of expressions you may use when asking someone to do an errand for you at the post office:

address	*la dirección* (lah dee-rehk-**syohn**)
airmail	*el correo aéreo* (ehl koh-**rreh**-oh ah-**eh**-reh-oh)
certified	*certificado* (sehr-tee-fee-**kah**-doh)
envelope	*el sobre* (ehl **soh**-breh)

express	*urgente* (oor-**hehn**-teh)
letter	*la carta* (lah **kahr**-tah)
mail carrier	*el cartero* (ehl kahr-**teh**-roh)
mailbox	*el buzón* (ehl boo-**sohn**)
money order	*el giro postal* (ehl **hee**-roh pohs-**tahl**)
package	*el paquete* (ehl pah-**keh**-teh)
post office box	*el apartado postal* (ehl ah-pahr-**tah**-doh pohs-**tahl**)
postcard	*la tarjeta postal* (lah tahr-**heh**-tah pohs-**tahl**)
sender	*el remitente* (ehl rreh-mee-**tehn**-teh)
shipping charge	*el costo de envío* (ehl **kohs**-toh deh ehn-**bee**-oh)
stamp	*la estampilla/el sello* (lah ehs-tahm-**pee**-yah/ehl **seh**-yoh)
zip code	*la zona postal* (lah **soh**-nah pohs-**tahl**)

Verbs

to deliver	*repartir* (rreh-pahr-**teer**)
to pick up	*recoger* (rreh-koh-**hehr**)
to mail	*echar al correo* (eh-**chahr** ahl koh-**rreh**-oh)
to send	*enviar/mandar* (ehn-**byahr**/mahn-**dahr**)
to take	*llevar* (yeh-**bahr**)

In the Barbershop/Beauty Salon
En la barbería/la peluquería
(ehn lah bahr-beh-**ree**-ah/lah peh-loo-keh-**ree**-ah)

Many barbershops and beauty salons are operated by Spanish speakers. You'll create an excellent impression if you can request services in Spanish. (Note that, as before, we list adjectives in their masculine singular form only.)

appointment	*la cita* (lah **see**-tah)
beard	*la barba* (lah **bahr**-bah)
curly	*rizado* (rree-**sah**-doh)
dry	*seco* (**seh**-koh)
gray hair	*la cana* (lah **kah**-nah)
greasy	*grasoso* (grah-**soh**-soh)
hair color	*el tinte* (ehl **teen**-teh)
hair	*el pelo/el cabello* (ehl **peh**-loh/ehl kah-**beh**-yoh)
hair conditioner	*el acondicionador de pelo* (ehl ah-kohn-dee-syoh-nah-**dohr** deh **peh**-loh)
hairbrush	*el cepillo de pelo* (ehl seh-**pee**-yoh deh **peh**-loh)
haircut	*el corte de pelo* (ehl **kohr**-teh deh **peh**-loh)
hairdresser	*el barbero; el peluquero/la peluquera* (ehl bahr-**beh**-roh; ehl peh-loo-**keh**-roh/lah peh-loo-**keh**-rah)
hairpin	*la horquilla* (lah ohr-**kee**-yah)
hairspray	*la laca para el pelo* (lah **lah**-kah **pah**-rah ehl **peh**-loh)
long	*largo* (**lahr**-goh)
manicure	*la manicura* (lah mah-nee-**koo**-rah)
massage	*el masaje* (ehl mah-**sah**-heh)
moustache	*el bigote* (ehl bee-**goh**-teh)
nail	*la uña* (lah **oo**-nyah)
nail file	*la lima de uñas* (lah **lee**-mah deh **oo**-nyahs)
nail polish	*la pintura de uñas* (lah peen-**too**-rah deh **oo**-nyahs)
pedicure	*la pedicura* (lah peh-dee-**koo**-rah)
shampoo	*el champú* (ehl chahm-**poo**)
short	*corto* (**kohr**-toh)
sideburn	*la patilla* (lah pah-**tee**-yah)
straight	*lacio* (**lah**-syoh)
trim	*el recorte* (ehl rreh-**kohr**-teh)

| wavy | *ondulado* (ohn-doo-**lah**-doh) |
| wet | *mojado* (moh-**hah**-doh) |

Verbs

to blow dry	*secar a mano* (seh-**kahr** ah **mah**-noh)
to curl	*rizar* (rree-**sahr**)
to cut	*cortar* (kohr-**tahr**)
to dry	*secar* (seh-**kahr**)
to dye	*teñir (i)* (teh-**nyeer**)
to file	*limar* (lee-**mahr**)
to paint	*pintar* (peen-**tahr**)
to shave	*afeitar* (ah-feh-ee-**tahr**)
to wash	*lavar* (lah-**bahr**)

At the Service/Gas Station
En el taller de reparaciones/ la gasolinera
(ehn ehl tah-**yehr** deh rreh-pah-rah-**syoh**-nehs/
lah gah-soh-lee-**neh**-rah)

Your employee may drive the family car, get gas, or take the car in for repairs. You may also find it is useful to communicate in Spanish with Spanish-speaking personnel at your service station or repair shop. In any of these situations, you will find the following vocabulary helpful:

Types of Vehicles
Tipos de vehículos
(**tee**-pohs deh beh-**ee**-koo-lohs)

car	*el carro/el coche* (ehl **kah**-rroh/ehl **koh**-cheh)
motorcycle	*la motocicleta/la moto* (lah moh-toh-see-**kleh**-tah/lah **moh**-toh)
SUV	*el SUV* (ehl **eh**-seh oo beh)
truck	*el camión* (ehl kah-**myohn**)
van	*la camioneta* (lah kah-myoh-**neh**-tah)

The Car (Inside and Out)
El coche/el carro (por dentro y por fuera)
(ehl **koh**-cheh/ehl **kah**-rroh pohr **dehn**-troh ee pohr **fweh**-rah)

baby seat	la sillita de seguridad para niños (lah see-**yee**-tah deh seh-goo-ree-**dahd** **pah**-rah **nee**-nyohs)
battery	la batería (lah bah-teh-**ree**-ah)
brakes	el freno (ehl **freh**-noh)
bumper	el parachoques (ehl pah-rah-**choh**-kehs)
car seat	el asiento (ehl ah-**syehn**-toh)
clutch	el embrague (ehl ehm-**brah**-geh)
cylinder	el cilindro (ehl see-**leen**-droh)
dashboard	el tablero de instrumentos (ehl tah-**bleh**-roh deh eens-troo-**mehn**-tohs)
distributor	el delco (ehl **dehl**-koh)
door	la puerta (lah **pwehr**-tah)
engine	el motor (ehl moh-**tohr**)
exhaust	el escape (ehl ehs-**kah**-peh)
fanbelt	la correa del ventilador (lah koh-**rreh**-ah dehl behn-tee-lah-**dohr**)
gear	el engranaje (ehl ehn-grah-**nah**-heh)
gear box	la caja de cambios (lah **kah**-hah deh **kahm**-byohs)
gearshift	la palanca de cambio (lah pah-**lahn**-kah deh **kahm**-byoh)
glove compartment	la guantera (lah gwahn-**teh**-rah)
grease	el engrase (ehl ehn-**grah**-seh)
hood	el capó (ehl kah-**poh**)
horn	la bocina (lah boh-**see**-nah)
horsepower	los caballos de fuerza (lohs kah-**bah**-yohs deh **fwehr**-sah)
hubcap	el tapacubos (ehl tah-pah-**koo**-bohs)
inner tube	la cámara (de aire) (lah **kah**-mah-rah [deh **ah**-ee-reh])
jack	el gato (ehl **gah**-toh)

license plate	*el número de la matrícula* (ehl **noo**-meh-roh deh lah mah-**tree**-koo-lah)
lights	*las luces* (lahs **loo**-sehs)
mirror	*el espejo* (ehl ehs-**peh**-hoh)
motor	*el motor* (ehl moh-**tohr**)
mudguard	*el guardafango* (ehl gwahr-dah-**fahn**-goh)
muffler	*el silenciador* (ehl see-lehn-syah-**dohr**)
piston	*el émbolo* (ehl **ehm**-boh-loh)
radiator	*el radiador* (ehl rrah-dyah-**dohr**)
roof	*el techo* (ehl **teh**-choh)
spare tire	*la llanta de repuesto* (lah **yahn**-tah deh rreh-**pwehs**-toh)
spark plug	*la bujía* (lah boo-**hee**-ah)
spring	*el muelle* (ehl **mweh**-yeh)
starter	*el motor de arranque* (ehl moh-**tohr** deh ah-**rrahn**-keh)
steering wheel	*el volante* (ehl boh-**lahn**-teh)
suspension	*la suspensión* (lah soos-pehn-**syohn**)
tire	*la llanta* (lah **yahn**-tah)
tire pressure	*la presión de los neumáticos* (lah preh-**syohn** deh lohs neh-oo-**mah**-tee-kohs)
transmission	*la transmisión* (lah trahns-mee-**syohn**)
transmission shaft	*el eje de transmisión* (ehl **eh**-heh deh trahns-mee-**syohn**)
trunk	*el maletero* (ehl mah-leh-**teh**-roh)
valve	*la válvula* (lah **bahl**-boo-lah)
wheel	*la rueda* (lah **rrweh**-dah)
windshield	*el parabrisas* (ehl pah-rah-**bree**-sahs)

Verbs

to accelerate	*acelerar* (ah-seh-leh-**rahr**)
to brake (stop)	*frenar* (freh-**nahr**)
to shift gears	*cambiar de velocidad* (kahm-**byahr** deh beh-loh-see-**dahd**)

to start (the car)	*poner (el coche/el carro) en marcha* (poh-**nehr** [ehl **koh**-cheh/ehl **kah**-rroh] ehn **mahr**-chah)
to throw into gear	*embragar* (ehm-brah-**gahr**)
to throw out of gear	*desembragar* (deh-sehm-brah-**gahr**)
to turn off	*apagar* (ah-pah-**gahr**)
to work	*funcionar* (foon-syoh-**nahr**)

At the Gas Station
En la gasolinera
(ehn lah gah-soh-lee-**neh**-rah)

antifreeze	*el anticongelante* (ehl ahn-tee-kohn-heh-**lahn**-teh)
brake fluid	*el líquido de frenos* (ehl **lee**-kee-doh deh **freh**-nohs)
gas can	*el bidón de gasolina* (ehl bee-**dohn** deh gah-soh-**lee**-nah)
gas pump	*la bomba de gasolina* (lah **bohm**-bah deh gah-soh-**lee**-nah)
gas tank	*el tanque de gasolina* (ehl **tahn**-keh deh gah-soh-**lee**-nah)
gasoline	*la gasolina* (lah gah-soh-**lee**-nah)
motor oil	*el aceite* (ehl ah-**seh**-ee-teh)

Things to Do at the Service/Gas Station
Lo que se hace en el taller de reparaciones/la gasolinera
(loh keh seh **ah**-seh ehn ehl tah-**yehr** deh rreh-pah-rah-**syoh**-nehs/lah gah-soh-lee-**neh**-rah)

Please . . .	*Haga el favor de...* (**ah**-gah ehl fah-**bohr** deh...)
change the oil.	*cambiar el aceite.* (kahm-**byahr** ehl ah-**seh**-ee-teh)

change the wind-shield wipers.	*cambiar los limpiaparabrisas.* (kahm-**byahr** lohs leem-pyah-pah-rah-**bree**-sahs)
change the tire.	*cambiar la llanta.* (kahm-**byahr** lah **yahn**-tah)
check the brakes.	*revisar los frenos.* (rreh-bee-**sahr** lohs **freh**-nohs)
check the oil level.	*revisar el nivel de aceite.* (rreh-bee-**sahr** ehl nee-**behl** deh ah-**seh**-ee-teh)
check the tires.	*revisar las llantas.* (rreh-bee-**sahr** lahs **yahn**-tahs)
clean the windshield.	*limpiar el parabrisas.* (leem-**pyahr** ehl pah-rah-**bree**-sahs)
fill the gas tank.	*llenar el tanque de gasolina.* (yeh-**nahr** ehl **tahn**-keh deh gah-soh-**lee**-nah)
fix the car.	*arreglar el coche/el carro.* (ah-rreh-**glahr** ehl **koh**-cheh/ehl **kah**-rroh)
park.	*estacionar.* (ehs-tah-syoh-**nahr**)
push the car.	*empujar el coche/el carro.* (ehm-poo-**hahr** ehl **koh**-cheh/ehl **kah**-rroh)
put air in the tires.	*inflar las llantas.* (een-**flahr** lahs **yahn**-tahs)
repair the car.	*reparar el coche/el carro.* (rreh-pah-**rahr** ehl **koh**-cheh/ehl **kah**-rroh)
replace the spark plugs.	*reemplazar las bujías.* (rrehm-plah-**sahr** lahs boo-**hee**-ahs)
start the car.	*poner el coche (el carro) en marcha.* (poh-**nehr** ehl **koh**-cheh [el **kah**-rroh] ehn **mahr**-chah)
turn off the lights.	*apagar las luces.* (ah-pah-**gahr** lahs **loo**-sehs)
turn off the motor.	*apagar el motor.* (ah-pah-**gahr** ehl moh-**tohr**)
turn on the lights.	*encender las luces.* (ehn-sehn-**dehr** lahs **loo**-sehs)

Check-Ups and Repairs of the Car
El mantenimiento y arreglo del coche
(ehl mahn-teh-nee-**myehn**-toh ee ah-**rreh**-gloh dehl **koh**-cheh)

All cars need to be checked from time to time to keep them running well. When a car is malfunctioning, it is important to explain clearly what you want done and to be specific about the problem. The following phrases will help you at the gas station or at the mechanic's shop. Let's hope you don't need them too often!

Is there a mechanic here?	*¿Hay un mecánico?* (**ah**-ee oon meh-**kah**-nee-koh)
Are you a mechanic?	*¿Es Ud. mecánico?* (ehs oos-**tehd** meh-**kah**-nee-koh)
The car doesn't run (well).	*El coche no anda (bien).* (ehl **koh**-cheh noh **ahn**-dah [byehn])
There is a knock in the motor.	*El motor tiene un ruido.* (ehl moh-**tohr** tyeh-neh oon **rrwee**-doh)
The battery is dead.	*La batería no funciona.* (lah bah-teh-**ree**-ah noh foon-**syoh**-nah)
Please check the car.	*Haga el favor de revisar el coche/el carro.* (**ah**-gah ehl fah-**bohr** deh rreh-bee-**sahr** ehl **koh**-cheh/ehl **kah**-rroh)
What's wrong?	*¿Qué tiene?* (keh **tyeh**-neh)
How long will it take to fix the problem?	*¿Cuánto tiempo necesita Ud. para arreglar el problema?* (**kwahn**-toh **tyehm**-poh neh-seh-**see**-tah oos-**tehd** **pah**-rah ah-rreh-**glahr** ehl proh-**bleh**-mah)
It is going to take X days.	*Va a tomar X días.* (bah ah toh-**mahr**... **dee**-ahs)

Verbs

to have a breakdown	*tener una avería* (teh-**nehr** **oo**-nah ah-beh-**ree**-ah)
to have a dent	*tener una abolladura* (teh-**nehr** **oo**-nah ah-boh-yah-**doo**-rah)

to have a flat tire	*tener un pinchazo/una llanta pinchada* (teh-**nehr** oon peen-**chah**-soh/**oo**-nah **yahn**-tah peen-**chah**-dah)
to have a leak in the tire	*tener un escape en la llanta* (teh-**nehr** oon ehs-**kah**-peh ehn lah **yahn**-tah)
to run out of gas	*quedarse sin gasolina* (keh-**dahr**-seh seen gah-soh-**lee**-nah)

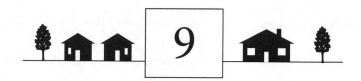

Shopping
De compras

(deh **kohm**-prahs)

Transactions
Las transacciones
(lahs trahn-sahk-**syoh**-nehs)

With the growing Hispanic population in the United States, you may at times need to communicate with Spanish-speaking personnel at a store. Wouldn't it be nice to go to the grocery store, *la bodega* (lah boh-**deh**-gah), and do your shopping in Spanish? Let's begin with some of the general questions needed for any kind of shopping, from the *bodega* to the department store.

A salesperson may ask you:

How can I help you?	*¿En qué puedo servirle?* (ehn keh **pweh**-doh sehr-**beer**-leh)

You'll need to learn a few ways to ask for a particular item.

Do you have . . . ?	*¿Tiene Ud...?* (**tyeh**-neh oos-**tehd**...)
I need . . .	*Necesito...* (neh-seh-**see**-toh...)
What brand is it?	*¿De qué marca es?* (deh keh **mahr**-kah ehs)

How much does it cost?	¿Cuánto cuesta? (**kwahn**-toh **kwehs**-tah)
Can I pay with . . .	¿Puedo pagar con... (**pweh**-doh pah-**gahr** kohn...)
a credit card?	una tarjeta de crédito? (**oo**-nah tahr-**heh**-tah deh **kreh**-dee-toh)
a check/a traveler's check?	un cheque/un cheque de viajero? (oon **cheh**-keh/oon **cheh**-keh deh byah-**heh**-roh)
Is tax included?	¿Está incluido el impuesto? (ehs-**tah** een-**klwee**-doh ehl eem-**pwehs**-toh)

Sometimes you may find that you have to return an item you have bought. First, try to find the right person to talk to.

I need to speak with the . . .	Necesito hablar con... (neh-seh-**see**-toh ah-**blahr** kohn...)
manager.	el/la gerente. (ehl/lah heh-**rehn**-teh)
owner.	el dueño/la dueña. (ehl **dweh**-nyoh/lah **dweh**-nyah)
person in charge.	el encargado/la encargada. (ehl ehn-kahr-**gah**-doh/lah ehn-kahr-**gah**-dah)
salesperson.	el dependiente/la dependienta. (ehl deh-pehn-**dyehn**-teh/lah deh-pehn-**dyehn**-tah)
Why do you want to return . . . ?	¿Por qué quiere devolver...? (pohr-**keh kyeh**-reh deh-bohl-**behr**...)
I want/need to return . . . because . . .	Quiero/Necesito devolver... porque... (**kyeh**-roh/neh-seh-**see**-toh deh-bohl-**behr**... **pohr**-keh...)
It is not the brand I want.	No es de la marca que quiero. (noh ehs deh lah **mahr**-kah keh **kyeh**-roh)
It is too . . .	Es demasiado... (ehs deh-mah-**syah**-doh...)
large.	grande. (**grahn**-deh)
small.	pequeño/pequeña. (peh-**keh**-nyoh/peh-**keh**-nyah)

I don't like it.	*No me gusta.* (noh meh **goos**-tah)
I want my money back.	*Quiero que me devuelva el dinero.* (**kyeh**-roh keh meh deh-**bwehl**-bah ehl dee-**neh**-roh)
Can you exchange it for another one?	*¿Me lo puede cambiar por otro/otra?* (meh loh **pweh**-deh kahm-**byahr** pohr **oh**-troh/**oh**-trah)

Shopping Vocabulary
Vocabulario para hacer las compras
(boh-kah-boo-**lah**-ryoh **pah**-rah ah-**sehr** lahs **kohm**-prahs)

Here is a list of vocabulary terms useful for any type of shopping:

aisle	*el pasillo* (ehl pah-**see**-yoh)
bag	*la bolsa* (lah **bohl**-sah)
bargain	*la ganga* (lah **gahn**-gah)
basket	*la cesta/la canasta* (lah **sehs**-tah/lah kah-**nahs**-tah)
bill (banknote)	*el billete* (ehl bee-**yeh**-teh)
bill (statement)	*la cuenta* (lah **kwehn**-tah)
box	*la caja* (lah **kah**-hah)
cart	*el carrito* (ehl kah-**rree**-toh)
cash register	*la caja* (lah **kah**-hah)
cashier	*el cajero/la cajera* (ehl kah-**heh**-roh/lah kah-**heh**-rah)
cent	*el centavo* (ehl sehn-**tah**-boh)
change (coins)	*el cambio* (ehl **kahm**-byoh)
change (money returned)	*la vuelta* (lah **bwehl**-tah)
check	*el cheque* (ehl **cheh**-keh)
checkout	*la caja* (lah **kah**-hah)
coin(s)	*la(s) moneda(s)/el cambio* (lah[s] moh-**neh**-dah[s]/ehl **kahm**-byoh)
counter	*el mostrador* (ehl mohs-trah-**dohr**)
coupon	*el cupón* (ehl koo-**pohn**)
credit card	*la tarjeta de crédito* (lah tahr-**heh**-tah deh **kreh**-dee-toh)

debit card	*la tarjeta de cargo automático/de débito* (lah tahr-**heh**-tah deh **kahr**-goh ah-oo-toh-**mah**-tee-koh/deh **deh**-bee-toh)
dime	*diez centavos* (dyehs sehn-**tah**-bohs)
discount	*el descuento* (ehl dehs-**kwehn**-toh)
dollar	*el dólar* (ehl **doh**-lahr)
money	*el dinero* (ehl dee-**neh**-roh)
nickel	*cinco centavos* (**seen**-koh sehn-**tah**-bohs)
penny	*el centavo* (ehl sehn-**tah**-boh)
price	*el precio* (ehl **preh**-syoh)
quarter	*veinte y cinco centavos* (**beh**-een-teh ee **seen**-koh sehn-**tah**-bohs)
receipt	*el recibo* (ehl rreh-**see**-boh)
sales (reductions)	*las rebajas* (lahs rreh-**bah**-hahs)
shopping list	*la lista de compras* (lah **lees**-tah deh **kohm**-prahs)
size	*la talla/el tamaño* (lah **tah**-yah/ehl tah-**mah**-nyoh)
store window	*la vitrina* (lah bee-**tree**-nah)

Verbs

to cost	*costar (ue)* (kohs-**tahr**)
to exchange	*cambiar* (kahm-**byahr**)
to need	*necesitar* (neh-seh-see-**tahr**)
to pay	*pagar* (pah-**gahr**)
to return	*devolver (ue)* (deh-bohl-**behr**)
to wrap	*envolver (ue)* (ehn-bohl-**behr**)

For more detailed lists relating to clothing, shoes, and jewelry, go to Chapter 10.

At the Grocery Store
En la tienda de comestibles
(ehn lah **tyehn**-dah deh koh-mehs-**tee**-blehs)

Although large supermarkets sell almost anything that you need to feed a family, specialized stores are still often available in many neighborhoods. They may include the following:

bakery	*la panadería* (lah pah-nah-deh-**ree**-ah)
butcher shop	*la carnicería* (lah kahr-nee-seh-**ree**-ah)
dairy store	*la lechería* (lah leh-cheh-**ree**-ah)
farmer's market	*el mercado al aire libre* (ehl mehr-**kah**-doh ahl **ah**-ee-reh **lee**-breh)
fish market	*la pescadería* (lah pehs-kah-deh-**ree**-ah)
fruit store	*la frutería* (lah froo-teh-**ree**-ah)
grocery store	*la bodega* (lah boh-**deh**-gah)
market	*el mercado* (ehl mehr-**kah**-doh)
pastry shop	*la pastelería* (lah pahs-teh-leh-**ree**-ah)
supermarket	*el supermercado* (ehl soo-pehr-mehr-**kah**-doh)
vegetable (produce) store	*la verdulería* (lah behr-doo-leh-**ree**-ah)

In addition to large supermarkets, your city may have *bodegas* (boh-**deh**-gahs), small grocery stores that are often owned and staffed by Hispanics. Regardless of where you shop, you'll enjoy having some vocabulary to communicate with Spanish-speaking employees. Review Chapter 4, which contains many lists of foods separated by categories. In the market, you'll also need to ask where the different sections are. Here are the basics:

bread	*el pan* (ehl pahn)
cleaning products	*los productos para la limpieza* (lohs proh-**dook**-tohs **pah**-rah lah leem-**pyeh**-sah)
condiments	*los condimentos* (lohs kohn-dee-**mehn**-tohs)
eggs	*los huevos* (lohs **weh**-bohs)
fish	*el pescado* (ehl pehs-**kah**-doh)

frozen food	*los alimentos congelados* (lohs ah-lee-**mehn**-tohs kohn-heh-**lah**-dohs)
meat	*la carne* (lah **kahr**-neh)
milk	*la leche* (lah **leh**-cheh)
pasta	*la pasta* (lah **pahs**-tah)
vegetables	*los vegetales* (lohs beh-heh-**tah**-lehs)

Verbs

to look bad (an item)	*tener mala pinta* (teh-**nehr mah**-lah **peen**-tah)
to look good (an item)	*tener buena pinta* (teh-**nehr bweh**-nah **peen**-tah)

Here are some basic questions and phrases:

How much do you need?	*¿Cuánto necesita?* (**kwahn**-toh neh-seh-**see**-tah)
How many do you need?	*¿Cuántos/Cuántas necesita?* (**kwahn**-tohs/**kwahn**-tahs neh-seh-**see**-tah)
I need . . .	*Necesito...* (neh-seh-**see**-toh...)
a bag of . . .	*una bolsa de...* (**oo**-nah **bohl**-sah deh...)
a bottle of . . .	*una botella de...* (**oo**-nah boh-**teh**-yah deh...)
a box of . . .	*una caja de...* (**oo**-nah **kah**-hah deh...)
a bunch of . . .	*un atado/un racimo de...* (oon ah-**tah**-doh/oon rrah-**see**-moh deh...)
a can of . . .	*una lata de...* (**oo**-nah **lah**-tah deh...)
a dozen (of) . . .	*una docena de...* (**oo**-nah doh-**seh**-nah deh...)
a jar of . . .	*un pote/un jarro de...* (oon **poh**-teh/oon **hah**-rroh deh...)
a package of . . .	*un paquete de...* (oon pah-**keh**-teh deh...)
a pair of . . .	*un par de...* (oon pahr deh...)
a pound of . . .	*una libra de...* (**oo**-nah **lee**-brah deh...)
one/two . . .	*uno/dos...* (**oo**-noh/dohs...)

A more detailed list of how to express quantities appears in Chapter 4 on page 58; numbers are presented in Chapter 14.

At the Pharmacy/Drugstore
En la farmacia
(ehn lah fahr-**mah**-syah)

The most important things sold at a pharmacy are prescription and over-the-counter medications. You may want your employee to pick up a prescription medication at the pharmacy for you or a family member. Here are some words and expressions that may be helpful. (Don't forget that your employee may require written permission or a phone call to your pharmacy in order to be able to pick up a prescription in your name.)

Take this prescription to the drugstore, give it to the pharmacist, and wait there.	*Lleve esta receta a la farmacia, désela al farmacéutico y espere allí.* (**yeh**-beh **ehs**-tah rre-**seh**-tah ah lah fahr-**mah**-syah, **deh**-seh-lah ahl fahr-mah-**seh**-oo-tee-koh ee ehs-**peh**-reh ah-**yee**)

Remedies/Cures
Los remedios
(lohs rreh-**meh**-dyohs)

antacids	*los antiácidos* (lohs ahn-**tyah**-see-dohs)
antibiotics	*los antibióticos* (lohs ahn-tee-**byoh**-tee-kohs)
antihistamines	*los antihistamínicos* (lohs ahn-tees-tah-**mee**-nee-kohs)
aspirin	*la aspirina* (lah ahs-pee-**ree**-nah)
bandages	*las vendas* (lahs **behn**-dahs)
band-aids	*las curitas* (lahs koo-**ree**-tahs)
cough syrup	*el jarabe para la tos* (ehl hah-**rah**-beh **pah**-rah lah tohs)
creams	*las pomadas* (lahs poh-**mah**-dahs)
lotions	*las lociones* (lahs loh-**syoh**-nehs)
penicillin	*la penicilina* (lah peh-nee-see-**lee**-nah)

pills	*las píldoras* (lahs **peel**-doh-rahs)
thermometer	*el termómetro* (ehl tehr-**moh**-meh-troh)
throat lozenges	*las pastillas para la garganta* (lahs pahs-**tee**-yahs **pah**-rah lah gahr-**gahn**-tah)
vitamins	*las vitaminas* (lahs bee-tah-**mee**-nahs)

Toiletries
Los artículos de tocador
(lohs ahr-**tee**-koo-lohs deh toh-kah-**dohr**)

blow dryer	*la secadora de pelo* (lah seh-kah-**doh**-rah deh **peh**-loh)
comb	*el peine* (ehl **peh**-ee-neh)
cotton	*el algodón* (ehl ahl-goh-**dohn**)
dental floss	*el hilo dental* (ehl **ee**-loh dehn-**tahl**)
deodorant	*el desodorante* (ehl deh-soh-doh-**rahn**-teh)
perfume	*el perfume* (ehl pehr-**foo**-meh)
powder (talcum)	*el talco* (ehl **tahl**-koh)
razor	*la navaja* (lah nah-**bah**-hah)
sanitary napkins	*los paños higiénicos* (lohs **pah**-nyohs ee-**hyeh**-nee-kohs)
scissors (small)	*las tijeritas* (lahs tee-heh-**ree**-tahs)
shampoo	*el champú* (ehl chahm-**poo**)
soap	*el jabón* (ehl hah-**bohn**)
tampon	*el tampón* (ehl tahm-**pohn**)
toilet paper	*el papel higiénico* (ehl pah-**pehl** ee-**hyeh**-nee-koh)
toothbrush	*el cepillo de dientes* (ehl seh-**pee**-yoh deh **dyehn**-tehs)
toothpaste	*la pasta de dientes* (lah **pahs**-tah deh **dyehn**-tehs)
tweezers	*las pinzas* (lahs **peen**-sahs)

Unlike in Spanish-speaking countries, in the United States most toiletries and personal hygiene items can be found at the drugstore, in addition to prescription and over-the-counter medications.

Make-Up
Los cosméticos
(lohs kohs-**meh**-tee-kohs)

eye shadow	*la sombra de ojos* (lah **sohm**-brah deh **oh**-hohs)
eyebrow pencil	*el lápiz de cejas* (ehl **lah**-pees deh **seh**-hahs)
eyeliner	*el lápiz de ojos* (ehl **lah**-pees deh **oh**-hohs)
face powder	*el polvo* (ehl **pohl**-boh)
lip gloss	*el brillo de labios* (ehl **bree**-yoh deh **lah**-byohs)
lipstick	*el lápiz de labios* (ehl **lah**-pees deh **lah**-byohs)
rouge	*el colorete* (ehl koh-loh-**reh**-teh)

Other Pharmacy Items
Otras cosas en la farmacia
(**oh**-trahs **koh**-sahs ehn lah fahr-**mah**-syah)

batteries	*las pilas* (lahs **pee**-lahs)
candles	*las velas* (lahs **beh**-lahs)
cigarettes	*los cigarrillos* (lohs see-gah-**rree**-yohs)
cigars	*los cigarros* (lohs see-**gah**-rrohs)
disposable cameras	*las cámaras desechables* (lahs **kah**-mah-rahs deh-seh-**chah**-blehs)
envelopes	*los sobres* (lohs **soh**-brehs)
film	*los rollos de película* (lohs **rroh**-yohs deh peh-**lee**-koo-lah)
flashlights	*las linternas* (lahs leen-**tehr**-nahs)
greeting cards	*las tarjetas* (las tahr-**heh**-tahs)
lightbulbs	*los bombillas* (lohs bohm-**bee**-yahs)
magazines	*las revistas* (lahs rreh-**bees**-tahs)
matches	*los fósforos* (lohs **fohs**-foh-rohs)
newspapers	*los periódicos* (lohs peh-**ryoh**-dee-kohs)

postcards	*las tarjetas postales/las postales* (lahs tahr-**heh**-tahs pohs-**tah**-lehs/lahs pohs-**tah**-lehs)
sunglasses	*los anteojos de sol* (lohs ahn-teh-**oh**-hohs deh sohl)
suntan lotion	*los bronceadores* (lohs brohn-seh-ah-**doh**-rehs)

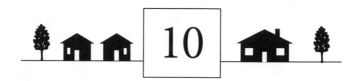

10

Clothing
La ropa
(lah **rroh**-pah)

With the exception of a few garments, men and women often wear the same types of clothing. This greatly simplifies vocabulary learning.

Articles of Clothing
Las prendas de vestir
(lahs **prehn**-dahs deh behs-**teer**)

bathing suit	*el traje de baño* (ehl **trah**-heh deh **bah**-nyoh)
blazer	*la americana* (lah ah-meh-ree-**kah**-nah)
coat	*el abrigo/el sobretodo* (ehl ah-**bree**-goh/ehl soh-breh-**toh**-doh)
jacket	*el saco/la chaqueta* (ehl **sah**-koh/lah chah-**keh**-tah)
jeans	*los blue jeans/los vaqueros* (lohs bloo yeens/lohs bah-**keh**-rohs)
overalls	*el overol* (ehl oh-beh-**rohl**)
pajamas	*el piyama* (ehl pee-**yah**-mah)

pants	*los pantalones* (lohs pahn-tah-**loh**-nehs)
raincoat	*la gabardina/el impermeable* (lah gah-bar-**dee**-nah/ehl eem-pehr-meh-**ah**-bleh)
shirt	*la camisa* (lah kah-**mee**-sah)
shorts	*los pantalones cortos* (lohs pahn-tah-**loh**-nehs **kohr**-tohs)
socks	*los calcetines* (lohs kahl-seh-**tee**-nehs)
suit	*el traje* (ehl **trah**-heh)
sweater	*el suéter* (ehl **sweh**-tehr)
sweatshirt	*la sudadera* (lah soo-dah-**deh**-rah)
tee shirt	*la camiseta* (lah kah-mee-**seh**-tah)
uniform	*el uniforme* (ehl oo-nee-**fohr**-meh)
vest	*el chaleco* (ehl chah-**leh**-koh)

For Women
Para las damas
(**pah**-rah lahs **dah**-mahs)

blouse	*la blusa* (lah **bloo**-sah)
bra	*el sostén* (ehl sohs-**tehn**)
dress	*el vestido* (ehl behs-**tee**-doh)
evening dress	*el traje de noche* (ehl **trah**-heh deh **noh**-cheh)
girdle	*la faja* (lah **fah**-hah)
panties	*las bragas* (lahs **brah**-gahs)
pantyhose	*los pantis/las pantimedias* (lohs **pahn**-tees/lahs pahn-tee-**meh**-dyahs)
skirt	*la falda* (lah **fahl**-dah)
slip	*la enagua* (lah eh-**nah**-gwah)
stockings (hose)	*las medias* (lahs **meh**-dyahs)
tights	*los leotardos* (lohs leh-oh-**tahr**-dohs)

For Men
Para los caballeros
(**pah**-rah lohs kah-bah-**yeh**-rohs)

briefs	*los calzoncillos* (lohs kahl-sohn-**see**-yohs)
tuxedo/black tie	*el traje de etiqueta* (ehl **trah**-heh deh eh-tee-**keh**-tah)
undershirt	*la camiseta* (lah kah-mee-**seh**-tah)

When you want to say "a pair," use *un par de* (oon pahr deh) + (name of article of clothing).

a pair of socks	*un par de calcetines* (oon pahr deh kahl-seh-**tee**-nehs)

To learn more vocabulary about the care and laundering of your clothing or how to take various articles to the dry cleaners, go to Chapter 3 on pages 39–42. Also, see later in this chapter, "Clothing Accessories," "Parts of Garments," and "Materials."

Clothing Accessories
Los complementos para la ropa
(lohs kohm-pleh-**mehn**-tohs **pah**-rah lah **rroh**-pah)

belt	*el cinturón* (ehl seen-too-**rohn**)
buckle	*la hebilla* (lah eh-**bee**-yah)
cap	*la gorra* (lah **goh**-rrah)
glove	*el guante* (ehl **gwahn**-teh)
handkerchief	*el pañuelo* (ehl pah-**nyweh**-loh)
hat	*el sombrero* (ehl sohm-**breh**-roh)
pocketbook	*el bolso/la cartera* (ehl **bohl**-soh/lah kahr-**teh**-rah)
purse	*el bolso/la cartera* (ehl **bohl**-soh/lah kahr-**teh**-rah)
scarf	*la bufanda* (lah boo-**fahn**-dah)
suspenders	*los tirantes* (lohs tee-**rahn**-tehs)

| tie | *la corbata* (lah kohr-**bah**-tah) |
| wallet | *la billetera/la cartera* (lah bee-yeh-**teh**-rah/lah kahr-**teh**-rah) |

Shoes
Los zapatos
(lohs sah-**pah**-tohs)

Some words and expressions that you may need are:

athletic shoes	*los zapatos deportivos* (lohs sah-**pah**-tohs deh-pohr-**tee**-bohs)
boots	*las botas* (lahs **boh**-tahs)
heel	*el tacón* (ehl tah-**kohn**)
pair	*el par* (ehl pahr)
sandals	*las sandalias* (lahs sahn-**dah**-lyahs)
shoe polish	*el betún* (ehl beh-**toon**)
shoelaces	*los cordones* (lohs kohr-**doh**-nehs)
size	*el número* (ehl **noo**-meh-roh)
sole	*la suela* (lah **sweh**-lah)

Parts of Garments
Las partes de las prendas de vestir
(lahs **pahr**-tehs deh lahs **prehn**-dahs deh behs-**teer**)

button	*el botón* (ehl boh-**tohn**)
collar	*el cuello* (ehl **kweh**-yoh)
cuff	*el puño* (ehl **poo**-nyoh)
hem	*el falso* (ehl **fahl**-soh)
pocket	*el bolsillo* (ehl bohl-**see**-yoh)
sleeve	*la manga* (lah **mahn**-gah)

Verbs

to fix	*arreglar* (ah-rreh-**glahr**)
to get dressed	*vestirse (i)* (behs-**teer**-seh)
to put on	*ponerse* (poh-**nehr**-seh)

to show	*mostrar (ue)* (mohs-**trahr**)
to take off	*quitarse* (kee-**tahr**-seh)
to undress	*desvestirse (i)* (dehs-behs-**teer**-seh)
to wear	*llevar* (yeh-**bahr**)

Note that many verbs used with clothing are reflexive. You may want to review how to use reflexive verbs in Appendix B on pages 187–88.

Shopping for Clothes
Para comprar ropa
(**pah**-rah kohm-**prahr rroh**-pah)

When you go shopping, you often have in mind the size, style, color, and material of the garment you want to buy. It will be important to know how to express your preferences to the salesperson. After all, as we say in Spanish, *"El hábito hace al monje"* (ehl **ah**-bee-toh **ah**-seh ahl **mohn**-heh), which loosely translates as "Clothes make the man."

Talking About Size
Para hablar de tamaño
(**pah**-rah ah-**blahr** deh tah-**mah**-nyoh)

What size is it?	*¿De qué tamaño es?* (deh keh tah-**mah**-nyoh ehs)
It is large/medium/small.	*Es grande/mediano/pequeño.* (ehs **grahn**-deh/meh-**dyah**-noh/peh-**keh**-nyoh)
What is the size of . . . ?	*¿De qué talla es...?* (deh keh **tah**-yah ehs...)
It is size . . .	*Es la talla número...* (ehs lah **tah**-yah **noo**-meh-roh...)

Describing Clothing
Para describir la ropa
(**pah**-rah dehs-kree-**beer** lah **rroh**-pah)

It is . . .	*Es...* (ehs...)
elegant.	*elegante.* (eh-leh-**gahn**-teh)
expensive.	*caro.* (**kah**-roh)
in bad taste.	*de mal gusto.* (deh mahl **goos**-toh)
in good taste.	*de buen gusto.* (deh bwehn **goos**-toh)
inexpensive.	*barato.* (bah-**rah**-toh)
pretty.	*lindo/bonito.* (**leen**-doh/boh-**nee**-toh)
ugly.	*feo.* (**feh**-oh)
It is . . .	*Está...* (ehs-**tah**...)
in style.	*de moda.* (deh **moh**-dah)
out of style.	*pasado de moda.* (pah-**sah**-doh deh **moh**-dah)

Verbs

to fit loosely	*quedarle ancho* (keh-**dahr**-leh **ahn**-choh)
to fit tightly	*quedarle estrecho* (keh-**dahr**-leh ehs-**treh**-choh)
to fit (well/badly)	*quedarle (bien/mal)* (keh-**dahr**-leh [byehn/mahl])
to match	*hacer juego con* (ah-**sehr hweh**-goh kohn)

Colors
Los colores
(lohs koh-**loh**-rehs)

To ask the color of an object in Spanish, use the following question:

What color is (the blouse)?	*¿De qué color es (la blusa)?* (deh keh koh-**lohr** ehs [lah **bloo**-sah])
(The blouse) is red.	*(La blusa) es roja.* ([lah **bloo**-sah] ehs **rroh**-hah)

Remember that colors are descriptive adjectives, and they must agree with the noun they describe in gender and number. Also note that color, like most adjectives, is placed after the noun.

Here is a list of some colors:

black	*negro* (**neh**-groh)
blue	*azul* (ah-**sool**)
brown	*marrón* (mah-**rrohn**)
gray	*gris* (grees)
green	*verde* (**behr**-deh)
navy blue	*azul marino* (ah-**sool** mah-**ree**-noh)
orange	*anaranjado* (ah-nah-rahn-**hah**-doh)
pink	*rosado* (rroh-**sah**-doh)
purple	*violeta* (byoh-**leh**-tah)
red	*rojo* (**rroh**-hoh)
violet	*morado* (moh-**rah**-doh)
white	*blanco* (**blahn**-koh)
yellow	*amarillo* (ah-mah-**ree**-yoh)

When expressing dark and light colors, use *oscuro* (ohs-**koo**-roh) for "dark," *claro* (**klah**-roh) for "light." For example: *azul oscuro* (ah-**sool** ohs-**koo**-roh), *verde claro* (**vehr**-deh **klah**-roh), etc.

Patterns
Los diseños
(lohs dee-**seh**-nyohs)

The material is . . .	*La tela es...* (lah **teh**-lah ehs...)
flowered.	*floreada/de florecitas.* (floh-re-**ah**-dah/deh floh-reh-**see**-tahs)
plaid.	*a cuadros.* (ah **kwah**-drohs)
polka dotted.	*de bolitas/de lunares.* (deh boh-**lee**-tahs/deh loo-**nah**-rehs)
printed.	*estampada.* (ehs-tahm-**pah**-dah)
striped.	*a rayas.* (ah **rrah**-yahs)

Materials
Las telas
(lahs **teh**-lahs)

Knowing the materials your clothes are made of is important, not only for comfort and durability, but also for their care.

What is it made of?	*¿De qué es?* (deh keh ehs)
It is made of . . .	*Es de...* (ehs deh...)
acrylic.	*acrílico.* (ah-**kree**-lee-koh)
corduroy.	*pana.* (**pah**-nah)
cotton.	*algodón.* (ahl-goh-**dohn**)
denim.	*mezclilla.* (mehs-**klee**-yah)
flannel.	*franela.* (frah-**neh**-lah)
fur.	*piel.* (pyehl)
lace.	*encaje.* (ehn-**kah**-heh)
leather.	*cuero.* (**kweh**-roh)
linen.	*lino.* (**lee**-noh)
nylon.	*nilón.* (nee-**lohn**)
polyester.	*poliéster.* (poh-**lyehs**-tehr)
rayon.	*rayón.* (rrah-**yohn**)
satin.	*satín.* (sah-**teen**)
silk.	*seda.* (**seh**-dah)
suede.	*ante.* (**ahn**-teh)
velvet.	*terciopelo.* (tehr-syoh-**peh**-loh)
wool.	*lana.* (**lah**-nah)

Jewelry
Las joyas
(lahs **hoh**-yahs)

Here are the names of some items of jewelry, for both men and women:

It goes well with that/those . . .	*Va bien con ese/esa/esos/esas...* (bah byehn kohn **eh**-seh/**eh**-sah/**eh**-sohs/**eh**-sahs...)
bracelet.	*(el) brazalete/(la) pulsera.* ([ehl] brah-sah-**leh**-teh/[lah] pool-**seh**-rah)

brooch.	*(el) broche.* ([ehl] **broh**-cheh)
chain.	*(la) cadena.* ([lah] kah-**deh**-nah)
cufflinks.	*(los) gemelos.* ([lohs] heh-**meh**-lohs)
earrings.	*(los) aretes/(los) pendientes.* ([lohs] ah-**reh**-tehs/[lohs] pehn-**dyehn**-tehs)
medallion.	*(la) medalla.* ([lah] meh-**dah**-yah)
necklace.	*(el) collar.* ([ehl] koh-**yahr**)
pendant.	*(la) medalla.* ([lah] meh-**dah**-yah)
pin.	*(el) alfiler.* ([ehl] ahl-fee-**lehr**)
ring.	*(el) anillo.* ([ehl] ah-**nee**-yoh)
wristwatch.	*(el) reloj de pulsera.* ([ehl] reh-**loh** deh pool-**seh**-rah)

You'll want to find out what your jewelry or proposed jewelry purchases are made of. To make sure you are getting what you want—and can afford—here is some useful vocabulary:

Of what (material) is it made?	*¿De qué es?* (deh keh ehs)
It is made of . . .	*Es de...* (ehs deh...)
diamonds.	*diamantes.* (dyah-**mahn**-tehs)
emeralds.	*esmeraldas.* (ehs-meh-**rahl**-dahs)
gold.	*oro.* (**oh**-roh)
pearls.	*perlas.* (**pehr**-lahs)
rubies.	*rubíes.* (rroo-**bee**-ehs)
sapphires.	*zafiros.* (sah-**fee**-rohs)
silver.	*plata.* (**plah**-tah)

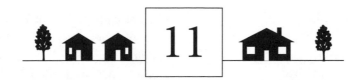

Family Health and Well-Being
La salud y el bienestar de la familia
(lah sah-**lood** ee ehl byehn-ehs-**tahr** deh lah fah-**mee**-lyah)

At the Doctor's Office
En el consultorio del médico
(ehn ehl kohn-sool-**toh**-ryoh dehl **meh**-dee-koh)

Whether a family member is going in for a routine medical checkup or someone gets sick and needs medical attention (especially if it is a child or an elder) it is essential to have all the information at hand and to be familiar with basic medical terminology.

Our doctor's/pediatrician's name is . . .	*Nuestro médico/Nuestra médica; Nuestro/Nuestra pediatra se llama...* (**nwehs**-troh **meh**-dee-koh/**nwehs**-trah **meh**-dee-kah; **nwehs**-troh/ **nwehs**-trah peh-**dyah**-trah seh **yah**-mah...)
His/Her phone number is . . .	*Su número de teléfono es...* (soo **noo**-meh-roh deh teh-**leh**-foh-noh ehs...)
(Name) is allergic . . .	*Es alérgico/alérgica...* (ehs ah-**lehr**-hee-koh/ah-**lehr**-hee-kah)
to aspirin.	*a la aspirina.* (ah lah ahs-pee-**ree**-nah)

to antibiotics.	*a los antibióticos.* (ah lohs ahn-tee-**byoh**-tee-kohs)
to bee stings.	*a la mordedura de las abejas.* (ah lah mohr-deh-**doo**-rah deh lahs ah-**beh**-hahs)
to dust.	*al polvo.* (ahl **pohl**-boh)
to grass.	*a la hierba.* (ah lah **yehr**-bah)
to peanuts.	*al maní/a los cacahuetes.* (ahl mah-**nee**/ah lohs kah-kah-**weh**-tehs)
to perfume.	*al perfume.* (ahl pehr-**foo**-meh)
to pollen.	*al polen.* (ahl **poh**-lehn)
to shellfish.	*a los mariscos.* (ah lohs mah-**rees**-kohs)
I'm sick.	*Estoy enfermo/enferma.* (ehs-**toh**-ee ehn-**fehr**-moh/ehn-**fehr**-mah)
Please call the doctor.	*Llame al médico, por favor.* (**yah**-meh ahl **meh**-dee-koh pohr fah-**bohr**)
I have to go . . .	*Tengo que ir...* (**tehn**-goh keh eer...)
to the doctor's office.	*a la consulta del médico/de la médica.* (ah lah kohn-**sool**-tah dehl **meh**-dee-koh/deh lah **meh**-dee-kah)
to the hospital.	*al hospital.* (ahl ohs-pee-**tahl**)

Additional words that you may need include:

allergy	*la alergia* (lah ah-**lehr**-hyah)
antidote	*el antídoto* (ehl ahn-**tee**-doh-toh)
appointment	*la cita* (lah **see**-tah)
contagious	*contagioso* (kohn-tah-**hyoh**-soh)
doctor	*el médico/la médica* (ehl **meh**-dee-koh/lah **meh**-dee-kah)
nurse	*el enfermero/la enfermera* (ehl ehn-fehr-**meh**-roh/lah ehn-fehr-**meh**-rah)
office hours	*las horas de consulta* (lahs **oh**-rahs deh kohn-**sool**-tah)
patient	*el/la paciente* (ehl/lah pah-**syehn**-teh)

prescription	*la receta* (lah rreh-**seh**-tah)
remedies	*los remedios* (los rreh-**meh**-dyohs)
specialist	*el/la especialista* (ehl/lah ehs-peh-syah-**lees**-tah)
vaccination	*la vacuna* (lah bah-**koo**-nah)
waiting room	*la sala de espera* (lah **sah**-lah deh ehs-**peh**-rah)
wound	*la herida* (lah eh-**ree**-dah)

Parts of the Body
Las partes del cuerpo
(lahs **pahr**-tehs dehl **kwehr**-poh)

ankle	*el tobillo* (ehl toh-**bee**-yoh)
arm	*el brazo* (ehl **brah**-soh)
back	*la espalda* (lah ehs-**pahl**-dah)
blood	*la sangre* (lah **sahn**-greh)
brain	*el cerebro* (ehl seh-**reh**-broh)
cheek	*la mejilla* (lah meh-**hee**-yah)
chest	*el pecho* (ehl **peh**-choh)
chin	*la barbilla* (lah bahr-**bee**-yah)
ear	*la oreja* (lah oh-**reh**-hah)
elbow	*el codo* (ehl **koh**-doh)
eye	*el ojo* (ehl **oh**-hoh)
eyebrow	*la ceja* (lah **seh**-hah)
face	*la cara* (lah **kah**-rah)
finger	*el dedo* (ehl **deh**-doh)
foot	*el pie* (ehl pyeh)
forehead	*la frente* (lah **frehn**-teh)
hair	*el pelo/el cabello* (ehl **peh**-loh/ehl kah-**beh**-yoh)
hand	*la mano* (lah **mah**-noh)
head	*la cabeza* (lah kah-**beh**-sah)
heart	*el corazón* (ehl koh-rah-**sohn**)
hip	*la cadera* (lah kah-**deh**-rah)
inner ear	*el oído* (ehl oh-**ee**-doh)

knee	*la rodilla* (lah rroh-**dee**-yah)
leg	*la pierna* (lah **pyehr**-nah)
lip	*el labio* (ehl **lah**-byoh)
mouth	*la boca* (lah **boh**-kah)
nail	*la uña* (lah **oo**-nyah)
neck	*el cuello* (el **kweh**-yoh)
nose	*la nariz* (lah nah-**rees**)
shoulder	*el hombro* (ehl **ohm**-broh)
skin	*la piel* (lah pyehl)
stomach	*el estómago* (ehl ehs-**toh**-mah-goh)
thigh	*el muslo* (ehl **moos**-loh)
throat	*la garganta* (lah gahr-**gahn**-tah)
toe	*el dedo del pie* (ehl **deh**-doh dehl pyeh)
tongue	*la lengua* (lah **lehn**-gwah)
tooth	*el diente* (ehl **dyehn**-teh)
waist	*la cintura* (lah seen-**too**-rah)
wrist	*la muñeca* (lah moo-**nyeh**-kah)

Symptoms
Los síntomas
(lohs **seen**-toh-mahs)

I have . . .	*Tengo...* (**tehn**-goh...)
chills.	*escalofríos.* (ehs-kah-loh-**free**-ohs)
a cough.	*tos.* (tohs)
diarrhea.	*diarrea.* (dyah-**rreh**-ah)
dizziness.	*mareos.* (mah-**reh**-ohs)
an earache.	*dolor de oído.* (doh-**lohr** deh oh-**ee**-doh)
fever.	*fiebre.* (**fyeh**-breh)
gas.	*gases.* (**gah**-sehs)
a headache.	*dolor de cabeza.* (doh-**lohr** deh kah-**beh**-sah)
indigestion.	*indigestión.* (een-dee-hehs-**tyohn**)
phlegm.	*flema.* (**fleh**-mah)
a rash.	*una erupción.* (**oo**-nah eh-roop-**syohn**)

a sore throat.	*dolor de garganta.* (doh-**lohr** deh gahr-**gahn**-tah)
a stomachache.	*dolor de estómago.* (doh-**lohr** deh ehs-**toh**-mah-goh)
I am . . .	*Estoy...* (ehs-**toh**-ee...)
anxious.	*ansioso.* (ahn-**syoh**-soh)
depressed.	*deprimido.* (deh-pree-**mee**-doh)
dizzy.	*mareado.* (mah-reh-**ah**-doh)
exhausted.	*agotado.* (ah-goh-**tah**-doh)
nauseous.	*mareado.* (mah-reh-**ah**-doh)
nervous.	*nervioso.* (nehr-**byoh**-soh)
out of breath.	*sin respiración.* (seen rrehs-pee-rah-**syohn**)
tired.	*cansado.* (kahn-**sah**-doh)
weak.	*débil.* (**deh**-beel)

Remember that for adjectives that end in -*o*, the -*o* changes to -*a* to form the feminine.

Verbs

to cough	*toser* (toh-**sehr**)
to faint	*desmayarse* (dehs-mah-**yahr**-seh)
to get dizzy	*marearse* (mah-reh-**ahr**-seh)
to sneeze	*estornudar* (ehs-tohr-noo-**dahr**)
to vomit	*vomitar* (boh-mee-**tahr**)

Illnesses
Las enfermedades
(lahs ehn-fehr-meh-**dah**-dehs)

acne	*el acné* (ehl ahk-**neh**)
asthma	*el asma* (ehl **ahs**-mah)
bronchitis	*la bronquitis* (lah brohn-**kee**-tees)
chicken pox	*la varicela* (lah bah-ree-**seh**-lah)
a cold	*el resfriado/el catarro* (ehl rrehs-**fryah**-doh/ehl kah-**tah**-rroh)

constipation	*el estreñimiento* (ehl ehs-treh-nyee-**myehn**-toh)
diabetes	*la diabetes* (lah dyah-**beh**-tehs)
flu	*la gripe* (lah **gree**-peh)
measles	*el sarampión* (ehl sah-rahm-**pyohn**)
mononucleosis	*la mononucleosis* (lah moh-noh-noo-kleh-**oh**-sees)
mumps	*las paperas* (lahs pah-**peh**-rahs)
pneumonia	*la pulmonía* (lah pool-moh-**nee**-ah)
rubella	*la rubiola* (lah rroo-**byoh**-lah)

Recommendations
Las recomendaciones
(lahs rreh-koh-mehn-dah-**syoh**-nehs)

In order to get better, you must . . .	*Para mejorarse, Ud. debe...* (**pah**-rah meh-hoh-**rahr**-seh oos-**tehd deh**-beh...)
stay in bed.	*guardar cama.* (gwahr-**dahr kah**-mah)
take care of yourself.	*cuidarse.* (kwee-**dahr**-seh)
Here is the prescription.	*Aquí tiene la receta.* (ah-**kee tyeh**-neh lah rreh-**seh**-tah)
You have to take . . .	*Tiene que tomar...* (**tyeh**-neh keh toh-**mahr**...)
antibiotics.	*antibióticos.* (ahn-tee-**byoh**-tee-kohs)
antihistamines.	*antihistamínicos.* (ahn-tees-tah-**mee**-nee-kohs)
antacids.	*antiácidos.* (ahn-**tyah**-see-dohs)
aspirin.	*aspirina.* (ahs-pee-**ree**-nah)
cough syrup.	*jarabe para la tos.* (hah-**rah**-beh **pah**-rah lah tohs)
penicillin.	*penicilina.* (peh-nee-see-**lee**-nah)
. . . tablets (lozenges).	*pastillas de....* (pahs-**tee**-yahs deh...)
vitamins.	*vitaminas.* (bee-tah-**mee**-nahs)

Put on . . .	*Póngase...* (**pohn**-gah-seh...)
this antiseptic.	*este antiséptico.* (**ehs**-teh ahn-tee-**sehp**-tee-koh)
this cream.	*esta pomada.* (**ehs**-tah poh-**mah**-dah)
iodine.	*yodo.* (**yoh**-doh)
this liniment.	*este linimento.* (**ehs**-teh lee-nee-**mehn**-toh)
this lotion.	*esta loción.* (**ehs**-tah loh-**syohn**)
this powder.	*este polvo.* (**ehs**-teh **pohl**-boh)
Drink a lot of water.	*Tome mucha agua.* (**toh**-meh **moo**-chah **ah**-gwah)

Giving Medication to Children
Para darles medicina a los niños
(**pah**-rah **dahr**-lehs meh-dee-**see**-nah ah lohs **nee**-nyohs)

It is very important to make it clear to the caretaker what medications can be given to a child, how much should be given, and when to give it.

Give him/her . . .	*Déle...* (**deh**-leh...)
Don't give him/her . . .	*No le dé...* (noh leh deh...)
How much should he/she take?	*¿Cuánto debe tomar?* (**kwahn**-toh **deh**-beh toh-**mahr**)
He/She should take . . .	*Debe tomar...* (**deh**-beh toh-**mahr**...)
one (two . . .) pill(s).	*una (dos...) píldora(s).* (**oo**-nah [dohs...] **peel**-doh-rah[s])
a teaspoonful.	*una cucharadita.* (**oo**-nah koo-chah-rah-**dee**-tah)
a tablespoonful.	*una cucharada.* (**oo**-nah koo-chah-**rah**-dah)
How often should he/she take the medicine?	*¿Cada cuánto tiempo tiene que tomar la medicina?* (**kah**-dah **kwahn**-toh **tyehm**-poh **tyeh**-neh keh toh-**mahr** lah meh-dee-**see**-nah)

He/She has to take the medicine . . .	*Tiene que tomar la medicina...* (**tyeh**-neh keh toh-**mahr** lah meh-dee-**see**-nah...)
every X hours.	*cada X horas.* (**kah**-dah... **oh**-rahs)
once a day.	*una vez al día.* (**oo**-nah behs ahl **dee**-ah)
X times a day.	*X veces al día.* (... **beh**-sehs ahl **dee**-ah)
X times a week.	*X veces a la semana.* (... **beh**-sehs ah lah seh-**mah**-nah)
in the morning.	*por la mañana.* (pohr lah mah-**nyah**-nah)
in the afternoon.	*por la tarde.* (pohr lah **tahr**-deh)
at night.	*por la noche.* (pohr lah **noh**-cheh)
between meals.	*entre comidas.* (**ehn**-treh koh-**mee**-dahs)
before breakfast/ lunch/dinner.	*antes del desayuno/del almuerzo/ de la cena.* (**ahn**-tehs dehl deh-sah-**yoo**-noh/dehl ahl-**mwehr**-soh/deh lah **seh**-nah)
with food.	*con comida.* (kohn koh-**mee**-dah)
after meals.	*después de las comidas.* (dehs-**pwehs** deh lahs koh-**mee**-dahs)

Accidents
Los accidentes
(lohs ahk-see-**dehn**-tehs)

Many of the verbs used to talk about accidents are reflexive verbs. For example:

to break	*romperse* (rrohm-**pehr**-seh)
to burn	*quemarse* (keh-**mahr**-seh)
to cut	*cortarse* (kohr-**tahr**-seh)
to fall	*caerse* (kah-**ehr**-seh)
to hit	*golpearse* (gohl-peh-**ahr**-seh)
to sprain	*torcerse* (tohr-**sehr**-seh)

To review the conjugation of reflexive verbs, go to Appendix B on pages 187–88. You will need to use the preterite tense to talk about what happened to you or to someone else. To review the Spanish preterite, see also Appendix B on pages 193–97.

What happened to him/her?	*¿Qué le pasó?* (keh leh pah-**soh**)
He/She broke his/her . . . (part of body)	*Se rompió el/la/los/las* (part of body) (seh rrohm-**pyoh** ehl/lah/lohs/lahs...)
He/She has a(n) . . . (part of body).	*Tiene el/la...* (part of body) (**tyeh**-neh ehl/lah...)
broken	*roto* (**rroh**-toh)
burned	*quemado* (keh-**mah**-doh)
infected	*infectado* (een-fehk-**tah**-doh)
swollen	*hinchado* (een-**chah**-doh)
twisted	*torcido* (tohr-**see**-doh)
It is necessary . . .	*Hay que...* (**ah**-ee keh...)
to bandage the wound.	*vendar la herida.* (behn-**dahr** lah eh-**ree**-dah)
to clean the wound.	*limpiar la herida.* (leem-**pyahr** lah eh-**ree**-dah)

Medical Equipment and Devices
Los aparatos médicos
(lohs ah-pah-**rah**-tohs **meh**-dee-kohs)

band-aid	*la curita* (lah koo-**ree**-tah)
bandage	*la venda* (lah **behn**-dah)
cane	*el bastón* (ehl bahs-**tohn**)
cast	*el yeso* (ehl **yeh**-soh)
crutches	*las muletas* (lahs moo-**leh**-tahs)
stitches	*los puntos* (lohs **poon**-tohs)
thermometer	*el termómetro* (ehl tehr-**moh**-meh-troh)
wheelchair	*la silla de ruedas* (lah **see**-yah deh **rrweh**-dahs)

In an Emergency
En una emergencia
(ehn **oo**-nah eh-mehr-**hehn**-syah)

We hope that you and your employees will never encounter any emergencies, but in the event that you do, it is important to have a routine in place. First, your family members and anyone who is involved in your family's well-being must know how to call 911 (or other local emergency numbers), give the relevant address, and state the problem. In case of fire, all members of the household should know what your plan of escape is. For example: everyone must get out of the house or apartment, meet at a certain place, and call 911, the fire department, or other emergency services (if they have not yet been summoned).

Call 911.	*Llame al 911.* (**yah**-meh ahl **nweh**-beh **ohn**-seh)
The address is . . .	*La dirección es...* (lah dee-rehk-**syohn** ehs...)
Call the police.	*Llame a la policía.* (**yah**-meh ah lah poh-lee-**see**-ah)
There is a fire at . . .	*Hay un fuego en...* (**ah**-ee oon **fweh**-goh ehn...)
Call the fire department.	*Llame a los bomberos.* (**yah**-meh ah lohs bohm-**beh**-rohs)
Someone has robbed the house.	*Alguien ha saqueado la casa.* (**ahl**-gyehn ah sah-keh-**ah**-doh lah **kah**-sah)
There has been an accident.	*Ha habido un accidente.* (ah ah-**bee**-doh oon ahk-see-**dehn**-teh)
He/She is . . .	*Está...* (ehs-**tah**...)
bleeding.	*sangrando.* (sahn-**grahn**-doh)
choking.	*asfixiándose.* (ahs-feek-**syahn**-doh-seh)
dizzy.	*mareado.* (mah-reh-**ah**-doh)
suffocating.	*asfixiándose.* (ahs-feek-**syahn**-doh-seh)
unconscious.	*inconsciente.* (een-kohn-**syehn**-teh)
vomiting.	*vomitando.* (boh-mee-**tahn**-doh)
wounded.	*herido.* (eh-**ree**-doh)

He/She can't breathe.	*No puede respirar.* (noh **pweh**-deh rrehs-pee-**rahr**)
He/She has . . .	*Tiene...* (**tyeh**-neh...)
a burn.	*una quemadura.* (**oo**-nah keh-mah-**doo**-rah)
convulsions.	*convulsiones.* (kohn-bool-**syoh**-nehs)
a rash.	*una erupción.* (**oo**-nah eh-roop-**syohn**)
A dog bit him/her.	*Un perro lo/la mordió.* (oon **peh**-rroh loh/lah mohr-**dyoh**)
He/She fell into the pool.	*Se cayó en la piscina.* (seh kah-**yoh** ehn lah pee-**see**-nah)
I need an ambulance.	*Necesito una ambulancia.* (neh-seh-**see**-toh **oo**-nah ahm-boo-**lahn**-syah)

Here are some words that can be shouted in an emergency.

Be careful!	*¡Cuidado!* (kwee-**dah**-doh)
Fire!	*¡Fuego!* (**fweh**-goh)
Help!	*¡Socorro!* (soh-**koh**-rroh)
Hurry up!	*¡Dese prisa!* (**deh**-seh **pree**-sah)
Listen!	*¡Escuche!* (ehs-**koo**-cheh)
Look!	*¡Mire!* (**mee**-reh)
Police!	*¡Policía!* (poh-lee-**see**-ah)

At the Dentist's Office
En el consultorio del dentista
(ehn ehl kohn-sool-**toh**-ryoh dehl dehn-**tees**-tah)

Nowadays, going to the dentist is not the unpleasant experience it used to be.

Here are some words and expressions related to dental care:

baby teeth	*los dientes de leche* (lohs **dyehn**-tehs deh **leh**-cheh)
brace	*el corrector* (ehl koh-**rrehk**-tohr)
cavity	*la caries* (lah **kah**-ryehs)

dental floss	*el hilo dental* (ehl **ee**-loh dehn-**tahl**)
dentist's office	*el consultorio del dentista* (ehl kohn-sool-**toh**-ryoh dehl dehn-**tees**-tah)
filling	*el empaste* (ehl ehm-**pahs**-teh)
gum	*la encía* (lah ehn-**see**-ah)
wisdom tooth	*la muela del juicio* (lah **mweh**-lah dehl **hwee**-syoh)
Ouch!	*¡Ay!* (**ah**-ee)

Verbs

to brush your teeth	*cepillarse los dientes* (seh-pee-**yahr**-seh lohs **dyehn**-tehs)
to extract a tooth	*sacar una muela* (sah-**kahr oo**-nah **mweh**-lah)
to fill a tooth	*empastar una muela* (ehm-pahs-**tahr oo**-nah **mweh**-lah)
to have a toothache	*tener dolor de muelas* (teh-**nehr** doh-**lohr** deh **mweh**-lahs)
to hurt	*doler (ue)* (doh-**lehr**)

Eye Care
El cuidado de los ojos
(ehl kwee-**dah**-doh deh lohs **oh**-hohs)

Here are some words and expressions related to eye care:

contact lenses	*los lentes de contacto* (lohs **lehn**-tehs deh kohn-**tahk**-toh)
eye doctor	*el oculista* (ehl oh-koo-**lees**-tah)
eyeglasses	*los anteojos* (lohs ahn-teh-**oh**-hohs)
sunglasses	*los anteojos de sol* (lohs ahn-teh-**oh**-hohs deh sohl)

You can study the verb *doler* (to hurt) in greater detail in Appendix B on pages 192–93.

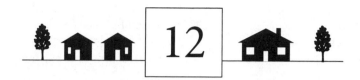

Taking Care of the Children
El cuidado de los niños
(ehl kwee-**dah**-doh deh lohs **nee**-nyohs)

Making sure that the children in the household are safe and sound (*sanos y salvos*) (**sah**-nohs ee **sahl**-bohs) is of utmost importance. You'll need some words to help your caretaker fulfill this important task.

In the Children's Bedroom
En el dormitorio de los niños
(ehn ehl dohr-mee-**toh**-ryoh deh lohs **nee**-nyohs)

Here are some things you may find in a young child's bedroom:

baby bottle	*el biberón* (ehl bee-beh-**rohn**)
baby carriage	*el cochecito* (ehl koh-cheh-**see**-toh)
baby wipes	*los trapitos para limpiar al bebé* (lohs trah-**pee**-tohs **pah**-rah leem-**pyahr** ahl bee-**beh**)
bib	*el babero* (ehl bah-**beh**-roh)
car seat	*el asiento de seguridad para niños* (ehl ah-**syehn**-toh deh seh-goo-ree-**dahd pah**-rah **nee**-nyohs)
crib	*la cuna* (lah **koo**-nah)

diaper	*el pañal* (ehl pah-**nyahl**)
diaper pin	*el imperdible* (ehl eem-pehr-**dee**-bleh)
disposable diaper	*el pañal desechable* (ehl pah-**nyahl** deh-seh-**chah**-bleh)
lotion	*la loción* (lah loh-**syohn**)
pacifier	*el chupete* (ehl choo-**peh**-teh)
rattle	*el sonajero* (ehl soh-nah-**heh**-roh)
rocking chair	*la mecedora* (lah meh-seh-**doh**-rah)
stroller	*el cochecito* (ehl koh-cheh-**see**-toh)
toy	*el juguete* (ehl hoo-**geh**-teh)

Verbs

to change a dirty diaper	*cambiar un pañal sucio* (kahm-**byahr** oon pah-**nyahl soo**-syoh)
to put on a clean diaper	*ponerle un pañal limpio* (poh-**nehr**-leh oon pah-**nyahl leem**-pyoh)

Toys and Playthings
Los juguetes y otras cosas para jugar
(lohs hoo-**geh**-tehs ee **oh**-trahs **koh**-sahs **pah**-rah hoo-**gahr**)

Children have many playthings, and it will be helpful to know what they are called, in English and in Spanish.

balloon	*el globo* (ehl **gloh**-boh)
blocks (wood)	*los bloques de madera* (lohs **bloh**-kehs deh mah-**deh**-rah)
coloring book	*el libro de colorear* (ehl **lee**-broh deh koh-loh-reh-**ahr**)
costume	*el disfraz* (ehl dees-**frahs**)
jump rope	*la cuerda de saltar* (lah **kwehr**-dah deh sahl-**tahr**)
kite	*la cometa* (lah koh-**meh**-tah)
puppet	*el títere* (ehl **tee**-teh-reh)
skates	*los patines* (lohs pah-**tee**-nehs)
stuffed animal	*el animal de peluche* (ehl ah-nee-**mahl** deh peh-**loo**-cheh)

| top | *el trompo* (ehl **trohm**-poh) |
| wagon | *el carretón* (ehl kah-rreh-**tohn**) |

It is common to refer to stuffed animals with the ending -*ito* (-*ita*), used to indicate affection or endearment. For example: toy bear *el osito* (ehl oh-**see**-toh), toy cat *el gatito* (ehl gah-**tee**-toh), toy dog *el perrito* (ehl peh-**rree**-toh), etc. The diminutive ending -*ito* (-*ita*) is also used with people's names to indicate endearment. You will hear, for example, *Juanito* for *Juan*, or *Teresita* for *Teresa*.

Children's Likes and Dislikes
Lo que les gusta o no les gusta a los niños
(loh keh lehs **goos**-tah oh noh lehs **goos**-tah ah lohs **nee**-nyohs)

It is important for a caretaker to know a child's likes, dislikes, and favorite activities. Here are some of the things a child may like to do at or near home:

He/She likes . . .	*Le gusta...* (leh **goos**-tah...)
to color.	*colorear.* (koh-loh-reh-**ahr**)
to draw.	*dibujar.* (dee-boo-**hahr**)
to go to the park.	*ir al parque.* (eer ahl **pahr**-keh)
to hear stories.	*oír cuentos.* (oh-**eer kwehn**-tohs)
to paint.	*pintar.* (peen-**tahr**)
to play . . .	*jugar (ue)...* (hoo-**gahr**...)
board games.	*juegos de mesa.* (**hweh**-gohs deh **meh**-sah)
cards.	*a las cartas.* (ah lahs **kahr**-tahs)
checkers.	*a las damas.* (ah lahs **dah**-mahs)
chess.	*al ajedrez.* (ahl ah-heh-**drehs**)
computer games.	*juegos de computadora.* (**hweh**-gohs deh kohm-poo-tah-**doh**-rah)
"dress up."	*a disfrazarse.* (ah dees-frah-**sahr**-seh)
"house."	*a la casita.* (ah lah kah-**see**-tah)
video games.	*juegos de vídeo.* (**hweh**-gohs deh **bee**-deh-oh)

to play in the yard.	*jugar en el patio.* (hoo-**gahr** ehn ehl **pah**-tyoh)
to put puzzles together.	*armar rompecabezas.* (ahr-**mahr** rrohm-peh-kah-**beh**-sahs)
to read stories.	*leer cuentos.* (leh-**ehr kwehn**-tohs)
to ride . . .	*montar...* (mohn-**tahr**...)
a bicycle.	*en bicicleta.* (ehn bee-see-**kleh**-tah)
a sled.	*en trineo.* (ehn tree-**neh**-oh)
a swing.	*en columpio.* (ehn koh-**loom**-pyoh)
a tricycle.	*en triciclo.* (ehn tree-**see**-kloh)
a skateboard.	*en monopatín.* (ehn moh-noh-pah-**teen**)
to rollerblade.	*patinar con patines en línea.* (pah-tee-**nahr** kohn pah-**tee**-nehs ehn **lee**-neh-ah)
to tell stories.	*contar cuentos.* (kohn-**tahr kwehn**-tohs)

Rules of Behavior for Children
Las reglas de comportamiento para los niños
(lahs **rreh**-glahs deh kohm-pohr-tah-**myehn**-toh **pah**-rah lohs **nee**-nyohs)

Each family has its own standards concerning what children ought to learn and how to teach it. To work as your ally in this most important task, a caretaker must know the behavior you expect from your children. He or she must also know what consequences there will be when family rules are not followed, and who will administer these consequences. You need to be able to explain your family's system of rewards and punishments. Do you expect your caretaker to administer them or explain to you what may have occurred? What type of rewards and punishments do you consider appropriate?

Daily Routine
La rutina diaria
(lah rroo-**tee**-nah **dyah**-ryah)

It's time . . .	*Es hora de...* (ehs **oh**-rah deh...)
to get up.	*levantarse.* (leh-bahn-**tahr**-seh)
to take a nap/rest.	*dormir (ue) la siesta/descansar.* (dohr-**meer** lah **syehs**-tah/dehs-kahn-**sahr**)

to go to bed.	*acostarse (ue).* (ah-kohs-**tahr**-seh)
Children have . . .	*Los niños tienen que...* (lohs **nee**-nyohs **tyeh**-nehn keh...)
to bathe.	*bañarse.* (bah-**nyahr**-seh)
to brush their teeth.	*cepillarse los dientes.* (seh-pee-**yahr**-seh lohs **dyehn**-tehs)
to comb their hair.	*peinarse.* (peh-ee-**nahr**-seh)
to do their homework.	*hacer la tarea.* (ah-**sehr** lah tah-**reh**-ah)
to dress themselves.	*vestirse.* (behs-**teer**-seh)
to play quietly before bedtime.	*jugar tranquilamente antes de la hora de acostarse (ue).* (hoo-**gahr** trahn-kee-lah-**mehn**-teh **ahn**-tehs deh lah **oh**-rah deh ah-kohs-**tahr**-seh)
to put on their shoes/ clothes.	*ponerse los zapatos/la ropa.* (poh-**nehr**-seh lohs sah-**pah**-tohs/lah **rroh**-pah)
to study.	*estudiar.* (ehs-too-**dyahr**)
to tie their shoelaces.	*abrocharse los cordones.* (ah-broh-**chahr**-seh lohs kohr-**doh**-nehs)
to wash up.	*lavarse.* (lah-**bahr**-seh)

Other Obligations
Otras obligaciones
(**oh**-trahs oh-blee-gah-**syoh**-nehs)

Children must . . .	*Los niños deben...* (lohs **nee**-nyohs **deh**-behn...)
have good manners.	*tener buenos modales.* (teh-**nehr bweh**-nohs moh-**dah**-lehs)
share.	*compartir sus cosas.* (kohm-pahr-**teer** soos **koh**-sahs)
treat others with respect.	*tratar a los demás con respeto.* (trah-**tahr** ah lohs deh-**mahs** kohn rrehs-**peh**-toh)

Be sure to inform your caretaker of any weekly or daily chores your children are supposed to do around the house. Here are some chores children may be involved in:

clean their room	*limpiar su cuarto* (leem-**pyahr** soo **kwahr**-toh)
clear the table	*quitar la mesa* (kee-**tahr** lah **meh**-sah)
make their bed	*hacer la cama* (ah-**sehr** lah **kah**-mah)
pick up their clothes	*recoger su ropa* (rre-koh-**hehr** soo **rroh**-pah)
put away their toys	*guardar sus juguetes* (gwahr-**dahr** soos hoo-**geh**-tehs)
set the table	*poner la mesa* (poh-**nehr** lah **meh**-sah)
take care of their pets	*cuidar de sus animales domésticos* (kwee-**dahr** deh soos ah-nee-**mah**-lehs doh-**mehs**-tee-kohs)
Children should not . . .	*Los niños no deben...* (lohs **nee**-nyohs noh **deh**-behn...)
bite.	*morder.* (mohr-**dehr**)
fight.	*pelear.* (peh-leh-**ahr**)
hit.	*dar golpes.* (dahr **gohl**-pehs)
kick.	*dar patadas.* (dahr pah-**tah**-dahs)
push.	*empujar.* (ehm-poo-**hahr**)
run in the house.	*correr dentro de la casa.* (koh-**rrehr** **dehn**-troh deh lah **kah**-sah)
say bad words.	*decir malas palabras.* (deh-**seer** **mah**-lahs pah-**lah**-brahs)
talk to strangers.	*hablar con desconocidos.* (ah-**blahr** kohn dehs-koh-noh-**see**-dohs)
watch . . . on TV.	*mirar... en la televisión.* (mee-**rahr**... ehn lah teh-leh-bee-**syohn**)

To find out if a child has behaved in the way you have outlined, ask:

Did he/she behave?	*¿Se portó bien?* (seh pohr-**toh** byehn)
How did he/she behave? Or:	*¿Cómo se portó?* (**koh**-moh seh pohr-**toh**)
What did he/she do today?	*¿Qué hizo hoy?* (keh **ee**-soh **oh**-ee)

One of the most important aspects of taking care of children is making sure that they stay healthy and that any illness is promptly addressed. For words and expressions that will help a caretaker do this, review "Accidents" and "In an Emergency" on pages 128–29 and 130–31 in Chapter 11.

What is expected on a day-to-day basis must be made clear to the caretaker. Here we list some things you may want (or not want) the caretaker to do:

Please . . .	*Haga el favor de...* (**ah**-gah ehl fah-**bohr** deh...)
bathe the children.	*bañar a los niños.* (bah-**nyahr** ah lohs **nee**-nyohs)
change their clothes.	*cambiarlos de ropa.* (kahm-**byahr**-lohs deh **rroh**-pah)
dress them.	*vestirlos.* (behs-**teer**-lohs)
feed them.	*darles de comer.* (**dahr**-lehs deh koh-**mehr**)
help them to . . .	*ayudarlos a...* (ah-yoo-**dahr**-lohs ah...)
pick them up at . . .	*recogerlos en...* (rreh-koh-**hehr**-lohs ehn...)
put them to bed at X.	*acostarlos a la/las X.* (ah-kohs-**tahr**-lohs ah lah/lahs...)
scold them if . . .	*regañarlos si...* (rreh-gah-**nyahr**-lohs see...)
take them to . . .	*llevarlos a...* (yeh-**bahr**-lohs ah...)
wake them up at X.	*despertarlos a la/las X.* (dehs-pehr-**tahr**-lohs ah lah/lahs...)

Good supervision is the key to avoiding accidents.

Please supervise them while they . . .	*Haga el favor de supervisarlos mientras...* (**ah**-gah ehl fah-**bohr** deh soo-pehr-bee-**sahr**-lohs **myehn**-trahs...)
bathe.	*se bañan.* (seh **bah**-nyahn)
do their homework.	*hacen la tarea.* (**ah**-sehn lah tah-**reh**-ah)
play.	*juegan.* (**hweh**-gahn)
play video/computer games.	*juegan con vídeos/la computadora.* (**hweh**-gahn kohn **bee**-deh-ohs/lah kohm-poo-tah-**doh**-rah)
watch TV.	*miran la tele.* (**mee**-rahn lah **teh**-leh)

It is also very important to make clear what not to do.

Please do not . . .	*Haga el favor de no...* (**ah**-gah ehl fah-**bohr** deh noh...)
leave the children alone.	*dejar a los niños solos.* (deh-**hahr** ah lohs **nee**-nyohs **soh**-lohs)

| leave the doors open. | *dejar las puertas abiertas.* (deh-**hahr** lahs **pwehr**-tahs ah-**byehr**-tahs) |
| let anyone in the house. | *permitir que nadie entre en la casa.* (pehr-mee-**teer** keh **nah**-dyeh **ehn**-treh ehn lah **kah**-sah) |

| Please do not let the children . . . | *Haga el favor de no permitir que los niños...* (**ah**-gah ehl fah-**bohr** deh noh pehr-mee-**teer** keh lohs **nee**-nyohs...) |

ride their bikes without a helmet.	*monten en bicicleta sin casco.* (**mohn**-tehn ehn bee-see-**kleh**-tah seen **kahs**-koh)
be near the pool by themselves.	*estén cerca de la piscina solos.* (ehs-**tehn** **sehr**-kah deh lah pee-**see**-nah **soh**-lohs)
swim by themselves.	*naden solos.* (**nah**-dehn **soh**-lohs)
talk to strangers.	*hablen con desconocidos.* (**ah**-blehn kohn dehs-koh-noh-**see**-dohs)
touch . . .	*toquen...* (**toh**-kehn...)
use the oven/ microwave by themselves.	*usen el horno/el microondas solos.* (**oo**-sehn ehl **ohr**-noh/ehl mee-kroh-**ohn**-dahs **soh**-lohs)

Dangers Around the House
Los peligros en la casa
(lohs peh-**lee**-grohs ehn lah **kah**-sah)

As you know, children get into everything, and every household contains things that are potentially dangerous. It is important to go over possible dangers with anyone who helps you at home. Three areas of the home are particularly dangerous: the kitchen, the bathroom, and the tool shed and yard.

ammonia	*el amoníaco* (ehl ah-moh-**nee**-ah-koh)
bleach	*el blanqueador/el cloro* (ehl blahn-keh-ah-**dohr**/ehl **kloh**-roh)
chemicals	*los productos químicos* (lohs proh-**dook**-tohs **kee**-mee-kohs)
electrical outlets	*los enchufes* (lohs ehn-**choo**-fehs)

pills   *las píldoras* (lahs **peel**-doh-rahs)

plastic bags   *las bolsas plásticas* (lahs **bohl**-sahs **plahs**-tee-kahs)

Talking About School
Para hablar sobre la escuela
(**pah**-rah ah-**blahr soh**-breh lah ehs-**kweh**-lah)

At times you may need to get some feedback from an employee who takes your child to school. You may even want to use your Spanish to speak with someone who works in the school.

When addressing a Spanish speaker, using the titles *señor* (seh-**nyohr**) (sir), *señora* (seh-**nyoh**-rah) (madam), or *señorita* (seh-nyoh-**ree**-tah) (miss) is a sign of respect (even if you are not using the individual's name). For example:

Yes, sir.   *Sí, señor.* (see seh-**nyohr**)

When talking (in the third person) about a teacher (or about any other person) in Spanish, use the definite article with the titles *señor* (seh-**nyohr**), *señora* (seh-**nyoh**-rah), or *señorita* (seh-nyoh-**ree**-tah).

Mister (Mr.) Díaz   *el señor (Sr.) Díaz* (ehl seh-**nyohr dee**-ahs)

Mrs. Nadel   *la señora (Sra.) Nadel* (lah seh-**nyoh**-rah nah-**dehl**)

Miss Mosco   *la señorita (Srta.) Mosco* (lah seh-nyoh-**ree**-tah **mohs**-koh)

For example:

Mr. Díaz is the Spanish teacher.   *El señor Díaz es el maestro de español.* (ehl seh-**nyohr dee**-ahs ehs ehl mah-**ehs**-troh deh ehs-pah-**nyohl**)

Here is some vocabulary you will need to talk about school-related subjects:

backpack   *la mochila* (lah moh-**chee**-lah)

book   *el libro* (ehl **lee**-broh)

chalkboard   *la pizarra* (lah pee-**sah**-rrah)

classroom	*el salón de clases/el aula* (ehl sah-**lohn** deh **klah**-sehs/ehl **ah**-oo-lah)
grade (level)[1]	*el grado* (ehl **grah**-doh)
grade (mark)	*la nota* (lah **noh**-tah)
homework	*la tarea* (lah tah-**reh**-ah)
lesson	*la lección* (lah lehk-**syohn**)
notebook	*el cuaderno* (ehl kwah-**dehr**-noh)
pencil	*el lápiz* (ehl **lah**-pees)
principal	*el director/la directora* (ehl dee-rehk-**tohr**/lah dee-rehk-**toh**-rah)
recess	*el recreo* (ehl rreh-**kreh**-oh)
report (paper)	*el informe* (ehl een-**fohr**-meh)
report card	*el boletín* (ehl boh-leh-**teen**)
schedule	*el horario* (ehl oh-**rah**-ryoh)
school year	*el año escolar* (ehl **ah**-nyoh ehs-koh-**lahr**)
student	*el/la estudiante* (ehl/lah ehs-too-**dyahn**-teh)
subject (course)	*la asignatura* (lah ah-seeg-nah-**too**-rah)
teacher	*el maestro/la maestra* (ehl mah-**ehs**-troh/lah mah-**ehs**-trah)
test	*el examen/la prueba* (ehl ehk-**sah**-mehn/lah **prweh**-bah)

School Subjects
Las asignaturas
(lahs ah-seeg-nah-**too**-rahs)

Art	*el arte* (ehl **ahr**-teh)
Computer Science	*la informática* (lah een-fohr-**mah**-tee-kah)
English	*el inglés* (ehl een-**glehs**)
French	*el francés* (ehl frahn-**sehs**)

1. For a list of ordinal numbers go to Chapter 14 on pages 158–159.

History	*la historia* (lah ees-**toh**-ryah)
Mathematics	*las matemáticas* (lahs mah-teh-**mah**-tee-kahs)
Physical Education	*la educación física* (lah eh-doo-kah-**syohn fee**-see-kah)
Science	*la ciencia* (lah **syehn**-syah)
Spanish	*el español* (ehl ehs-pah-**nyohl**)

Verbs

to attend	*asistir a* (ah-sees-**teer** ah)
to be absent	*estar ausente* (ehs-**tahr** ah-oo-**sehn**-teh)
to behave badly	*portarse mal* (pohr-**tahr**-seh mahl)
to behave well	*portarse bien* (pohr-**tahr**-seh byehn)
to know (information or facts)	*saber* (sah-**behr**)
to know (to be familiar with a person/place/subject)	*conocer*[2] (koh-noh-**sehr**)
to learn	*aprender* (ah-prehn-**dehr**)
to teach	*enseñar* (ehn-seh-**nyahr**)
to understand	*comprender* (kohm-prehn-**dehr**)

2. For more on the use of *saber* and *conocer* go to Appendix B on pages 190–91.

Social and Cultural Activities
Las actividades sociales y culturales
(lahs ahk-tee-bee-**dah**-dehs soh-**syah**-lehs ee kool-too-**rah**-lehs)

People of all cultures value their family and friends and gather on special occasions to celebrate together. Whatever the program of activities, it is important for everyone to have a good time.

Have a good time!

¡Que se diviertan!/¡Que lo pasen bien! (keh seh dee-**byehr**-tahn/keh loh **pah**-sehn byehn)

Family Celebrations/Parties
Las celebraciones familiares/las fiestas
(lahs seh-leh-brah-**syoh**-nehs fah-mee-**lyah**-rehs/lahs **fyehs**-tahs)

Each family has its own customs and days when they celebrate. Your employees will appreciate your remembering their special dates. You will appreciate their learning something about yours.

anniversaries
los aniversarios (lohs ah-nee-behr-**sah**-ryohs)

births
los nacimientos (lohs nah-see-**myehn**-tohs)

birthday(s)	*el/los cumpleaños* (ehl/lohs koom-pleh-**ah**-nyohs)
graduations	*las graduaciones* (lahs grah-dwah-**syoh**-nehs)
weddings	*las bodas* (lahs **boh**-dahs)

To express congratulations, say:

Congratulations!	*¡Felicidades!/¡Enhorabuena!* (feh-lee-see-**dah**-dehs/eh-noh-rah-**bweh**-nah)
Happy anniversary!	*¡Feliz aniversario!* (feh-**lees** ah-nee-behr-**sah**-ryoh)
Happy birthday!	*¡Feliz cumpleaños!* (feh-**lees** koom-pleh-**ah**-nyohs)

National and Religious Holidays
Las fiestas nacionales y religiosas
(lahs **fyehs**-tahs nah-syoh-**nah**-lehs ee rreh-lee-**hyoh**-sahs)

Celebrating national and religious holidays is an important part of any culture. Some of the holidays we celebrate in the United States are:

Christmas	*la Navidad* (lah nah-bee-**dahd**)
Columbus Day	*el día de la Raza* (ehl **dee**-ah deh lah **rrah**-sah)
Easter	*la Pascua de Resurrección* (lah **pahs**-kwah deh rreh-soo-rrehk-**syohn**)
Halloween	*la víspera de Todos los Santos* (lah **bees**-peh-rah deh **toh**-dohs lohs **sahn**-tohs)
Hanukkah	*la Fiesta de las Luces* (lah **fyehs**-tah deh lahs **loo**-sehs)
Labor Day	*el día del trabajador* (ehl **dee**-ah dehl trah-bah-hah-**dohr**)
New Year's Day	*el día de Año Nuevo* (ehl **dee**-ah deh **ah**-nyoh **nweh**-boh)
Presidents' Day	*el día de los Presidentes* (ehl **dee**-ah deh lohs preh-see-**dehn**-tehs)
Ramadan	*Ramadán* (rrah-mah-**dahn**)

Rosh Hashanah	*el día de Año Nuevo Judío* (ehl **dee**-ah deh **ah**-nyoh **nweh**-boh hoo-**dee**-oh)
Thanksgiving	*el día de Acción de Gracias* (ehl **dee**-ah deh ahk-**syohn** deh **grah**-syahs)
Valentine's Day	*el día de los Enamorados* (ehl **dee**-ah deh lohs eh-nah-moh-**rah**-dohs)

To express good wishes, say:

Happy Easter!	*¡Felices Pascuas!* (feh-**lee**-sehs **pahs**-kwahs)
Merry Christmas!	*¡Feliz Navidad!* (feh-**lees** nah-bee-**dahd**)
Happy New Year!	*¡Feliz/Próspero Año Nuevo!* (feh-**lees**/**prohs**-peh-roh **ah**-nyoh **nweh**-boh)

Renting Videos
Para alquilar vídeos
(**pah**-rah ahl-kee-**lahr bee**-deh-ohs)

Watching videos and DVDs at home is a favorite family pastime. Here are some words that will come in handy:

actor	*el actor* (ehl ahk-**tohr**)
actress	*la actriz* (lah ahk-**trees**)
adventure films	*las películas de aventuras* (lahs peh-**lee**-koo-lahs deh ah-behn-**too**-rahs)
DVD	*el DVD* (ehl deh beh deh)
comedies	*las comedias* (lahs koh-**meh**-dyahs)
horror films	*las películas de horror* (lahs peh-**lee**-koo-lahs deh oh-**rrohr**)
popcorn	*las palomitas de maíz* (lahs pah-loh-**mee**-tahs deh mah-**ees**)
movies	*las películas* (lahs peh-**lee**-koo-lahs)
musicals	*las comedias musicales* (lahs koh-**meh**-dyahs moo-see-**kah**-lehs)

videos	*los vídeos* (lohs **bee**-deh-ohs)
video store	*la tienda de vídeos* (lah **tyehn**-dah deh **bee**-deh-ohs)

Verbs

to rent	*alquilar* (ahl-kee-**lahr**)
to return	*devolver (ue)* (deh-bohl-**behr**)

To describe a movie, say:

The movie is . . .	*La película es...* (lah peh-**lee**-koo-lah ehs...)
boring.	*aburrida.* (ah-boo-**rree**-dah)
funny.	*cómica.* (**koh**-mee-kah)
exciting.	*emocionante.* (eh-moh-syoh-**nahn**-teh)
interesting.	*interesante.* (een-teh-reh-**sahn**-teh)
long.	*larga.* (**lahr**-gah)
sad.	*triste.* (**trees**-teh)

Verbs

to be about	*tratarse de* (trah-**tahr**-seh deh)
to watch	*mirar* (mee-**rahr**)

At the Museum
En el museo
(ehn ehl moo-**seh**-oh)

There are many different types of museums. In your city, or when you travel, you may visit . . .

an art museum.	*un museo de arte.* (oon moo-**seh**-oh deh **ahr**-teh)
a natural history museum.	*un museo de historia natural.* (oon moo-**seh**-oh deh ees-**toh**-ryah nah-too-**rahl**)
a science museum.	*un museo de ciencia.* (oon moo-**seh**-oh deh **syehn**-syah)

Discussing Art
Para hablar de arte
(**pah**-rah ah-**blahr** deh **ahr**-teh)

art	*el arte* (ehl **ahr**-teh)
artist	*el/la artista* (ehl/lah ahr-**tees**-tah)
drawing	*el dibujo* (ehl dee-**boo**-hoh)
exhibit	*la exposición* (lah ehs-poh-see-**syohn**)
gallery	*la galería* (lah gah-leh-**ree**-ah)
painting	*la pintura/el cuadro* (lah peen-**too**-rah/ehl **kwah**-droh)

Sports and Exercise
Los deportes y el ejercicio
(lohs deh-**pohr**-tehs ee ehl eh-hehr-**see**-syoh)

Many people like to practice a sport, attend games, or watch sports events on TV. Is anyone in your family interested in the following?

(Name) likes to play . . .	*A... le gusta jugar al...* (ah... leh **goos**-tah hoo-**gahr** ahl...)
basketball.	*básquetbol.* (**bahs**-keht-bohl)
baseball.	*béisbol.* (**beh**-ees-bohl)
football.	*fútbol americano.* (**foot**-bohl ah-meh-ree-**kah**-noh)
ice hockey.	*hockey sobre el hielo.* (**hoh**-kee **soh**-breh ehl **yeh**-loh)
soccer.	*fútbol.* (**foot**-bohl)
tennis.	*tenis.* (**teh**-nees)
volleyball.	*volibol.* (boh-lee-**bohl**)

Did you notice the similarities in the English and Spanish names of the sports?

Sports- and Fitness-Related Vocabulary
El vocabulario deportivo
(ehl boh-kah-boo-**lah**-ryoh deh-pohr-**tee**-boh)

baseball	*la pelota de béisbol* (lah peh-**loh**-tah deh **beh**-ees-bohl)
basketball	*el balón de básquetbol* (ehl bah-**lohn** deh **bahs**-keht-bohl)
basket	*la canasta* (lah kah-**nahs**-tah)
bat	*el bate* (ehl **bah**-teh)
court	*la cancha* (lah **kahn**-chah)
field	*el campo deportivo* (ehl **kahm**-poh deh-pohr-**tee**-boh)
golf club	*el palo* (ehl **pah**-loh)
gym	*el gimnasio* (ehl heem-**nah**-syoh)
helmet	*el casco* (ehl **kahs**-koh)
match (game)	*el partido* (ehl pahr-**tee**-doh)
net	*la red* (lah rrehd)
player	*el jugador/la jugadora* (ehl hoo-gah-**dohr**/lah hoo-gah-**doh**-rah)
racket	*la raqueta* (lah rrah-**keh**-tah)
referee	*el árbitro* (ehl **ahr**-bee-troh)
soccer ball	*el balón de fútbol* (ehl bah-**lohn** deh **foot**-bohl)
stadium	*el estadio* (ehl ehs-**tah**-dyoh)
team	*el equipo* (ehl eh-**kee**-poh)
tennis ball	*la pelota de tenis* (lah peh-**loh**-tah deh **teh**-nees)
tournament	*el torneo* (ehl tohr-**neh**-oh)

Verbs

to do aerobics	*hacer ejercicios aeróbicos* (ah-**sehr** eh-hehr-**see**-syohs ah-eh-**roh**-bee-kohs)
to exercise	*hacer ejercicios* (ah-**sehr** eh-hehr-**see**-syohs)
to go to the gym	*ir al gimnasio* (eer ahl heem-**nah**-syoh)

to hike	*dar una caminata* (dahr **oo**-nah kah-mee-**nah**-tah)
to jog	*trotar* (troh-**tahr**)
to jump	*saltar* (sahl-**tahr**)
to lift weights	*levantar pesas* (leh-bahn-**tahr peh**-sahs)
to lose	*perder (ie)* (pehr-**dehr**)
to practice	*practicar* (prahk-tee-**kahr**)
to run	*correr* (koh-**rrehr**)
to score (a goal)	*marcar (un tanto)* (mahr-**kahr** [oon **tahn**-toh])
to shoot	*tirar* (tee-**rahr**)
to sweat	*sudar* (soo-**dahr**)
to throw	*lanzar* (lahn-**sahr**)
to win	*ganar* (gah-**nahr**)

In addition to the team sports listed on page 149, some other popular sports are:

to box	*boxear* (bohk-seh-**ahr**)
to bowl	*bolear* (boh-leh-**ahr**)
to fish	*pescar* (pehs-**kahr**)
to golf	*jugar (ue) golf* (hoo-**gahr** gohlf)
to hunt	*cazar* (kah-**sahr**)
to ride horses	*montar a caballo* (mohn-**tahr** ah kah-**bah**-yoh)
to sail	*navegar en barco de vela* (nah-beh-**gahr** ehn **bahr**-koh deh **beh**-lah)
to skate	*patinar* (pah-tee-**nahr**)
to ski	*esquiar* (ehs-kee-**ahr**)
to swim	*nadar* (nah-**dahr**)
to surf	*correr las olas* (koh-**rrehr** lahs **oh**-lahs)

Talking About the Weather
Para hablar del tiempo
(**pah**-rah ah-**blahr** dehl **tyehm**-poh)

If you want to discuss the weather, keep in mind that most of the Spanish expressions you will need make use of the verb *hacer* (ah-**sehr**). To talk about what the weather is like, you can say:

How is the weather?	*¿Qué tiempo hace?* (keh **tyehm**-poh **ah**-seh)
The weather is good.	*Hace buen tiempo.* (**ah**-seh bwehn **tyehm**-poh)
The weather is bad.	*Hace mal tiempo.* (**ah**-seh mahl **tyehm**-poh)
It is . . .	*Hace...* (**ah**-seh...)
(very) cold.	*(mucho) frío.* ([**moo**-choh] **free**-oh)
(very) hot.	*(mucho) calor.* ([**moo**-choh] **kah**-lohr)
cool.	*fresco.* (**frehs**-koh)
sunny.	*sol.* (sohl)
windy.	*viento.* (**byehn**-toh)

If you want to talk about the weather in the past, it is easy to remember to use *hizo* (**ee**-soh) instead of *hace* (**ah**-seh).

Yesterday it was hot.	*Ayer hizo calor.* (ayehr **ee**-soh kah-**lohr**)

Now, if you want to talk about what the weather will be like in the future, substitute *va a hacer* (bah ah ah-**sehr**) whenever you use *hace* (**ah**-seh) in the present. If you want to learn or review the simple future construction, go to Appendix B on pages 197–98.

What is the weather going to be like tomorrow?	*¿Qué tiempo va a hacer mañana?* (keh **tyehm**-poh bah ah ah-**sehr** mah-**nyah**-nah)
Tomorrow it is going to be windy.	*Mañana va a hacer viento.* (mah-**nyah**-nah bah ah ah-**sehr** **byehn**-toh)

With the following expressions of weather you'll need to use the verb *estar* (ehs-**tahr**) (to be):

It is . . .	*Está...* (ehs-**tah**...)
cloudy.	*nublado.* (noo-**blah**-doh)
clear.	*despejado.* (dehs-peh-**hah**-doh)

sunny.	*soleado.* (soh-leh-**ah**-doh)
rainy.	*lluvioso.* (yoo-**byoh**-soh)

These two expressions of weather have their own verb:

to rain	*llover (ue)* (yoh-**behr**)
It is raining.	*Llueve./Está lloviendo.* (**yweh**-beh/ehs-**tah** yoh-**byehn**-doh)
to snow	*nevar (ie)* (neh-**bahr**)
It is snowing.	*Nieva./Está nevando.* (**nyeh**-bah/ehs-**tah** neh-**bahn**-doh)

The Seasons
Las estaciones
(lahs ehs-tah-**syoh**-nehs)

You may find it interesting to talk with your employee about the climate of his or her home country. Here are the seasons in Spanish:

autumn	*el otoño* (ehl oh-**toh**-nyoh)
spring	*la primavera* (lah pree-mah-**beh**-rah)
summer	*el verano* (ehl beh-**rah**-noh)
winter	*el invierno* (ehl een-**byehr**-noh)

It will be useful for you to know some other terms dealing with climate and the weather:

fog	*la neblina* (lah neh-**blee**-nah)
hail	*el granizo* (ehl grah-**nee**-soh)
lightening	*el relámpago* (ehl reh-**lahm**-pah-goh)
rain	*la lluvia* (lah **yoo**-byah)
shower (heavy)	*el aguacero* (ehl ah-gwah-**seh**-roh)
snow	*la nieve* (lah **nyeh**-beh)
thunder	*el trueno* (ehl **trweh**-noh)
weather forecast	*el pronóstico del tiempo* (ehl proh-**nohs**-tee-koh dehl **tyehm**-poh)

Natural Disasters
Los desastres naturales
(lohs deh-**sahs**-trehs nah-too-**rah**-lehs)

Depending on the part of the country you live in, hopefully the following events will never occur!

blackouts	*los apagones* (lohs ah-pah-**goh**-nehs)
earthquakes	*los terremotos* (lohs teh-rreh-**moh**-tohs)
floods	*las inundaciones* (lahs ee-noon-dah-**syoh**-nehs)
hurricanes	*los huracanes* (lohs oo-rah-**kah**-nehs)
snowstorms	*las nevadas* (lahs neh-**bah**-dahs)
thunderstorms	*las tormentas* (lahs tohr-**mehn**-tahs)
tornados	*los tornados* (lohs tohr-**nah**-dohs)

Numbers
Los números

(lohs **noo**-meh-rohs)

Cardinal Numbers
Los números cardinales
(lohs **noo**-meh-rohs kahr-dee-**nah**-lehs)

zero	0	*cero* (**seh**-roh)
one	1	*un(o)/una* (oon, **oo**-noh/**oo**-nah)
two	2	*dos* (dohs)
three	3	*tres* (trehs)
four	4	*cuatro* (**kwah**-troh)
five	5	*cinco* (**seen**-koh)
six	6	*seis* (**seh**-ees)
seven	7	*siete* (**syeh**-teh)
eight	8	*ocho* (**oh**-choh)
nine	9	*nueve* (**nweh**-beh)
ten	10	*diez* (dyehs)
eleven	11	*once* (**ohn**-seh)
twelve	12	*doce* (**doh**-seh)
thirteen	13	*trece* (**treh**-seh)
fourteen	14	*catorce* (kah-**tohr**-seh)
fifteen	15	*quince* (**keen**-seh)

sixteen	16	*dieciséis* (dyeh-see-**seh**-ees)
seventeen	17	*diescisiete* (dyeh-see-**syeh**-teh)
eighteen	18	*dieciocho* (dyeh-see-**oh**-choh)
nineteen	19	*diecinueve* (dyeh-see-**nweh**-beh)
twenty	20	*veinte* (**beh**-een-teh)
twenty-one	21	*veinte y uno* (**beh**-een-teh ee **oo**-noh)
twenty-two	22	*veinte y dos* (**beh**-een-teh ee dohs)
twenty-three	23	*veinte y tres* (**beh**-een-teh ee trehs)
twenty-four	24	*veinte y cuatro* (**beh**-een-teh ee **kwah**-troh)
twenty-five	25	*veinte y cinco* (**beh**-een-teh ee **seen**-koh)
twenty-six	26	*veinte y seis* (**beh**-een-teh ee **seh**-ees)
twenty-seven	27	*veinte y siete* (**beh**-een-teh ee **syeh**-teh)
twenty-eight	28	*veinte y ocho* (**beh**-een-teh ee **oh**-choh)
twenty-nine	29	*veinte y nueve* (**beh**-een-teh ee **nweh**-beh)
thirty	30	*treinta* (**treh**-een-tah)
forty	40	*cuarenta* (kwah-**rehn**-tah)
fifty	50	*cincuenta* (seen-**kwen**-tah)
sixty	60	*sesenta* (seh-**sehn**-tah)
seventy	70	*setenta* (seh-**tehn**-tah)
eighty	80	*ochenta* (oh-**chehn**-tah)
ninety	90	*noventa* (noh-**behn**-tah)
one hundred	100	*ciento/cien* (**syehn**-toh/syehn)
one hundred one	101	*ciento un(o)/una* (**syehn**-toh oon/**oo**-noh/**oo**-nah)
one hundred two	102	*ciento dos* (**syehn**-toh dohs)
two hundred	200	*doscientos/doscientas* (doh-**syehn**-tohs/doh-**syehn**-tahs)
three hundred	300	*trescientos/trescientas* (treh-**syehn**-tohs/treh-**syehn**-tahs)

four hundred	400	*cuatrocientos/cuatrocientas* (kwah-troh-**syehn**-tohs/kwah-troh-**syehn**-tahs)
five hundred	500	*quinientos/quinientas* (kee-**nyehn**-tohs/kee-**nyehn**-tahs)
six hundred	600	*seiscientos/seiscientas* (seh-ee-**syehn**-tohs/seh-ee-**syehn**-tahs)
seven hundred	700	*setecientos/setecientas* (seh-teh-**syehn**-tohs/seh-teh-**syehn**-tahs)
eight hundred	800	*ochocientos/ochocientas* (oh-choh-**syehn**-tohs/oh-choh-**syehn**-tahs)
nine hundred	900	*novecientos/novecientas* (noh-**beh**-syehn-tohs/noh-beh-**syehn**-tahs)
one (a) thousand	1,000	*mil* (meel)
two thousand	2,000	*dos mil* (dohs meel)
one hundred thousand	100,000	*cien mil* (syehn meel)
two hundred thousand	200,000	*doscientos/doscientas mil* (dohs-**syehn**-tohs/dohs-**syehn**-tahs meel)
one (a) million	1,000,000	*un millón (de* + noun*)* (oon mee-**yohn** [deh +...])
two million	2,000,000	*dos millones (de* + noun*)* (dohs mee-**yoh**-nehs [deh +...])
one (a) billion	1,000,000,000	*mil millones (de* + noun*)* (meel mee-**yoh**-nehs [deh +...])

Fractions
Las fracciones
(lahs frahk-**syoh**-nehs)

one-half	½	*un medio* (oon **meh**-dyoh)
one and one-half	1½	*uno y medio* (**oo**-noh ee **meh**-dyoh)
two and one-half . . .	2½ . . .	*dos y medio...* (dohs ee **meh**-dyoh...)
one-third	⅓	*un tercio* (oon **tehr**-syoh)
two-thirds	⅔	*dos tercios* (dohs **tehr**-syohs)
three-thirds . . .	⅗ . . .	*tres tercios...* (trehs **tehr**-syohs...)
one-fourth	¼	*un cuarto* (oon **kwar**-toh)
two-fourths	¾	*dos cuartos* (dohs **kwahr**-tohs)

three-fourths . . .	¾ . . .	*tres cuartos...* (trehs **kwahr**-tohs...)
one-fifth	⅕	*un quinto* (oon **keen**-toh)
two-fifths	⅖	*dos quintos* (dohs **keen**-tohs)
three-fifths . . .	⅗ . . .	*tres quintos...* (trehs **keen**-tohs...)
one-sixth	⅙	*un sexto* (oon **sehs**-toh)
two-sixths	2/6	*dos sextos* (dohs **sehs**-tohs)
three-sixths . . .	3/6 . . .	*tres sextos...* (trehs **sehs**-tohs...)
one-seventh	⅐	*un séptimo* (oon **sehp**-tee-moh)
two-sevenths	2/7	*dos séptimos* (dohs **sehp**-tee-mohs)
three-sevenths . . .	3/7 . . .	*tres séptimos...* (trehs **sehp**-tee-mohs...)
one-eighth	⅛	*un octavo* (oon ohk-**tah**-boh)
two-eighths	2/8	*dos octavos* (dohs ohk-**tah**-bohs)
three-eighths . . .	⅜ . . .	*tres octavos...* (trehs ohk-**tah**-bohs...)
one-ninth	⅑	*un noveno* (oon noh-**beh**-noh)
two-ninths	2/9	*dos novenos* (dohs noh-**beh**-nohs)
three-ninths . . .	3/9 . . .	*tres novenos...* (trehs noh-**beh**-nohs...)
one-tenth	1/10	*un décimo* (oon **deh**-see-moh)
two-tenths	2/10	*dos décimos* (dohs **deh**-see-mohs)
three-tenths . . .	3/10 . . .	*tres décimos...* (trehs **deh**-see-mohs...)

Ordinal Numbers
Los números ordinales
(lohs **noo**-meh-rohs ohr-dee-**nah**-lehs)

first	*primer; primero/primera* (pree-**mehr**; pree-**meh**-roh/pree-**meh**-rah)
second	*segundo/segunda* (seh-**goon**-doh/seh-**goon**-dah)
third	*tercer; tercero/tercera* (tehr-**sehr**; tehr-**seh**-roh/tehr-**seh**-rah)
fourth	*cuarto/cuarta* (**kwahr**-toh/**kwahr**-tah)
fifth	*quinto/quinta* (**keen**-toh/**keen**-tah)
sixth	*sexto/sexta* (**sehs**-toh/**sehs**-tah)
seventh	*séptimo/séptima* (**sehp**-tee-moh/**sehp**-tee-mah)
eighth	*octavo/octava* (ohk-**tah**-boh/ohk-**tah**-bah)
ninth	*noveno/novena* (noh-**beh**-noh/noh-**beh**-nah)
tenth	*décimo/décima* (**deh**-see-moh/**deh**-see-mah)

Days and Dates
Los días y las fechas
(lohs **dee**-ahs ee lahs **feh**-chahs)

Working out the schedule (*el horario* [ehl oh-**rah**-ryoh]) with your employee is of the utmost importance. In this section you will learn how to talk about the days of the week and dates and how to tell time. You will also find a list of idiomatic expressions dealing with time.

In Spanish all the days of the week are masculine and are not capitalized.

Can you come on Mondays?	*¿Puede Ud. venir los lunes?* (**pweh**-deh oos-**tehd** beh-**neer** lohs **loo**-nehs)
Monday	*lunes* (**loo**-nehs)
Tuesday	*martes* (**mahr**-tehs)
Wednesday	*miércoles* (**myehr**-koh-lehs)
Thursday	*jueves* (**hweh**-behs)
Friday	*viernes* (**byehr**-nehs)
Saturday	*sábado* (**sah**-bah-doh)
Sunday	*domingo* (doh-**meen**-goh)

To express dates in Spanish, you will first need to learn the months of the year:

January	*enero* (eh-**neh**-roh)
February	*febrero* (feh-**breh**-roh)
March	*marzo* (**mahr**-soh)
April	*abril* (ah-**breel**)
May	*mayo* (**mah**-yoh)
June	*junio* (**hoo**-nyoh)
July	*julio* (**hoo**-lyoh)
August	*agosto* (ah-**gohs**-toh)
September	*septiembre* (sehp-**tyehm**-breh)
October	*octubre* (ohk-**too**-breh)
November	*noviembre* (noh-**byehm**-breh)
December	*diciembre* (dee-**syehm**-breh)

If you need to find out today's date in Spanish, here are some questions you may use:

What is today's date?	*¿A cómo estamos hoy?* (ah **koh**-moh ehs-**tah**-mohs **oh**-ee)
Today is December fourteenth.	*Hoy estamos a catorce de diciembre.* (**oh**-ee ehs-**tah**-mohs ah kah-**tohr**-seh deh dee-**syehm**-breh)

The date of an event can be found by asking:

What is the date of . . . ?	*¿Cuál es la fecha de...?* (kwahl ehs lah **feh**-chah deh...)
It's July twenty-fifth.	*Es el veinte y cinco de julio.* (ehs ehl **beh**-een-teh ee **seen**-koh deh **hoo**-lyoh)

Did you notice that in Spanish the cardinal numbers (1, 2, 3, etc.) are used for the dates? The only time you will need to use an ordinal number (first, second, third, etc.) is to express the first of the month.

It's the first of January.	*Es el primero de enero.* (ehs ehl pree-**meh**-roh deh eh-**neh**-roh)

Time
La hora
(lah **oh**-rah)

You'll need to be able to set an exact schedule with your employee. Of course, that will include the time of day. The verb *ser* (sehr) is always used to tell time in Spanish. If you need to find out the exact time at a given moment, you may ask:

What time is it?	*¿Qué hora es?* (keh **oh**-rah ehs)
It's one o'clock.	*Es la una.* (ehs lah **oo**-nah)
It's two o'clock.	*Son las dos.* (sohn lahs dohs)

Note that you use *es* (ehs) when it is one o'clock and *son* (sohn) for all other hours. *Y* (ee) (and) is used to tell time between the hour and half past the hour.

It is three ten.	*Son las tres y diez.* (sohn lahs trehs ee dyehs)

After the half hour you usually use *menos* (**meh**-nohs) (minus).

It's seven thirty-five.	*Son las ocho menos veinte y cinco.* (sohn lahs **oh**-choh **meh**-nohs **beh**-een-tee ee **seen**-koh)

The quarter and half hour in Spanish can be expressed by using:

quarter	*cuarto* (**kwahr**-toh)
half	*media* (**meh**-dyah)
It's a quarter after one.	*Es la una y cuarto.* (ehs lah **oo**-nah ee **kwar**-toh)
It's half past five.	*Son las cinco y media.* (sohn lahs **seen**-koh ee **meh**-dyah)

When stating the time, use the following to specify morning, afternoon, or evening:

in the morning	*de la mañana* (deh lah mah-**nyah**-nah)
in the afternoon	*de la tarde* (deh lah **tahr**-deh)
in the evening	*de la noche* (deh lah **noh**-cheh)

For example:

It is three o'clock in the afternoon.	*Son las tres de la tarde.* (sohn lahs trehs deh lah **tahr**-deh)

You will also need to find out at what time your employee is going to start to do certain things, and you will want to tell your employee at what time you want him or her to be at a certain place. Here is the appropriate question:

At what time (can you begin)?	*¿A qué hora (puede Ud. empezar)?* (ah keh **oh**-rah [**pweh**-deh oos-**tehd** ehm-peh-**sahr**])

And some possible replies:

I can begin . . .	*Puedo empezar...* (**pweh**-doh ehm-peh-**sahr**)
at noon.	*al mediodía.* (ahl meh-dyoh-**dee**-ah)
at midnight.	*a la medianoche.* (ah lah meh-dyah-**noh**-cheh)
at about . . .	*a eso de...* (ah **eh**-soh deh...)

To ask the question "when?" use *¿cuándo?* (**kwahn**-doh). To express "sharp" or "on the dot," use *en punto* (ehn **poon**-toh).

When do we start?	*¿Cuándo empezamos?* (**kwahn**-doh ehm-peh-**sah**-mohs)
We begin at two o'clock sharp.	*Empezamos a las dos en punto.* (ehm-peh-**sah**-mos ah lahs dohs ehn **poon**-toh)

Here are some more phrases you can use to express time:

at once/immediately	*en seguida/inmediatamente* (ehn seh-**gee**-dah/een-meh-**dyah**-tah-mehn-teh)
at the beginning of	*a principios de* (ah preen-**see**-pyohs deh)
at the end of	*a fines de* (ah **fee**-nehs deh)
early	*temprano* (tehm-**prah**-noh)
from time to time	*de vez en cuando* (deh behs ehn **kwahn**-doh)
in or about the middle of	*a mediados de* (ah meh-**dyah**-dohs deh)
last month	*el mes pasado* (ehl mehs pah-**sah**-doh)
last week	*la semana pasada* (lah seh-**mah**-nah pah-**sah**-dah)
last year	*el año pasado* (ehl **ah**-nyoh pah-**sah**-doh)
late	*tarde* (**tahr**-deh)
later	*más tarde* (mahs **tahr**-deh)
next month	*el mes próximo* (ehl mehs **prohk**-see-moh)

next week	*la semaña próxima* (lah seh-**mah**-nah **prohk**-see-mah)
next year	*el año próximo* (ehl **ah**-nyoh **prohk**-see-moh)
not yet	*todavía no* (toh-dah-**bee**-ah noh)
often	*a menudo* (ah meh-**noo**-doh)
right now	*ahora mismo* (ah-**oh**-rah **mees**-moh)
sometimes	*a veces* (ah **beh**-sehs)
starting from/on	*a partir de* (ah pahr-**teer** deh)
today	*hoy* (**oh**-ee)
tomorrow	*mañana* (mah-**nyah**-nah)
tomorrow afternoon	*mañana por la tarde* (mah-**nyah**-nah pohr lah **tahr**-deh)
tomorrow morning	*mañana por la mañana* (mah-**nyah**-nah pohr lah mah-**nyah**-nah)
tomorrow night	*mañana por la noche* (mah-**nyah**-nah pohr lah **noh**-cheh)
whenever you can	*cuando pueda* (**kwahn**-doh **pweh**-dah)
whenever you have time	*cuando tenga tiempo* (**kwahn**-doh **tehn**-gah **tyehm**-poh)
whenever you like	*cuando quiera* (**kwahn**-doh **kyeh**-rah)
yesterday	*ayer* (ah-**yehr**)
yesterday afternoon	*ayer por la tarde* (ah-**yehr** pohr lah **tahr**-deh)
yesterday morning	*ayer por la mañana* (ah-**yehr** pohr lah mah-**nyah**-nah)
last night	*ayer por la noche* (ah-**yehr** pohr lah **noh**-cheh)

Appendix A
The Sounds of Spanish

Good news! Spanish pronunciation is much more uniform than English. With few exceptions, Spanish consonants and vowels have one sound and one length. Once you know the correct pronunciation of each letter, you can simply put them together into syllables to build each full word.

When you speak, remember to use body language in addition to spoken language. Even if you mispronounce a word, body language will help to get your meaning across. So, don't be afraid of trying!

All Spanish words, expressions, and sentences given in this book are followed by their pronunciation transcribed in parentheses. Each Spanish word has one stressed syllable. The stressed syllable appears in bold-face characters in the transcription of the pronunciation.

Listen closely to any native speakers of Spanish you encounter, as well as to radio and TV broadcasts, films, and videos. Imitate the pronunciation and intonation patterns that you hear. The more you listen, the more comprehensible your speech will become.

Pronouncing Spanish Vowels

Pronouncing the vowels correctly is essential to authentic Spanish pronunciation and, therefore, to communication. Spanish vowels are crisper and shorter than English vowels. In order to obtain clipped vowels, it is a good idea to add an "h" (not pronounced) after *a*, *e*, and *o* (ah, eh, oh). The Spanish vowels *i* and *u* will be represented in our transcriptions by "ee" and "oo." This phonetic spelling may look a little awkward to you at first. For instance, the Spanish words *sábado* (Saturday), *libro* (book), and *computadora* (computer) are transcribed as "**sah**-bah-doh," "**lee**-broh," and "kohm-poo-tah-**doh**-rah." However, you may find that once you have fully learned the basic pronunciation rules, you will not need to refer to the transcriptions very often.

a   The Spanish *a* is pronounced like the "a" in the English word "father." Examples: *habla* (**ah**-blah), *terraza* (teh-**rrah**-sah).

e   The Spanish *e* is pronounced like a shortened version of the "e" in the English word "café." Examples: *mesa* (**meh**-sah), *teléfono* (teh-**leh**-foh-noh).

When followed by a consonant in the same syllable, *e* is pronounced like the "e" in "met." Examples: *el* (ehl), *usted* (oos-**tehd**).

i   The Spanish *i* is pronounced like the "ee" in the English word "see." Examples: *silla* (**see**-yah), *día* (**dee**-ah).

o   The Spanish *o* is pronounced like the "o" in the English word "obey," but it is clipped short. Examples: *no* (noh), *mucho* (**moo**-choh).

When followed by a consonant in the same syllable, *o* is pronounced like the "o" in "for." Examples: *postre* (**pohs**-treh), *mostaza* (mohs-**tah**-sah).

u   The Spanish *u* is pronounced like the "u" in the English word "rule." Examples: *una* (**oo**-nah), *azul* (ah-**sool**).

Pronouncing Spanish Diphthongs

The so-called "weak" vowels (*i*, [*y*], *u*) may combine with strong vowels (*a*, *e*, *o*) or with each other to form diphthongs. Their vowel sounds do not change, but they blend together to form a single syllable. Note, however, that in some of the pronunciation examples given, the sounds are expressed as two separate syllables to show that each vowel retains its own individual sound.

-ai/ay   The Spanish diphthong *-ai/ay* is pronounced like the "i" in the English word "mine." Examples: *hay* (**ah**-ee), *vainilla* (bah-ee-**nee**-yah).

-au   The Spanish diphthong *-au* is pronounced like the "ow" in the English word "owl." Examples: *autobús* (ah-oo-toh-**boos**), *restaurante* (rrehs-tah-oo-**rahn**-teh).

-ei/ey   The Spanish diphthong -*ei/ey* is pronounced like the "a" in the English word "late." Examples: *seis* (**seh**-ees), *afeitar* (ah-feh-ee-**tahr**).

-eu   The Spanish diphthong -*eu* has no close English equivalent. It sounds like a combination of the clipped English "e" in "eh" and the "oo" in the English word "boot." Examples: *reunión* (rreh-oo-**nyohn**), *Europa* (eh-oo-**roh**-pah).

-oi/oy   The Spanish diphthong -*oi/oy* is pronounced like the "oy" in the English word "boy." Examples: *soy* (**soh**-ee), *estoy* (ehs-**toh**-ee).

-ou   The Spanish diphthong -*ou* is pronounced like the "o" in the English word "note." Example: *lo usamos* (loh oo-**sah**-mos).

-ia   The Spanish diphthong -*ia* has no close English equivalent. The sound can be closely reproduced by combining the sound of a weak English "y" in the English word "yes" with the sound of the "a" in the English word "papa." Examples: *gracias* (**grah**-syahs), *Colombia* (koh-**lohm**-byah).

-ie   The Spanish diphthong -*ie* is pronounced somewhat like the English word "yea!" Examples: *bien* (byehn), *invierno* (een-**byehr**-noh).

-io   The Spanish diphthong -*io* is pronounced like the "eo" in the English word "video." Examples: *adiós* (ah-**dyohs**), *rubio* (**rroo**-byoh).

-iu   The Spanish diphthong -*iu* is pronounced similarly to the English word "you." Example: *ciudad* (syoo-**dahd**).

-ua   The Spanish diphthong -*ua* has no close English equivalent. The sound can be closely reproduced by combining the sound of the "w" in the English word "wet" with the sound of the "a" in the English word "papa." Examples: *cuarto* (**kwahr**-toh), *situación* (see-twah-**syohn**).

-ue   The Spanish diphthong -*ue* has no English equivalent. Pronouncing the "we" in the English word "wet" as a single sound closely reproduces the sound of -*ue*. Examples: *nueve* (**nweh**-beh), *puerta* (**pwehr**-tah).

-ui/uy   The Spanish diphthong -*ui/uy* is pronounced like the English word "we." Examples: *ruido* (**rrwee**-doh), *cuidado* (kwee-**dah**-doh).

-uo   The Spanish diphthong *-uo* has no real English equivalent. The sound can be closely reproduced by combining the sound of the "w" in the English word "wet" with the sound of the "o" in the English word "note." Be sure to combine these two sounds into a single sound. Examples: *antiguo* (ahn-**tee**-gwoh), *cuota* (**kwoh**-tah).

When they come together, two strong vowels (*a, e, o*) form two separate syllables. Examples: *correo* (koh-**rreh**-oh), *aéreo* (ah-**eh**-reh-oh).

When a weak vowel (*i, u*) is adjacent to a strong vowel (*a, e, o*), note the following:

- If there is a written accent on the weak vowel, the diphthong is broken and the two vowels are pronounced separately. Examples: *día* (**dee**-ah), *dúo* (**doo**-oh).
- If there is a written accent on the strong vowel, it simply indicates the stressed syllable, and the two vowels are pronounced together. Examples: *adiós* (ah-**dyohs**), *también* (tahm-**byehn**).

Pronouncing Spanish Consonants

Spanish consonants are not pronounced as strongly as English consonants and are never followed by the "h" sound that often follows English consonants.

b/v   The Spanish *b* and *v* are pronounced exactly alike. These letters have two distinct sounds:

     At the beginning of a word and after *m* or *n*, they closely resemble the "b" in the word "boy." Examples: *banco* (**bahn**-koh), *voy* (**boh**-ee), hombre (**ohm**-breh).

     In other positions, especially between vowels, *b* and *v* are pronounced like an English "b" in which the lips touch very lightly. (This is a sound that does not exist in English.) Examples: *vivir* (bee-**beer**), *escribo* (ehs-**kree**-boh).

c   The Spanish *c* has two separate sounds:

     Before *e* or *i*, in Latin America and in southern Spain, it is pronounced like the "s" in the English word "sent." In central and northern Spain it is pronounced like the "th" in the English word "thin." In this book, we will use only the first (largely Latin American) pronunciation. Examples: *césped* (**sehs**-pehd), *cocinar* (koh-see-**nahr**).

When appearing in the combinations *ca*, *co*, and *cu*, the pronunciation of *c* closely resembles the English "k" sound. The difference is that when the hard Spanish *c* is pronounced, there is no puff of air, as there is with the English "k." Examples: *casa* (**kah**-sah), *balcón* (bahl-**kohn**), *cubiertos* (koo-**byehr**-tohs).

Before *e* and *i*, the hard Spanish *c* sound is represented by *qu*. Examples: *queso* (**keh**-soh), *mantequilla* (mahn-teh-**kee**-yah).

ch   The Spanish *ch* is pronounced like the "ch" in the English word "chief." Examples: *chimenea* (chee-meh-**neh**-ah), *techo* (**teh**-choh).

d   The Spanish *d* has two separate sounds:

At the beginning of a word and after *n* or *l*, the Spanish *d* closely resembles the "d" in the word "dog," but with the tip of the tongue touching the inner surface of the upper front teeth. Examples: *dorar* (doh-**rahr**), *diente* (**dyehn**-teh).

In other cases, particularly between two vowels, the tongue drops even lower and the sound resembles the "th" sound in the English word "this." Examples: *entrada* (ehn-**trah**-dah), *batidora* (bah-tee-**doh**-rah).

f   The Spanish *f* is pronounced like the English "f." Examples: *grifo* (**gree**-foh), *frenos* (**freh**-nohs).

g   The Spanish *g* has three separate sounds:

Before *e* or *i*, *g* is pronounced like the "h" in the English word "halt," but with a raspier, throatier sound. Example: *gengibre* (hehn-**hee**-breh).

After a pause and when followed by *a*, *o*, *u*, and also when it follows the letter *n*, the Spanish *g* closely resembles the "g" in the English word "go." Examples: *albóndiga* (ahl-**bohn**-dee-gah), *langosta* (lahn-**gohs**-tah), *vengo* (**behn**-goh). Spanish *gu* followed by *e* or *i* also closely resembles the "g" in the English word "go." Examples: *guisado* (gee-**sah**-doh), *juguete* (hoo-**geh**-teh).

Between two vowels the *g* sound is much weaker and does not resemble any English sound. Examples: *digo* (**dee**-goh), *luego* (**lweh**-goh).

h   The Spanish letter *h* is always silent. Examples: *hoy* (**oh**-ee), *hablar* (ah-**blahr**).

j   The Spanish *j* is pronounced like the "h" in the English word "halt," except that it is a raspier, throatier sound. Examples: *cajón* (kah-**hohn**), *verja* (**behr**-hah).

l   The Spanish *l* is similar to, but not exactly like, the "l" in the English word "call." Examples: *papel* (pah-**pehl**), *alarma* (ah-**lahr**-mah).

ll   The Spanish *ll* is pronounced like the "y" in the English word "yes" in most of Latin America and in some regions of Spain. In other parts of Spain it is pronounced like the "lli" in the English word "million." In this book we will use only the first (largely Latin American) pronunciation. Examples: *bombilla* (bohm-**bee**-yah), *tortilla* (tohr-**tee**-yah).

m   The Spanish *m* is pronounced like the English "m." Examples: *mesa* (**meh**-sah), *alfombra* (ahl-**fohm**-brah).

n   The Spanish *n* is usually pronounced like the "n" in the English word "no." Examples: *poner* (poh-**nehr**), *una* (**oo**-nah).

However, before *b*, *v*, and *p*, *n* is pronounced like an English "m." Examples: *convenir* (kohm-beh-**neer**), *convertir* (kohm-behr-**teer**).

Before *c*, *gu*, *g*, and *j*, *n* is pronounced like "n" in the English word "sing." Examples: *blanco* (**blahn**-koh), *congelado* (kohn-heh-**lah**-doh).

ñ   The Spanish *ñ* is pronounced somewhat like the "ny" in the English word "canyon." Examples: *soñar* (soh-**nyahr**), *bañarse* (bah-**nyahr**-seh).

p   The Spanish *p* is pronounced like the English "p" but without the puff of air that often accompanies the "p" in English. Examples: *papel* (pah-**pehl**), *pico* (**pee**-koh).

q   The Spanish *q*—which always appears in combination with the letter *u*—is pronounced like the "c" in the word "cat," but without the puff of air that often accompanies the hard "c" in

English. Examples: *queso* (**keh**-soh), *mantequilla* (mahn-teh-**kee**-yah).

r The Spanish *r* has two separate sounds, depending on whether or not it is the first (initial) letter of a word:

When it is at the beginning of a word, the Spanish *r* is pronounced like the Spanish *rr* (see **rr** below).

When *r* is not the first letter of a word, it is pronounced much like the "dd" of the English word "ladder." (Well, it's not exactly the same, but it's much closer to this "dd" sound than it is to the English "r" sound.) Examples: *harina* (ah-**ree**-nah), *merendar* (meh-rehn-**dahr**).

rr The Spanish double *rr* is a vibrating or trilling sound. (Remember that the single "r" is also pronounced this way when it is the first letter of a Spanish word.) Examples: *arroz* (ah-**rrohs**), *radio* (**rrah**-dyoh).

s The Spanish *s* is pronounced like the "s" in the English word "salt," except that the sound is more clipped, a bit shorter. Examples: *jugoso* (hoo-**goh**-soh), *secar* (seh-**kahr**).

However, when *s* comes before *b, d, g, l, ll, m, n, r, v,* and *y*, it is pronounced like the "s" in the English word "rose." Examples: *mismo* (**mees**-moh), *desde* (**dehs**-deh).

t The Spanish *t* is pronounced with the tip of the tongue touching the back of the upper front teeth (instead of the ridge above the teeth as in English), but without the puff of air that accompanies the "t" in English. Examples: *techo* (**teh**-choh), *gusta* (**goos**-tah).

v See *b/v* above.

x The Spanish *x* has three separate sounds:

Before a consonant, *x* is pronounced like the "s" in the English word "sent." Examples: *explicar* (ehs-plee-**kahr**), *experiencia* (ehs-peh-**ryehn**-syah).

Between vowels, *x* usually has a double sound that is like the "ks" in the English word "talks." Examples: *examen* (ehks-**sah**-mehn), *existir* (ehks-sees-**teer**).

X is pronounced like the English letter "h" in certain words. Examples: *México* (**meh**-hee-koh), *mexicano* (meh-hee-**kah**-noh).

y   Depending upon the region, the Spanish *y* might sound like the
          "y" in the English word "yes" or the "j" in the English word
          "joy." In this book we will use the first pronunciation (yes).
          Examples: *mayonesa* (mah-yoh-**neh**-sah), *yema* (**yeh**-mah).
z   The Spanish *z* has two different pronunciations:
               In Latin America and in southern Spain, *z* is pronounced like
          the "s" in the English word "sent." Examples: *lápiz* (**lah**-pees),
          zapato (sah-**pah**-toh).
               In central and northern Spain, *z* is pronounced like the "th"
          in the English word "thin." This book does not use this
          pronunciation.

Note: In Spanish, the letters *k* and *w* are found only in foreign words. The
k is pronounced like an English "k" without the puff of air. Example:
kilogramo (kee-loh-**grah**-moh). The Spanish *w* is pronounced like the
Spanish *b/v* when it occurs between vowels.

General Guidelines for Speaking Spanish

"Stress" refers to the emphasis—in practical terms, the loudness—of a syllable. Stress is important in Spanish because it can completely change the
meaning of a word. Note the similarity of the following words, except for
the location of the stressed syllable. Note also the differences in meaning:

father	*papá* (pah-**pah**)	he bought	*compró* (kohm-**proh**)
potato	*papa* (**pah**-pah)	I buy	*compro* (**kohm**-proh)

In Spanish, note the following:

- Most words ending in a vowel or *n* or *s* are stressed on the next to the
  last syllable. Examples: *banco* (**bahn**-koh), *hablas* (**ah**-blahs).
- Most words ending in a consonant other than *n* or *s* are stressed on
  the last syllable. Examples: *colador* (koh-lah-**dohr**), *mantel* (mahn-
  tehl).
- Words that are not pronounced according to the above rules use a
  written accent to show where the word is stressed. Examples: *desván*
  (dehs-**bahn**), *árbol* (**ahr**-bohl), *higiénico* (ee-**hyeh**-nee-koh).

The written accent—there is a single, acute written accent in Spanish—is also used:

- to distinguish between some words that are spelled alike but have different meanings:
  el (ehl) the   él (ehl) he
  si (see) if   sí (see) yes
- on the stressed vowel of all question words:
  qué (keh) what   cuándo (**kwan**-doh) when

"Intonation" refers to pitch, or the rise and fall of one's voice at the level of a sentence or question. Intonation is important because it can change the meaning of an utterance. In Spanish,

- Normal statements end in a falling pitch.
  I want salad.   Quiero ensalada. (**kyeh**-roh ehn-
                                          sah-**lah**-dah)
- Questions that elicit information end in a falling pitch. This is the same pattern as normal statements in Spanish. However, information questions are never confused with statements because they always begin with question words.
  What do you want?   ¿Qué quieres? (keh **kyeh**-rehs)
- Simple yes/no questions end in a rising pitch, which convey a sense of uncertainty.
  Do you want salad?   ¿Quieres ensalada? (**kyeh**-rehs ehn-
                                          sah-**lah**-dah)
- When a question elicits an answer that is a choice between two or more alternatives, the pitch rises with each choice, and then falls with the final option.
  Do you want salad or   ¿Quieres ensalada o papas?
  potatoes?   (**kyeh**-rehs ehn-sah-**lah**-dah oh
                                          pah-pahs)

Linking Groups of Spanish Words

In speaking and in reading out loud, Spanish words are linked together so that two or more words may sound like one long word. The sounds of the final letters of a word often depend on the initial letter of the following word:

- When the last letter of one word is the same as the first letter of the next word, they are pronounced as a single sound. Example: *la alfombra* (lahl-**fohm**-brah).
- When a word that ends in a vowel is followed by a word that begins with a vowel or *h* followed by a vowel, those vowels are "linked" into one syllable, even if they are different. Example: *su hijo* (**swee**-hoh).
- When a word that ends in a consonant is followed by a word that begins with a vowel, the final consonant is "linked" with the initial vowel sound. Example: *el papel higiénico* (ehl pah-peh-lee-**hyeh**-nee-koh). In the examples given in this book the words are not linked.

Division of Words into Syllables

Some general rules for dividing Spanish words into syllables are:

- A single consonant (including *ch*, *ll*, and *rr*) is pronounced with the vowel that follows it. Examples: *ca-sa* (**kah**-sah), *no-che* (**noh**-cheh), *bu-rro* (**boo**-rroh).
- Two consonants are usually divided. Examples: *tar-de* (**tahr**-deh), *es-pa-ñol* (ehs-pah-**nyohl**).

However, consonants followed by *l* or *r* are generally pronounced together and go with the following vowel. Examples: *po-si-ble* (poh-**see**-bleh), *a-brir* (ah-**breer**).

- Three or more consonants in a row are divided in the following way: the final consonant in the series begins a new syllable. Example: *ins-crip-ción* (eens-kreep-**syohn**).
- When the final consonant in a series is *l* or *r*, it is pronounced with the consonant that immediately precedes. Examples: *en-trar* (ehn-**trahr**), *in-glés* (een-**glehs**).
- Two adjacent strong vowels (*a*, *e*, *o*) occur in separate syllables. Examples: *ve-o* (**beh**-oh), *tra-e* (**trah**-eh).

- Combinations of a weak (*i, u*) and a strong vowel (*a, e, o*) or of two weak vowels are part of the same syllable. Examples: *ciu-dad* (syoo-**dahd**), *bue-nos* (**bweh**-nohs), *gra-cias* (**grah**-syahs).

In combinations of a weak and a strong vowel or two weak vowels, note the following:
- If there is a written accent on the weak vowel, the two vowels are pronounced separately. Examples: *dí-a* (**dee**-ah), *tí-o* (**tee**-oh).
- If there is a written accent on the strong vowel, the two vowels are pronounced together. Examples: *a-diós* (ah-**dyohs**), *lección* (lehk-**syohn**).

Appendix B
Grammar Essentials

Nouns and Articles
Gender of Nouns

Unlike English nouns, all Spanish nouns are either masculine or feminine. In most cases the gender of a noun has to be memorized, but there are some helpful guidelines:

- Nouns that refer to males are masculine. Example: *el hombre* (the man).
- Nouns that refer to females are feminine. Example: *la mujer* (the woman).
- Nouns ending in *-ista* are both feminine and masculine. Examples: *el dentista/la dentista* (the dentist).
- Nouns ending in *-dad*, *-tad*, *-tud*, *-ción*, and *-sión* are feminine. Examples: *la libertad* (the liberty), *la televisión* (the television).
- Nouns ending in *-o* are usually masculine. Example: *el vaso* (the glass).
- Nouns ending in *-a* are usually feminine. Example: *la casa* (the house).

To remember the gender of a noun, always learn it with its definite article (meaning "the"). In Spanish, both definite and indefinite articles also have masculine and feminine forms, according to the gender of the noun they modify.

Definite Articles

The definite article has four forms in Spanish (all of which mean "the"):

two singular: *el* (masculine) and *la* (feminine)
two plural: *los* (masculine) and *las* (feminine)

el	masculine singular	*el árbol*	the tree
la	feminine singular	*la casa*	the house
los	masculine plural	*los árboles*	the trees
las	feminine plural	*las casas*	the houses

Note the following contractions with *el*:

a + el = al	*Voy **al** cine.*	I'm going to the movies.
de + el = del	*Es la casa **del** doctor.*	It is the doctor's house.

Indefinite Articles

The indefinite article ("a"/"an," "some") has four forms in Spanish:

two singular: *un* (masculine) and *una* (feminine), meaning "a"/"an."
two plural: *unos* (masculine) and *unas* (feminine), meaning "some."

un	masculine singular	*un árbol*	a tree
una	feminine singular	*una casa*	a house
unos	masculine plural	*unos árboles*	some trees
unas	feminine plural	*unas casas*	some houses

Adjectives

Adjectives are words that describe nouns. Unlike English adjectives, Spanish adjectives usually follow the noun. For example: *el abrigo rojo* (the red coat).

Note that, in Spanish, adjectives also have masculine and feminine forms, according to the gender of the noun they describe. Here are some general guidelines for adjectives:

- Adjectives ending in *-o* in the masculine singular change the *-o* to *-a* in the feminine singular.

  the tall man   *el hombre alto*   the tall woman   *la mujer alta*
- Adjectives of nationality ending in a consonant add *-a* for the feminine form.

  the Spanish man   *el hombre español*

  the Spanish woman   *la mujer española*
- Most other adjectives have the same form for the masculine and the feminine.

  the brave man   *el hombre valiente*

  the brave woman   *la mujer valiente*

Plural of Nouns and Adjectives

For nouns, number (i.e., whether the word is singular or plural) works exactly as in English: the singular form is used when referring to one person, place, or thing and the plural form is used when referring to two or more. But, unlike in English, in Spanish, the article and the adjective are also number sensitive (i.e., singular or plural).

To form the plural of nouns and adjectives in Spanish, add *-s* to those that end in a vowel.

a black blouse   *una blusa negra*

some black blouses   *unas blusas negras*

Or add *-es* to those that end in a consonant.

the easy lesson   *la lección fácil*

the easy lessons   *las lecciones fáciles*

Possessive Adjectives

Both English and Spanish use possessive adjectives to indicate ownership. Furthermore, in Spanish, as in English, possessive adjectives precede the noun. But, like all Spanish adjectives, possessive adjectives agree in gender and number with the noun they are limiting (i.e., with the possession, not with the owner).

One Possession		More than One Possession	
my toy	*mi juguete*	my toys	*mis juguetes*
your (*familiar*) toy	*tu juguete*	your (*familiar*) toys	*tus juguetes*
your (*formal*) toy	*su juguete*	your (*formal*) toys	*sus juguetes*
his/her toy	*su juguete*	his/her toys	*sus juguetes*
our toy	*nuestro juguete*	our toys	*nuestros juguetes*
their toy	*su juguete*	their toys	*sus juguetes*

The only possessive adjective listed above that changes according to gender is *nuestro/nuestros* which changes to *nuestra/nuestras* when the possession is feminine.

our home	*nuestra casa*	our homes	*nuestras casas*

Another way Spanish speakers express ownership is by using the verb *ser* + the possession + *de* + the owner. For example:

It is María's computer.	*Es la computadora de María.*
I am Juan's sister.	*Yo soy la hermana de Juan.*

Ser means "to be" and in the present tense is conjugated as follows: *yo soy, tú eres, él/ella es, Ud. es, nosotros/nosotras somos, ellos/ellas son, Uds. son.*

Demonstrative Adjectives

Demonstrative adjectives point out specific people and things. They precede the noun they are pointing out and agree with it in gender and number.

The demonstrative adjective "this" has four forms in Spanish:

este	masculine singular	*este vaso*	this glass
esta	feminine singular	*esta taza*	this cup
estos	masculine plural	*estos vasos*	these glasses
estas	feminine plural	*estas tazas*	these cups

There are two ways to say "that" in Spanish:

- When referring to something or someone relatively far from you, but near the person to whom you are speaking, use *ese*.
- When referring to something or someone far from both you and the person with whom you are speaking, use *aquel*.

Ese and *aquel* have four forms each:

ese	masculine singular	*ese periódico*	that newspaper
esa	feminine singular	*esa revista*	that magazine
esos	masculine plural	*esos periódicos*	those newspapers
esas	feminine plural	*esas revistas*	those magazines
aquel	masculine singular	*aquel periódico*	that newspaper
aquella	feminine singular	*aquella revista*	that magazine
aquellos	masculine plural	*aquellos periódicos*	those newspapers
aquellas	feminine plural	*aquellas revistas*	those magazines

Adverbs

Many Spanish adverbs are formed by adding *-mente* (equivalent to "-ly" in English) to the feminine singular of adjectives. Note that adverbs, unlike adjectives, have only one form. For example:

slow   *lento* (masculine)   *lenta* (feminine)   slowly *lentamente*

Subject Pronouns

Since verb endings in Spanish indicate the person about whom one is speaking, Spanish speakers very rarely use subject pronouns. As you begin learning Spanish, however, we recommend that you use them. These pronouns will help the listener know who the subject is, even if (at first) your verb endings are not perfectly correct.

I	*yo*	we	*nosotros*
you (*informal*)	*tú*	we (*all females*)	*nosotras*
he	*él*	they	*ellos*
she	*ella*	they (*all females*)	*ellas*
you (*formal*)	*usted (Ud.)*	you (*plural*)	*ustedes (Uds.)*

In this book, we generally recommend that you use the more formal *usted* (*Ud.*) when speaking to a person in Spanish. It is always appropriate (some Spanish-speaking parents also use it when talking to their children), and using it limits the number of forms you need to learn.

In the verb section we have included the informal *tú* forms for the present, past, and future tenses. You will also find a section on using the informal *tú* commands. Over time, you will gradually learn to use the *tú* forms with your most intimate friends, many of your family members, young children, and pets.

Remember always to use *ustedes* (*Uds.*) when talking to more than one person. There is an informal way to address more than one person in Spanish, but it is rarely used in the Americas. We have not included it here.

Verbs

Present Tense

Meanings and Uses of the Present Tense

The present tense in Spanish can be translated into several meanings in English:

Yo trabajo mucho.	I work a lot.
	I am working a lot.
	I do work a lot.

Regular Verbs

When talking about what you do, are doing, or will do in the near future, and to describe, use the present tense. For example:

The soup is cold.	*La sopa está fría.*
She is washing the car.	*Ella lava el coche.*
I'll dust the rooms later.	*(Yo) Sacudo los cuartos luego.*

In the third example above, the word *luego* makes the meaning clearer. See a list of words and expressions on pages 197–98 that indicate that the action will take place in the future.

The present tense can also be used in a question to ask for instructions:

Shall I close the window? *¿Cierro la ventana?*

The infinitive of verbs in English is expressed by "to + verb." The infinitive of verbs in Spanish ends in either *-ar*, *-er*, or *-ir*.

The present tense of regular Spanish verbs is formed by dropping the infinitive endings (*-ar*, *-er*, *-ir*) and adding the following endings:

For verbs ending in *-ar*:

For	Add	For	Add
yo	*-o*	*nosotros/nosotras*	*-amos*
tú	*-as*		
él/ella	*-a*	*ellos/ellas*	*-an*
Ud.	*-a*	*Uds.*	*-an*

comprar (to buy)

yo compro	I buy	*nosotros/ nosotras compramos*	we buy
tú compras	you buy		
él/ella compra	he/she buys	*ellos/ellas compran*	they buy
Ud. compra	you buy	*Uds. compran*	you (*plural*) buy

For verbs ending in *-er*:

For	Add	For	Add
yo	*-o*	*nosotros/ nosotras*	*-emos*
tú	*-es*		
él/ella	*-e*	*ellos/ellas*	*-en*
Ud.	*-e*	*Uds.*	*-en*

vender (to sell)

yo vendo	I sell	*nosotros/ nosotras vendemos*	we sell
tú vendes	you sell		
él/ella vende	he/she sells	*ellos/ellas venden*	they sell
Ud. vende	you sell	*Uds. venden*	you (*plural*) sell

For verbs ending in -*ir*:

For	Add	For	Add
yo	*-o*	*nosotros/nosotras*	*-imos*
tú	*-es*		
él/ella	*-e*	*ellos/ellas*	*-en*
Ud.	*-e*	*Uds.*	*-en*

abrir (**to open**)

yo abro	I open	*nosotros/nosotras abrimos*	we open
tú abres	you open		
él/ella abre	he/she opens	*ellos/ellas abren*	they open
Ud. abre	you open	*Uds. abren*	you (*plural*) open

Irregular Verbs

Verbs that do not follow the patterns shown above are called irregular verbs. Some important verbs that are irregular in the *yo* form are:

dar (**to give**)

yo doy	I give	*nosotros/ nosotras damos*	we give
tú das	you give		
él/ella da	he/she gives	*ellos/ellas dan*	they give
Ud. da	you give	*Uds. dan*	you (*plural*) give

poner (**to put/place**)

yo pongo	I put	*nosotros/ nosotras ponemos*	we put
tú pones	you put		
él/ella pone	he/she puts	*ellos/ellas ponen*	they put
Ud. pone	you put	*Uds. ponen*	you (*plural*) put

hacer (**to do/make**)

yo hago	I do	*nosotros/ nosotras hacemos*	we do
tú haces	you do		
él/ella hace	he/she does	*ellos/ellas hacen*	they do
Ud. hace	you do	*Uds. hacen*	you (*plural*) do

salir (to leave/go out)

yo salgo	I leave	*nosotros/ nosotras salimos*	we leave
tú sales	you leave		
él/ella sale	he/she leaves	*ellos/ellas salen*	they leave
Ud. sale	you leave	*Uds. salen*	you (*plural*) leave

traer (to bring)

yo traigo	I bring	*nosotros/ nosotras traemos*	we bring
tú traes	you bring		
él/ella trae	he/she brings	*ellos/ellas traen*	they bring
Ud. trae	you bring	*Uds. traen*	you (*plural*) bring

ver (to see)

yo veo	I see	*nosotros/ nosotras vemos*	we see
tú ves	you see		
él/ella ve	he/she sees	*ellos/ellas ven*	they see
Ud. ve	you see	*Uds. ven*	you (*plural*) see

The following verbs are irregular in the present tense:

decir (to say)

yo digo	I say	*nosotros/ nosotras decimos*	we say
tú dices	you say		
él/ella dice	he/she says	*ellos/ellas dicen*	they say
Ud. dice	you say	*Uds. dicen*	you (*plural*) say

ir (to go)

yo voy	I go	*nosotros/ nosotras vamos*	we go
tú vas	you go		
él/ella va	he/she goes	*ellos/ellas van*	they go
Ud. va	you go	*Uds. van*	you (*plural*) go

Note that the verb *ir* is often followed by *a* (meaning "to") and a place. If the place is masculine in gender, the combination *a* + *el* forms the contraction *al*, as in the following examples:

I'm going to the movies.	*Yo **voy al** cine.*
John is going to the beach.	*Juan **va a la** playa.*

tener (to have)

yo tengo	I have	*nosotros/*	we have
		nosotras tenemos	
tú tienes	you have		
él/ella tiene	he/she has	*ellos/ellas tienen*	they have
Ud. tiene	you have	*Uds. tienen*	you (*plural*) have

venir (to come)

yo vengo	I come	*nosotros/*	we come
		nosotras venimos	
tú vienes	you come		
él/ella viene	he/she comes	*ellos/ellas vienen*	they come
Ud. viene	you come	*Uds. vienen*	you (*plural*) come

Verbs with Special Changes

When you remove the *-ar*, *-er*, or *-ir* from the infinitive of a Spanish verb, the remaining portion is called "the stem." In the present tense, there are many common Spanish verbs that have the following changes in the stem of all the forms except *nosotros/nosotras*: *e* to *ie*, *o* to *ue*, *e* to *i*.

In this book, when these verbs appear in the infinitive form they will be followed by (*ie*), (*ue*), or (*i*). For example: *cerrar* (*ie*) (to close), *dormir* (*ue*) (to sleep), *servir* (*i*) (to serve).

When you use these verbs in the present tense you need to make the stem change in all persons except *nosotros/nosotras*. For example:

cerrar (*ie*) (to close)

yo cierro	I close	*nosotros/*	we close
		nosotras cerramos	
tú cierras	you close		
él/ella cierra	he/she closes	*ellos/ellas cierran*	they close
Ud. cierra	you close	*Uds. cierran*	you (*plural*) close

dormir (ue) (to sleep)

yo duermo	I sleep	*nosotros/* *nosotras dormimos*	we sleep
tú duermes	you sleep		
él/ella *duerme*	he/she sleeps	*ellos/ellas* *duermen*	they sleep
Ud. duerme	you sleep	*Uds. duermen*	you (*plural*) sleep

servir (i) (to serve)

yo sirvo	I serve	*nosotros/* *nosotras servimos*	we serve
tú sirves	you serve		
él/ella sirve	he/she serves	*ellos/ellas sirven*	they serve
Ud. sirve	you serve	*Uds. sirven*	you (*plural*) serve

Reflexive Verbs

When you talk about many day-to-day activities, you will find that in Spanish you will need to use reflexive verbs. These verbs are called "reflexive" because they indicate that the subject is acting upon himself or herself. How can you tell the difference between a reflexive verb and verbs that are not reflexive? Look at the ending of the infinitive. In Spanish, when reflexive verbs appear in the infinitive form, *-se* is attached to the end. Here are some useful examples:

to get up	*levantarse*
to wash up	*lavarse*
to brush one's teeth	*cepillarse los dientes*
to get dressed	*vestirse (i)*

As you use this book you will discover useful verbs related to the particular theme of a given section. Remember that reflexive verbs will have *-se* attached to the end of the infinitive. When you use these verbs, don't forget to use the following reflexive pronouns. The pronouns precede the conjugated verb unless you are ordering someone to do something.

me	myself	*nos*	ourselves
te	yourself (*familiar*)		
se	himself/herself	*se*	themselves
se	yourself (*formal*)	*se*	yourselves

For example:

***levantarse* (to get up [to raise oneself])**

(yo) me levanto	I get up	*(nosotros/nosotras)*	we get up
		nos levantamos	
(tú) te levantas	you get up		
(él/ella) se	he/she gets up	*(ellos/ellas) se*	they get up
levanta		*levantan*	
(Ud.) se levanta	you get up	*(Uds.) se levantan*	you (*plural*) get up

By the way, once you learn these pronouns you can also use them with reflexive verbs to talk about the past and the future (you will learn more about the past and the future tenses later on in this appendix). For example:

Yesterday I got up early.	*Ayer me levanté temprano.*
Tomorrow I am going to get up late.	*Mañana me voy a levantar tarde.*

There Is/There Are

Hay means "There is . . ." and "There are . . ." *¿Hay...?* means "Is there . . . ?" and "Are there . . . ?" For example:

Are there books on the bookshelves?	*¿Hay libros en los estantes?*
Yes, there are many.	*Sí, hay muchos.*

The Verb "to Be" in Spanish

Ser/Estar

There are two ways to translate the verb "to be" into Spanish: *ser* or *estar*. These two Spanish verbs (*ser* and *estar*) are not interchangeable, that is, each one has its own uses.

***ser* (to be)**

yo soy	I am	*nosotros/*	we are
		nosotras somos	
tú eres	you are		
él/ella es	he/she is	*ellos/ellas son*	they are
Ud. es	you are	*Uds. son*	you (*plural*) are

To express "It is" ("It's") using the verb *ser*, say *es*.
Use the verb *ser*:

- to find out or state the identity of people, places, and things:

What is it?	¿Qué es?
It's a book.	Es un libro.
Who is it/he/she?	¿Quién es?
It is Elena.	Es Elena.

- to find out or state ownership:

Whose is it?	¿De quién es?
It is my brother's.	Es de mi hermano.

- to find out or state the origin or nationality of someone or something:

Where is it/he/she from?	¿De dónde es?
It/He/She is from Mexico.	Es de México.
What nationality is he/she?	¿De qué nacionalidad es?
He/She is Mexican.	Es mexicano/mexicana.

- to find out or state what material something is made of:

What is it made of?	¿De qué es?
It's made of wood.	Es de madera.

- to find out or state the characteristics of someone or something:

What is it/he/she like?	¿Cómo es?
It's/He's/She's very interesting.	Es muy interesante.

For a list of adjectives that can be used with the verb *ser*, go to Chapter 2 on pages 23–25.

estar (to be)

yo estoy	I am	nosotros/ nosotras estamos	we are
tú estás	you are		
él/ella está	he/she is	ellos/ellas están	they are
Ud. está	you are	Uds. están	you (plural) are

To express "It is" (It's) using the verb *estar*, say *está*.
Use the verb *estar*:

- to find out or state where someone or something is located:

Where is he/she/it?	¿Dónde está?
He/She/It is at work.	Está en el trabajo.

- to find out or state the temporary physical or emotional condition of a person or thing:

How are they?	*¿Cómo están?*
They are nervous.	*Están nerviosos.*
How's the soup?	*¿Cómo está la sopa?*
It's delicious.	*Está deliciosa.*

For a list of adjectives that can be used with the verb *estar*, go to Chapter 2 on pages 25–26.

Idioms with Tener

When talking about physical and emotional states, in addition to using the verb *estar*, Spanish speakers use the verb *tener* (*yo tengo, tú tienes, él/ella/Ud. tiene, nosotros/nosotras tenemos, ellos/ellas/Uds. tienen*) with certain nouns. In these idioms the verb *tener* is translated as "to be" or "to feel."

Some important idioms are:

to be (feel) hungry	*tener hambre*	to be (feel) thirsty	*tener sed*
to be (feel) cold	*tener frío*	to be (feel) hot	*tener calor*
to be (feel) afraid	*tener miedo*	to be in a hurry	*tener prisa*
to be lucky	*tener suerte*	to be (feel) sleepy	*tener sueño*

The Verb "to Know" in Spanish: Saber/Conocer

There are two ways to translate the verb "to know" into Spanish: *saber* or *conocer*. These two Spanish verbs (*saber* and *conocer*) are not interchangeable; that is, each one has its own uses.

The verb *saber* means "to know information or facts," such as names, dates, telephone numbers, etc. It can never be used to say that you know (= are acquainted with) a person or a place. Note that *saber* and *conocer* are irregular in the *yo* form of the present tense:

saber (**to know**)

yo sé	I know	*nosotros/* *nosotras sabemos*	we know
tú sabes	you know		
él/ella sabe	he/she knows	*ellos/ellas saben*	they know
Ud. sabe	you know	*Uds. saben*	you (*plural*) know

For example:

I know that the store is open.	*Yo sé que la tienda está abierta.*
She knows my address.	*Ella sabe mi dirección.*

When talking about what you know how to do, use the verb *saber* followed by an infinitive. For example:

I know how to drive but I don't know how to park the car.	*Yo sé manejar pero no sé estacionar el coche.*

The verb *conocer* means "to know" in the sense of "to be acquainted (i.e., familiar) with a person or a place."

conocer (**to know**)

yo conozco	I know	*nosotros/* *nosotras conocemos*	we know
tú conoces	you know		
él/ella conoce	he/she knows	*ellos/ellas conocen*	they know
Ud. conoce	you know	*Uds. conocen*	you (*plural*) know

For example:

Do you know Juan's mother?	*¿Conoces a la mamá de Juan?*
She knows New York.	*Ella conoce Nueva York.*

When *conocer* is followed by a person, you must add *a* after the verb as in the first example above.

Talking About What You Like: Gustar

When Spanish speakers talk about the things they like and what they like to do, they use the verb *gustar* (meaning "to please, be pleasing to"). Note that the pronouns *me, te, le, nos,* and *les* are always used with *gustar:*

Singular		Plural	
I like . . .	*Me gusta...*	We like . . .	*Nos gusta...*
You (*familiar*) like . . .	*Te gusta...*		
He/She likes . . .	*Le gusta...*	They like . . .	*Les gusta...*
You like . . .	*Le gusta...*	You (*plural*) like . . .	*Les gusta...*

For example:

I like to listen to music.	*Me gusta escuchar música.*
I like Cuban music.	*Me gusta la música cubana.*

When you like more than one thing, *gusta* changes to *gustan*.

I like flowers.	*Me gustan las flores.*

When talking about what you or others don't like, put *no* before *me, te, le, nos, les.*

I don't like to arrive late.	*No me gusta llegar tarde.*
He/She doesn't like eggs.	*No le gustan los huevos.*

Talking About What Hurts (Aches): Doler

When Spanish speakers talk about what hurts, they use the verb *doler (ue)* followed by the part of the body that hurts. For a list of parts of the body go to Chapter 11 on pages 123–24. Note that the pronouns *me, te, le, nos,* and *les* are always used with *doler:*

My (part of body) hurts.	*Me duele* + part of the body (with its definite article).
Your (part of body) hurts.	*Te duele* + part of the body (with its definite article).
His/Her/Your (*formal*) (part of body) hurts.	*Le duele* + part of the body (with its definite article).
Our (part of body) hurts.	*Nos duele* + part of the body (with its definite article).
Their/Your (*plural*) (part of body) hurts.	*Les duele* + part of the body (with its definite article).

For example:

My head hurts. (I have a headache.)	*Me duele la cabeza.*
His stomach hurts. (He has a stomachache.)	*Le duele el estómago.*

When more than one part of the body hurts, *duele* changes to *duelen*. For example:

My legs hurt.	*Me duelen las piernas.*
Their arms hurt.	*Les duelen los brazos.*

Talking About Something That Just Happened: Acabar De

When talking about something that just happened or something you just did, use the following expression: *acabar de* + infinitive.

I have just + verb	*Yo acabo de* + infinitive
You have just + verb	*Tú acabas de* + infinitive
He/She has just + verb	*Él/Ella acaba de* + infinitive
You (*formal*) have just + verb	*Ud. acaba de* + infinitive
We have just + verb	*Nosotros/Nosotras acabamos de* + infinitive
They have just + verb	*Ellos/Ellas acaban de* + infinitive
You (*plural*) have just + verb	*Uds. acaban de* + infinitive

For example:

I have just eaten.	*Yo acabo de comer.*
You have just slept.	*Tú acabas de dormir.*
She has just arrived.	*Ella acaba de llegar.*
We have just gone.	*Nosotros acabamos de ir.*

Preterite Tense

Uses of the Preterite Tense

The preterite tense expresses an action or state completed within a definite period of time in the past.

The following words and expressions are useful when using the preterite to talk about the past:

yesterday	*ayer*
the day before yesterday	*anteayer*
last night	*anoche*
the night before last	*anteanoche*
last week	*la semana pasada*
last weekend	*el fin de semana pasado*
last Monday	*el lunes pasado*
last summer	*el verano pasado*

Regular Verbs

The preterite tense of regular Spanish verbs is formed by dropping the infinitive endings (*-ar, -er, -ir*) and adding the following endings:

For verbs ending in *-ar*:

For	**Add**	**For**	**Add**
yo	*-é*	*nosotros/nosotras*	*-amos*
tú	*-aste*		
él/ella	*-ó*	*ellos/ellas*	*-aron*
Ud.	*-ó*	*Uds.*	*-aron*

trabajar (to work)

yo trabajé	I worked	*nosotros/nosotras trabajamos*	we worked
tú trabajaste	you worked		
él/ella trabajó	he/she worked	*ellos/ellas trabajaron*	they worked
Ud. trabajó	you worked	*Uds. trabajaron*	you (*plural*) worked

For verbs ending in *-er*:

For	**Add**	**For**	**Add**
yo	*-í*	*nosotros/nosotras*	*-imos*
tú	*-iste*		
él/ella	*-ió*	*ellos/ellas*	*-ieron*
Ud.	*-ió*	*Uds.*	*-ieron*

barrer (to sweep)

yo barrí	I swept	nosotros/nosotras barrimos	we swept
tú barriste	you swept		
él/ella barrió	he/she swept	ellos/ellas barrieron	they swept
Ud. barrió	you swept	Uds. barrieron	you (*plural*) swept

For verbs ending in *-ir*:

For	Add	For	Add
yo	-í	nosotros/nosotras	-imos
tú	-iste		
él/ella	-ió	ellos/ellas	-ieron
Ud.	-ió	Uds.	-ieron

escribir (to write)

yo escribí	I wrote	nosotros/nosotras escribimos	we wrote
tú escribiste	you wrote		
él/ella escribió	he/she wrote	ellos/ellas escribieron	they wrote
Ud. escribió	you wrote	Uds. escribieron	you (*plural*) wrote

Irregular Verbs

Some verbs that are irregular in the preterite are:

dar (to give)

yo di	I gave	nosotros/nosotras dimos	we gave
tú diste	you gave		
él/ella dio	he/she gave	ellos/ellas dieron	they gave
Ud. dio	you gave	Uds. dieron	you (*plural*) gave

ir (to go)

yo fui	I went	nosotros/nosotras fuimos	we went
tú fuiste	you went		
él/ella fue	he/she went	ellos/ellas fueron	they went
Ud. fue	you went	Uds. fueron	you (*plural*) went

ser (**to be**)

yo fui	I was	*nosotros/nosotras fuimos*	we were
tú fuiste	you were		
él/ella fue	he/she was	*ellos/ellas fueron*	they were
Ud. fue	you were	*Uds. fueron*	you (*plural*) were

ver (**to see**)

yo vi	I saw	*nosotros/nosotras vimos*	we saw
tú viste	you saw		
él/ella vio	he/she saw	*ellos/ellas vieron*	they saw
Ud. vio	you saw	*Uds. vieron*	you (*plural*) saw

Verbs with Special Changes

Some Spanish verbs have irregular stems in the preterite. For example:

Verb		**Preterite Stem**
estar	to be	*estuv-*
hacer	to do/make	*hic-*
poner	to put	*pus-*
venir	to come	*vin-*

To form the preterite of these verbs, add the following to the irregular stem:

For	**Add**	**For**	**Add**
yo	*-e*	*nosotros/nosotras*	*-imos*
tú	*-iste*		
él/ella	*-o*	*ellos/ellas*	*-ieron*
Ud.	*-o*	*Uds.*	*-ieron*

For example:

I was at the museum yesterday.	*Yo estuve en el museo ayer.*
You did the chores.	*Tú hiciste los quehaceres.*
He put the books on the shelf.	*Él puso los libros en el estante.*
We came to the party at eight.	*Nosotros vinimos a la fiesta a las ocho.*

The following verbs also have an irregular stem:

Verb		Irregular Stem
decir	to say/tell	*dij-*
traer	to bring	*traj-*

To form the preterite of these verbs, add the following to the irregular stem:

For	Add	For	Add
yo	*-e*	*nosotros/nosotras*	*-imos*
tú	*-iste*		
él/ella	*-o*	*ellos/ellas*	*-eron*
Ud.	*-o*	*Uds.*	*-eron*

For example:

We told the truth.	*Nosotros dijimos la verdad.*
They brought the food.	*Ellos trajeron la comida.*

The Future

Spanish speakers use the present tense of the verb *ir* + *a* + an infinitive to talk about what they are going to do in the future. For example:

When are you going to iron?	*¿Cuándo vas a planchar?*
I am going to iron tomorrow.	*Voy a planchar mañana.*

Remember that when using a reflexive verb in any tense, you must also use the reflexive pronouns (*me*, *te*, *se*, *nos*, and *se*). Note the following example using the verb *vestirse*:

Are you going to get dressed for the party?	*¿Te vas a vestir para la fiesta?*

The following words and expressions are useful when talking about the future:

this morning	*esta mañana*
this afternoon	*esta tarde*
this month	*este mes*

next month	*el mes próximo*
tonight (this evening)	*esta noche*
today	*hoy*
tomorrow	*mañana*
the day after tomorrow	*pasado mañana*
this year	*este año*
next year	*el año próximo*
this spring	*esta primavera*
next spring	*la primavera próxima*

Commands

Telling Someone to Do Something (Ud./Uds.)

When addressing someone formally (*Ud./Uds.*), one way of telling him or her to do something is to give a direct command.

To give this type of command in Spanish, remove the *-o* ending from the *yo* form of the present tense, and add one of the following endings:

For *-ar* verbs, add:

-e if the command is given to one person.
-en if the command is given to more than one person.

For *-er* and *-ir* verbs, add:

-a if the command is given to one person.
-an if the command is given to more than one person.

Verb	*Yo* Form	Singular Command	Plural Command
cortar	*corto*	*corte*	*corten*
barrer	*barro*	*barra*	*barran*
escribir	*escribo*	*escriba*	*escriban*

For example:

Mow the lawn.	*Corten (Uds.) el césped.*
Write a list.	*Escriba (Ud.) una lista.*

If the *yo* form of the present tense does not end in *-o*, the command form is irregular. The following verbs are irregular in the command form:

Infinitive	Present Tense *Yo* Form	*Ud.* Command	*Uds.* Command
dar	*doy*	*dé*	*den*
estar	*estoy*	*esté*	*estén*
ir	*voy*	*vaya*	*vayan*
ser	*soy*	*sea*	*sean*
saber	*sé*	*sepa*	*sepan*

For example:

Go to the grocery store.	*Vaya (Ud.) a la bodega.*
Be here early.	*Estén (Uds.) aquí temprano.*

Telling Someone Not to Do Something *(Ud./Uds.)*

To tell someone not to do something, put *no* before the command.

Don't put the wineglasses in the dishwasher.	*No ponga (Ud.) las copas en el lavaplatos.*
Don't open the windows.	*No abran (Uds.) las ventanas.*

Telling Someone to Do Something (with *Tú*)

If you want to use the more informal *tú* singular command, use the *él* form of the present tense (without the *él*).

Eat the vegetables.	*Come los vegetales.*
Drink milk every day.	*Toma leche todos los días.*

Several important verbs are irregular in the *tú* command:

be	*sé*	Be good.	*Sé bueno.*
come	*ven*	Come here.	*Ven acá.*
do	*haz*	Do the homework.	*Haz la tarea.*
go	*ve*	Go to the library.	*Ve a la biblioteca.*
leave	*sal*	Leave early.	*Sal temprano.*
put	*pon*	Put the books in the backpack.	*Pon los libros en la mochila.*
tell	*di*	Tell the truth.	*Di la verdad.*

Telling Someone Not to Do Something (with *Tú*)

To tell someone (*tú* singular) not to do something, add *-s* to the negative *Ud.* command.

For example:

English Command	Negative *Ud.* Command	Negative *Tú* Command
Don't come late.	*No venga tarde.*	*No vengas tarde.*
Don't open the door.	*No abra la puerta.*	*No abras la puerta.*

Other Ways to Tell Someone to Do Something

There are many expressions that can be used with an infinitive to give commands. Some important ones are:

Do me the favor of . . .	*Haga el favor de* + infinitive
It is necessary to . . .	*Es necesario* + infinitive
It is important to . . .	*Es importante* + infinitive
. . . must be done	*Hay que* + infinitive
It is better to . . .	*Es mejor* + infinitive
Would you . . . ?	*¿Podría* + infinitive?

For example:

Do me the favor of arriving early tomorrow.	*Haga el favor de llegar temprano mañana.*
It is better to wash the dishes.	*Es mejor fregar los platos.*

Of course, "please" (*por favor*) and "thank you" (*gracias*) always go a long way.

Asking Questions

Yes/No Questions

The simplest way to ask yes/no questions is to raise the pitch of your voice at the end of the sentence:

Are you coming tomorrow?	*¿Viene Ud. mañana?*

When asking for confirmation/rejection of a statement, the question words *¿verdad?* or *¿no?* (meaning "right?") are added at the end of the statement. Raise the pitch of your voice when saying *¿verdad?* or *¿no?*

You like hamburgers, right?   *Te gustan las hamburguesas, ¿verdad?*

Questions Asking for a Specific Piece of Information

Use the following question words to obtain specific information:

To Ask	Use	To Ask	Use
Where?	*¿Dónde?*	Who?	*¿Quién?/¿Quiénes?*
From where?	*¿De dónde?*	Whose?	*¿De quién/quiénes?*
To where?	*¿Adónde?*	With whom?	*¿Con quién/quiénes?*
When?	*¿Cuándo?*	For whom?	*¿Para quién/quiénes?*
For when?	*¿Para cuándo?*	Why?	*¿Por qué?*
What?	*¿Qué?*	How?	*¿Cómo?*
With what?	*¿Con qué?*	How many?	*¿Cuántos?/¿Cuántas?*
For what?	*¿Para qué?*	How much?	*¿Cuánto?/¿Cuánta?*

For example:

Where are you going?	*¿Adónde va Ud.?*
When does Sonia arrive?	*¿Cuándo llega Sonia?*
Whose computer is it?	*¿De quiénes es la computadora?*

Negative Sentences

To make a sentence negative in Spanish, place *no* before the verb.

I do not travel by subway.   *No viajo en metro.*

Other negative words that can be placed before the verb are:

nada	nothing	*nunca*	never
nadie	no one/nobody	*tampoco*	neither
ninguno(a)	none/no one		

These negative words can also be placed after the verb but, if they are, the sentence must have another negative word before the verb. The meaning is exactly the same.

Nobody is going.   *Nadie va. = No va nadie.*

The affirmative counterparts of the negative words are:

Negative		**Affirmative**	
nada	nothing	*algo*	something
nadie	no one/nobody	*alguien*	someone/anybody
ninguno(a)	none/no one	*alguno(a)*	some/someone
		algunos(as)	some/any
nunca	never	*siempre*	always
tampoco	neither	*también*	also

Appendix C
Dictionary

English-Spanish

A

a/an: un/una (oon/**oo**-nah)
able (to be): poder (ue) (poh-**dehr**)
accident: el accidente (ehl ahk-see-**dehn**-teh)
add (to): añadir (ah-nyah-**deer**)
address: la dirección (lah dee-rehk-**syohn**)
afraid (to be [feel]): tener miedo (teh-**nehr myeh**-doh)
after: después (dehs-**pwehs**)
afternoon: la tarde (lah **tahr**-deh)
again: de nuevo/otra vez (deh **nweh**-boh/**oh**-trah behs)
agree (to): estar de acuerdo (ehs-**tahr** deh ah-**kwehr**-doh)
air conditioner: el aire acondicionado (ehl **ah**-ee-reh ah-kohn-dee-syoh-**nah**-doh)
alarm: la alarma (lah ah-**lahr**-mah)
alive: vivo (**bee**-boh)
allergy: la alergia (lah ah-**lehr**-hyah)
allow (to): permitir (pehr-mee-**teer**)
also: también (tahm-**byehn**)
always: siempre (**syehm**-preh)
ambulance: la ambulancia (lah ahm-boo-**lahn**-syah)
and: y (ee)
ankle: el tobillo (ehl toh-**bee**-yoh)
another: otro (**oh**-troh)
apartment: el apartamento (ehl ah-pahr-tah-**mehn**-toh)

apple: la manzana (lah mahn-**sah**-nah)
application: la solicitud (lah soh-lee-see-**tood**)
appointment: la cita (lah **see**-tah)
arm: el brazo (ehl **brah**-soh)
arrive (to): llegar (yeh-**gahr**)
ask for (to)/request (to): pedir (i) (peh-**deer**)
aspirin: la aspirina (lah ahs-pee-**ree**-nah)
at least: por lo menos (pohr loh **meh**-nohs)
ATM: el cajero automático (ehl kah-**heh**-roh ah-oo-toh-**mah**-tee-koh)
attend (to): asistir a (ah-sees-**teer** ah)
attic: el desván (ehl dehs-**bahn**)
aunt: la tía (lah **tee**-ah)
autumn: el otoño (ehl oh-**toh**-nyoh)
available: disponible (dees-poh-**nee**-bleh)
avenue: la avenida (lah ah-beh-**nee**-dah)

B

baby bottle: el biberón (ehl bee-beh-**rohn**)
back (body): la espalda (lah ehs-**pahl**-dah)
back (bottom): el fondo (ehl **fohn**-doh)
backpack: la mochila (lah moh-**chee**-lah)
backyard: el patio (ehl **pah**-tyoh)
bacon: el tocino (ehl toh-**see**-noh)
badly: mal (mahl)
bag: la bolsa (lah **bohl**-sah)
bakery: la panadería (lah pah-nah-deh-**ree**-ah)
balcony: el balcón (ehl bahl-**kohn**)
bald: calvo (**kahl**-boh)
ball: la pelota/el balón (lah peh-**loh**-tah/ehl bah-**lohn**)
ballpoint pen: el bolígrafo (ehl boh-**lee**-grah-foh)
banana: el plátano (ehl **plah**-tah-noh)
bandage (to): vendar (behn-**dahr**)
band-aid: la curita (lah koo-**ree**-tah)
bank: el banco (ehl **bahn**-koh)
barbershop: la barbería (lah bahr-beh-**ree**-ah)
bargain: la ganga (lah **gahn**-gah)
basement: el sótano (ehl **soh**-tah-noh)

basket: la cesta/la canasta (lah **sehs**-ta/lah kah-**nahs**-tah)

bathroom: el baño (ehl **bah**-nyoh)

bathtub: la bañera (lah bah-**nyeh**-rah)

battery: la batería/la pila (lah bah-teh-**ree**-ah/lah **pee**-lah)

be (to): ser (*irr.*) (sehr)/estar (*irr.*) (ehs-**tahr**)

beach: la playa (lah **plah**-yah)

bean: el frijol (ehl free-**hohl**)

bear: el oso (ehl **oh**-soh)

beard: la barba (lah **bahr**-bah)

beauty salon: la peluquería (lah peh-loo-keh-**ree**-ah)

because: porque (**pohr**-keh)

bed: la cama (lah **kah**-mah)

bedroom: el dormitorio/el cuarto de dormir (ehl dohr-mee-**toh**-ryoh/ehl **kwahr**-toh deh dohr-**meer**)

beef: la carne de vaca (lah **kahr**-neh deh **bah**-kah)

beer: la cerveza (lah sehr-**beh**-sah)

before: antes (**ahn**-tehs)

begin (to): empezar (ie) (ehm-peh-**sahr**)

behave (to): portarse (pohr-**tahr**-seh)

behavior: el comportamiento (ehl kohm-pohr-tah-**myehn**-toh)

behind: detrás (deh-**trahs**)

belt: el cinturón (ehl seen-too-**rohn**)

bench: el banco (ehl **bahn**-koh)

between: entre (**ehn**-treh)

bib: el babero (ehl bah-**beh**-roh)

bicycle: la bicicleta (lah bee-see-**kleh**-tah)

big: grande (**grahn**-deh)

bill (account): la cuenta (lah **kwehn**-tah)

bird: el pájaro (ehl **pah**-hah-roh)

black: negro (**neh**-groh)

blanket: la frazada: (lah frah-**sah**-dah)

bleach: el blanqueador/el cloro/la lejía (ehl blahn-keh-ah-**dohr**/ehl **kloh**-roh/lah leh-**hee**-ah)

block (toy): el bloque (ehl **bloh**-keh)

blond: rubio (**rroo**-byoh)

blood: la sangre (lah **sahn**-greh)

blouse: la blusa (lah **bloo**-sah)

blue: azul (ah-**sool**)
body: el cuerpo (ehl **kwehr**-poh)
boil (to): hervir (ie) (ehr-**beer**)
book: el libro (ehl **lee**-broh)
bookcase: el estante (ehl ehs-**tahn**-teh)
bookstore: la librería (lah lee-breh-**ree**-ah)
borrow (to): pedir (i) prestado (peh-**deer** prehs-**tah**-doh)
boss: el jefe/la jefa (ehl **heh**-feh/lah **heh**-fah)
bottle: la botella (lah boh-**teh**-yah)
bottom: el fondo (ehl **fohn**-doh)
boulevard: el paseo (ehl pah-**seh**-oh)
bowl: el tazón/el sopero (ehl tah-**sohn**/ehl soh-**peh**-roh)
box: la caja (lah **kah**-hah)
brace: el corrector (ehl koh-rrehk-**tohr**)
branch: la rama (lah **rrah**-mah)
brand: la marca (lah **mahr**-kah)
brave: valiente (bah-**lyehn**-teh)
bread: el pan (ehl pahn)
break (to): romper (rrohm-**pehr**)
breakfast: el desayuno (ehl deh-sah-**yoo**-noh)
breathe (to): respirar (rrehs-pee-**rahr**)
bridge: el puente (ehl **pwehn**-teh)
bring (to): traer (*irr.*) (trah-**ehr**)
broccoli: el brécol (ehl **breh**-kohl)
broken: roto (**rroh**-toh)
broom: la escoba (lah ehs-**koh**-bah)
broth: el caldo (ehl **kahl**-do)
brother: el hermano (ehl ehr-**mah**-noh)
brother-in-law: el cuñado (ehl koo-**nyah**-doh)
brown: marrón (mah-**rrohn**)
brush (to): cepillar (seh-pee-**yahr**)
brush: el cepillo (ehl seh-**pee**-yoh)
bucket: el cubo (ehl **koo**-boh)
building: el edificio (ehl eh-dee-**fee**-syoh)
bulb: la bombilla (lah bohm-**bee**-yah)
bunch: el atado/el manojo/el racimo (ehl ah-**tah**-doh/ehl mah-**noh**-hoh/ehl rrah-**see**-moh)

burn: la quemadura (lah keh-mah-**doo**-rah)
burn (to): quemar (keh-**mahr**)
bus: el autobús (ehl ah-oo-toh-**boos**)
bus stop: la parada de autobuses (lah pah-**rah**-dah deh ah-oo-toh-**boo**-sehs)
bush: el arbusto (ehl ahr-**boos**-toh)
busy: ocupado (oh-koo-**pah**-doh)
butcher shop: la carnicería (lah kahr-nee-seh-**ree**-ah)
butter: la mantequilla (lah mahn-teh-**kee**-yah)
button: el botón (ehl boh-**tohn**)
buy (to): comprar (kohm-**prahr**)

C

cab: el taxi (ehl **tahk**-see)
cabinet (display): la vitrina (lah bee-**tree**-nah)
cage: la jaula (lah **ha**-oo-lah)
call (to): llamar (yah-**mahr**)
calm: tranquilo/quieto (trahn-**kee**-loh/**kyeh**-toh)
can: la lata (lah **lah**-tah)
can opener: el abrelatas (ehl ah-breh-**lah**-tahs)
candle: la vela (lah **beh**-lah)
cap: la gorra (lah **goh**-rrah)
car: el coche/el carro (ehl **koh**-cheh/ehl **kah**-rroh)
car seat: la sillita de seguridad para niños (lah see-**yee**-tah deh seh-goo-ree-**dahd pah**-rah **nee**-nyohs)
care: el cuidado (ehl kwee-**dah**-doh)
carpenter: el carpintero/la carpintera (ehl kahr-peen-**teh**-roh/lah kahr-peen-**teh**-rah)
carpet: la alfombra (lah ahl-**fohm**-brah)
carrot: la zanahoria (lah sah-nah-**oh**-ryah)
carry (to): llevar (yeh-**bahr**)
cart: el carrito (ehl kah-**rree**-toh)
cash: el dinero en efectivo (ehl dee-**neh**-roh ehn eh-fehk-**tee**-boh)
cash register: la caja (lah **kah**-hah)
cat: el gato (ehl **gah**-toh)
ceiling: el techo (ehl **teh**-choh)
celery: el apio (ehl **ah**-pyoh)

cell phone: el teléfono celular (ehl teh-**leh**-foh-noh seh-loo-**lahr**)

cement: el cemento (ehl seh-**mehn**-toh)

cent: el centavo (ehl sehn-**tah**-boh)

cereal: el cereal (ehl seh-reh-**ahl**)

certified: certificado (sehr-tee-fee-**kah**-doh)

chair: la silla (lah **see**-yah)

change (to): cambiar (kahm-**byahr**)

check: el cheque (ehl **cheh**-keh)

checking account: la cuenta corriente (lah **kwehn**-tah koh-**rryehn**-teh)

cheek: la mejilla (lah meh-**hee**-yah)

cheese: el queso (ehl **keh**-soh)

cherry: la cereza (lah seh-**reh**-sah)

chest (body): el pecho (ehl **peh**-choh)

chicken: el pollo (ehl **poh**-yoh)

chimney: la chimenea (lah chee-meh-**neh**-ah)

chin: la barbilla (lah bahr-**bee**-yah)

choose (to): escoger (*irr.*) (ehs-koh-**hehr**)

chores: los quehaceres (lohs keh-ah-**seh**-rehs)

church: la iglesia (lah ee-**gleh**-syah)

cinnamon: la canela (lah kah-**neh**-lah)

clamp: la abrazadera (lah ah-brah-sah-**deh**-rah)

clean (to): limpiar (leem-**pyahr**)

clean: limpio (**leem**-pyoh)

clinic: la clínica (lah **klee**-nee-kah)

clock: el reloj (ehl rreh-**loh**)

clogged: atascado (ah-tahs-**kah**-doh)

close (to): cerrar (ie) (seh-**rrahr**)

closed: cerrado (seh-**rrah**-doh)

closet: el armario (ehl ahr-**mah**-ryoh)

clothes: la ropa (lah **rroh**-pah)

clutch (car): el embrague (ehl ehm-**brah**-geh)

coat: el abrigo/el sobretodo (ehl ah-**bree**-goh/ehl soh-breh-**toh**-doh)

coffee: el café (ehl kah-**feh**)

coffee filter: el filtro de café (ehl **feel**-troh deh kah-**feh**)

coffee pot: la cafetera (lah kah-feh-**teh**-rah)

coffee shop: el café (ehl kah-**feh**)

coffee table: la mesita de centro (lah meh-**see**-tah deh **sehn**-troh)

coin: la moneda (lah moh-**neh**-dah)
cold (illness): el resfriado/el catarro (ehl rrehs-**fryah**-doh/ehl kah-**tah**-rroh)
cold (temperature): frío (**free**-oh)
collar: el collar (ehl koh-**yahr**)
college (university): la universidad (lah oo-nee-behr-see-**dahd**)
color: el color (ehl koh-**lohr**)
comb: el peine (ehl **peh**-ee-neh)
comb (to): peinar (peh-ee-**nahr**)
come (to): venir (*irr.*) (beh-**neer**)
compost (fertilizer): el abono (ehl ah-**boh**-noh)
computer: la computadora (lah kohm-poo-tah-**doh**-rah)
concrete: el hormigón/el concreto (ehl ohr-mee-**gohn**/ehl kohn-**kreh**-toh)
condiment: el condimento (ehl kohn-dee-**mehn**-toh)
confused: confundido (kohn-foon-**dee**-doh)
container: el envase/el recipiente (ehl ehn-**bah**-seh/ehl rreh-see-**pyehn**-teh)
contract: el contrato (ehl kohn-**trah**-toh)
contractor: el/la contratista (ehl/lah kohn-trah-**tees**-tah)
cook (to): cocinar (koh-see-**nahr**)
cookie: la galleta (lah gah-**yeh**-tah)
cool: fresco (**frehs**-koh)
corkscrew: el sacacorchos (ehl sah-kah-**kohr**-chohs)
corn: el maíz (ehl mah-**ees**)
corner (inside): el rincón (ehl rreen-**kohn**)
corner (outside): la esquina (lah ehs-**kee**-nah)
cornmeal: la harina de maíz (lah ah-**ree**-nah deh mah-**ees**)
cost (to): costar (ue) (kohs-**tahr**)
cotton: el algodón (ehl ahl-goh-**dohn**)
cough: la tos (lah tohs)
cough (to): toser (toh-**sehr**)
counter (store): el mostrador (ehl mohs-trah-**dohr**)
country: el país (ehl pah-**ees**)
coupon: el cupón (ehl koo-**pohn**)
courteous: cortés (kohr-**tehs**)
cousin: el primo/la prima (ehl **pree**-moh/lah **pree**-mah)

cover: la cubierta (lah koo-**byehr**-tah)

cow: la vaca (lah **bah**-kah)

crack: la grieta (lah **gryeh**-tah)

cracker: la galleta salada (lah gah-**yeh**-tah sah-**lah**-dah)

crazy: loco (**loh**-koh)

cream: la crema (lah **kreh**-mah)

credit card: la tarjeta de crédito (lah tahr-**heh**-tah deh **kreh**-dee-toh)

crib: la cuna (lah **koo**-nah)

criticize (to): criticar (kree-tee-**kahr**)

cucumber: el pepino (ehl peh-**pee**-noh)

cuff (shirt): el puño (ehl **poo**-nyoh)

cup: la taza (lah **tah**-sah)

cupboard: el armario/la alacena (ehl ahr-**mah**-ryoh/lah ah-lah-**seh**-nah)

cure: el remedio (ehl rreh-**meh**-dyoh)

curtain: la cortina (lah kohr-**tee**-nah)

cushion: el cojín (ehl koh-**heen**)

cut (to): cortar (kohr-**tahr**)

cutlery: los cubiertos (lohs koo-**byehr**-tohs)

cutting board: la tabla para cortar (lah **tah**-blah **pah**-rah kohr-**tahr**)

D

dandelion: el diente de león (ehl **dyehn**-teh deh leh-**ohn**)

dangerous: peligroso (peh-lee-**groh**-soh)

dark: oscuro (ohs-**koo**-roh)

date (on calendar): la fecha (lah **feh**-chah)

date (with a person): la cita (lah **see**-tah)

daughter: la hija (lah **ee**-hah)

daughter-in-law: la nuera (lah **nweh**-rah)

day: el día (ehl **dee**-ah)

dead: muerto (**mwehr**-toh)

deadbolt (lock): el pestillo (ehl pehs-**tee**-yoh)

debit card: la tarjeta de cobro automático (lah tahr-**heh**-tah deh **koh**-broh ah-oo-toh-**mah**-tee-koh)

delicious: delicioso/rico (deh-lee-**syoh**-soh/**rree**-koh)

deliver (to): repartir (rreh-pahr-**teer**)

denim: la mezclilla (lah mehs-**klee**-yah)

deodorant: el desodorante (ehl deh-soh-doh-**rahn**-teh)

department store: el almacén (ehl ahl-mah-**sehn**)
describe (to): describir (dehs-kree-**beer**)
desk: el escritorio (ehl ehs-kree-**toh**-ryoh)
dessert: el postre (ehl **pohs**-treh)
detergent: el detergente (ehl deh-tehr-**gehn**-teh)
device: el aparato (ehl ah-pah-**rah**-toh)
dial tone: el tono de marcar (ehl **toh**-noh deh mahr-**kahr**)
diaper: el pañal (ehl pah-**nyahl**)
die (to): morir (ue) (moh-**reer**)
dig (to): excavar (ehs-kah-**bahr**)
dine (to): cenar (seh-**nahr**)
dining room: el comedor (ehl koh-meh-**dohr**)
dinner: la cena (lah **seh**-nah)
dirty: sucio (**soo**-syoh)
discount: el descuento (ehl dehs-**kwehn**-toh)
discover (to): descubrir (dehs-koo-**breer**)
discuss (to): discutir (dees-koo-**teer**)
dishwasher: el lavaplatos (ehl lah-bah-**plah**-tohs)
disinfect (to): desinfectar (deh-seen-fehk-**tahr**)
disinfectant: el desinfectante (ehl deh-seen-fehk-**tahn**-teh)
disorganized: desorganizado (deh-sohr-gah-nee-**sah**-doh)
disposable: desechable (deh-seh-**chah**-bleh)
do (to): hacer (*irr.*) (ah-**sehr**)
doctor: el médico/la médica (ehl **meh**-dee-koh/lah **meh**-dee-kah)
doctor's office: el consultorio del médico(ehl kohn-sool-**toh**-ryoh dehl **meh**-dee-koh)
dog: el perro (ehl **peh**-rroh)
dog food: la comida para perros (lah koh-**mee**-dah **pah**-rah **peh**-rrohs)
dollar: el dólar (ehl **doh**-lahr)
door: la puerta (lah **pwehr**-tah)
doorbell: el timbre (ehl **teem**-breh)
doorknob: el tirador (ehl tee-rah-**dohr**)
doorman: el portero (ehl pohr-**teh**-roh)
downstairs: abajo (ah-**bah**-hoh)
downtown: el centro (ehl **sehn**-troh)
dozen: la docena (lah doh-**seh**-nah)
drain: el desagüe (ehl deh-**sah**-gweh)

drawer: el cajón (ehl kah-**hohn**)
dress: el vestido (ehl behs-**tee**-doh)
dress (to): vestirse (i) (behs-**teer**-se)
dresser: la cómoda (lah **koh**-moh-dah)
drill: el taladro (ehl tah-**lah**-droh)
drink (to): beber/tomar (beh-**behr**/toh-**mahr**)
drink: la bebida (lah beh-**bee**-dah)
drive (to): conducir (*irr.*) (kohn-doo-**seer**)
driver: el conductor (ehl kohn-dook-**tohr**)
driver's license: el permiso de conducir (ehl pehr-**mee**-soh deh kohn-doo-**seer**)
driveway: la entrada (para carros) (lah ehn-**trah**-dah [**pah**-rah kah-rrohs])
drop (liquid): la gota (lah **goh**-tah)
drugstore: la farmacia (lah fahr-**mah**-syah)
dry: seco (**seh**-koh)
dry (to): secar (seh-**kahr**)
dry cleaners: la tintorería (lah teen-toh-reh-**ree**-ah)
dryer (clothes): la secadora (lah seh-kah-**doh**-rah)
duct: el conducto (ehl kohn-**dook**-toh)
dumb: tonto (**tohn**-toh)
dump: el basurero (ehl bah-soo-**reh**-roh)
dust (to): sacudir el polvo (sah-koo-**deer** ehl **pohl**-boh)
dust: el polvo (ehl **pohl**-boh)
DVD: el DVD (ehl deh beh deh)

E

each: cada (**kah**-dah)
ear: la oreja (lah oh-**reh**-hah)
ear (inner): el oído (ehl oh-**ee**-doh)
earache: el dolor de oído (ehl doh-**lohr** deh oh-**ee**-doh)
early: temprano (tehm-**prah**-noh)
east: el este (ehl **ehs**-teh)
eat (to): comer (koh-**mehr**)
edge: el borde (ehl **bohr**-deh)
egg: el huevo (ehl **weh**-boh)
egg white: la clara (lah **klah**-rah)

egg yolk: la yema (lah **yeh**-mah)
eight: ocho (**oh**-choh)
elbow: el codo (ehl **koh**-doh)
electrical: eléctrico (eh-**lehk**-tree-koh)
electrical cord: el cordón eléctrico (ehl kohr-**dohn** eh-**lehk**-tree-koh)
electrical outlet: el enchufe (ehl ehn-**choo**-feh)
elevator: el ascensor (ehl ah-sehn-**sohr**)
emergency: la emergencia (lah eh-mehr-**hehn**-syah)
employee: el empleado (ehl ehm-pleh-**ah**-doh)
employment: el empleo (ehl ehm-**pleh**-oh)
empty: vacío (bah-**see**-oh)
empty (to): vaciar (bah-see-**ahr**)
end: el fin (ehl feen)
engine: el motor (ehl moh-**tohr**)
entrance: la entrada (lah ehn-**trah**-dah)
envelope: el sobre (ehl **soh**-breh)
estimate: el presupuesto (ehl preh-soo-**pwehs**-toh)
evening: la noche (lah **noh**-cheh)
exercise: el ejercicio (ehl eh-hehr-**see**-syoh)
exhaust (car): el escape (ehl ehs-**kah**-peh)
exit: la salida (lah sah-**lee**-dah)
expensive: caro (**kah**-roh)
experience: la experiencia (lah ehs-peh-**ryehn**-syah)
exterminator: el fumigador (ehl foo-mee-gah-**dohr**)
eye: el ojo (ehl **oh**-hoh)
eyebrow: la ceja (lah **seh**-hah)
eyeglasses: los anteojos (lohs ahn-teh-**oh**-hohs)

F

face: la cara (lah **kah**-rah)
facing: frente a (**frehn**-teh ah)
fall (to): caerse (*irr.*) (kah-**ehr**-seh)
family: la familia (lah fah-**mee**-lyah)
fan: el ventilador (ehl behn-tee-lah-**dohr**)
far: lejos (**leh**-hohs)
farm: la finca (lah **feen**-kah)
fast: rápido (**rrah**-pee-doh)

fat: gordo/grueso (**gohr**-doh/**grweh**-soh)

fat-free: sin grasa (seen **grah**-sah)

father: el padre (ehl **pah**-dreh)

father-in-law: el suegro (ehl **sweh**-groh)

faucet: la llave/el grifo (lah **yah**-beh/ehl **gree**-foh)

feather: la pluma (lah **ploo**-mah)

feed (to): dar de comer/alimentar (dahr deh koh-**mehr**/ah-lee-mehn-**tahr**)

fence: la cerca (lah **sehr**-kah)

fertilizer: el abono (ehl ah-**boh**-noh)

fever: la fiebre (lah **fyeh**-breh)

field: el campo (ehl **kahm**-poh)

file cabinet: el fichero (ehl fee-**cheh**-roh)

filter: el filtro (ehl **feel**-troh)

finally: por fin (pohr feen)

finger: el dedo (ehl **deh**-doh)

finish (to): terminar (tehr-mee-**nahr**)

fire: el fuego (ehl **fweh**-goh)

fire extinguisher: el extintor (ehl ehs-teen-**tohr**)

fireplace: la chimenea (lah chee-meh-**neh**-ah)

first: primer/primero (pree-**mehr**/pree-**meh**-roh)

first aid kit: la caja de primeros auxilios (lah **kah**-hah deh pree-**meh**-rohs ah-oo-**see**-lyohs)

fish (live): el pez (ehl pehs)

fish (in a meal): el pescado (ehl pehs-**kah**-doh)

five: cinco (**seen**-koh)

fix (to): arreglar (ah-rreh-**glahr**)

flagstone: la losa (lah **loh**-sah)

flannel: la franela (lah frah-**neh**-lah)

flashlight: la linterna (lah leen-**tehr**-nah)

flat tire: la llanta pinchada (lah **yahn**-tah peen-**chah**-dah)

floor (story): el piso (ehl **pee**-soh)

flour: la harina (lah ah-**ree**-nah)

flower: la flor (lah flohr)

flower bed: el cantero (ehl kahn-**teh**-roh)

flowerpot: la maceta/el tiesto (lah mah-**seh**-tah/ehl **tyehs**-toh)

flu: la gripe (lah **gree**-peh)

fold (to): doblar (doh-**blahr**)
food: la comida (lah koh-**mee**-dah)
food store: la tienda de comestibles (lah **tyehn**-dah deh koh-mehs-**tee**-blehs)
foot: el pie (ehl pyeh)
fork: el tenedor (ehl teh-neh-**dohr**)
foundation: la fundación/el cimiento (lah foon-dah-**syohn**/ehl see-**myehn**-toh)
fountain: la fuente (lah **fwehn**-teh)
four: cuatro (**kwah**-troh)
frame: la armadura (lah ahr-mah-**doo**-rah)
free: libre (**lee**-breh)
fresh: fresco (**frehs**-koh)
Friday: el viernes (ehl **byehr**-nehs)
fried: frito (**free**-toh)
friendly: amistoso (ah-mees-**toh**-soh)
from: de (deh)
front: el frente (ehl **frehn**-teh)
frozen: congelado (kohn-heh-**lah**-doh)
fruit: la fruta (lah **froo**-tah)
fry (to): freír (*irr.*) (freh-**eer**)
frying pan: la sartén (lah sahr-**tehn**)
full: lleno (**yeh**-noh)
fun: divertido (dee-behr-**tee**-doh)
fur: la piel (lah pyehl)
furniture: los muebles (lohs **mweh**-blehs)
fuse box: la caja de fusibles (lah **kah**-hah deh foo-**see**-blehs)

G

gallon: el galón (ehl gah-**lohn**)
garage door: la puerta del garaje (lah **pwehr**-tah dehl gah-**rah**-heh)
garbage: la basura (lah bah-**soo**-rah)
garbage can: el cubo de basura (ehl **koo**-boh deh bah-**soo**-rah)
garden: el jardín (ehl hahr-**deen**)
gardener: el jardinero/la jardinera (ehl hahr-dee-**neh**-roh/lah hahr-dee-**neh**-rah)
garlic: el ajo (ehl **ah**-hoh)

gas: el gas (ehl gahs)
gas station: la gasolinera (lah gah-soh-lee-**neh**-rah)
gasoline: la gasolina (lah gah-soh-**lee**-nah)
gate (garden): la verja (lah **behr**-hah)
gear (car): el engranaje (ehl ehn-grah-**nah**-heh)
gearshift: la palanca de cambio (lah pah-**lahn**-kah deh **kahm**-byoh)
generous: generoso (heh-neh-**roh**-soh)
get (to): conseguir (*irr.*)/obtener (*irr.*) (kohn-seh-**geer**/ob-teh-**nehr**)
get off (to): bajarse de (bah-**hahr**-seh deh)
get on (to): subir a (soo-**beer** ah)
get up (to): levantarse (leh-bahn-**tahr**-seh)
give (to): dar (*irr.*) (dahr)
glass (material): el vidrio (ehl **bee**-dryoh)
glass (drinking): el vaso (ehl **bah**-soh)
glove: el guante (ehl **gwahn**-teh)
glove compartment: la guantera (lah gwahn-**teh**-rah)
glue: la cola/la goma (lah **koh**-lah/lah **goh**-mah)
go (to): ir (*irr.*) (eer)
go down (descend) (to): bajar (bah-**hahr**)
go out (to): salir (*irr.*) (sah-**leer**)
go shopping (to): ir de compras (eer deh **kohm**-prahs)
go to bed (to): acostarse (ue) (ah-kohs-**tahr**-seh)
godfather: el padrino (ehl pah-**dree**-noh)
godmother: la madrina (lah mah-**dree**-nah)
gold: el oro (ehl **oh**-roh)
golf (to): jugar golf (hoo-**gahr** gohlf)
good: bueno (**bweh**-noh)
good-bye: adiós (ah-**dyohs**)
grain: el grano (ehl **grah**-noh)
gram: el gramo (ehl **grah**-moh)
granddaughter: la nieta (lah **nyeh**-tah)
grandfather: el abuelo (ehl ah-**bweh**-loh)
grandmother: la abuela (lah ah-**bweh**-lah)
grandson: el nieto (ehl **nyeh**-toh)
grape: la uva (lah **oo**-bah)
grapefruit: la toronja (lah toh-**rohn**-hah)
grass: la hierba (lah **yehr**-bah)
gravel: la grava (lah **grah**-bah)

gray: gris (grees)
great: estupendo (ehs-too-**pehn**-doh)
green: verde (**behr**-deh)
greet (to): saludar (sah-loo-**dahr**)
grill: la parrilla (lah pah-**rree**-yah)
grocery store: la bodega (lah boh-**deh**-gah)
ground beef: la carne molida (lah **kahr**-neh moh-**lee**-dah)
guest: el invitado/la invitada (ehl een-bee-**tah**-doh/lah een-bee-**tah**-dah)
gym: el gimnasio (ehl heem-**nah**-syoh)

H

hair: el pelo/el cabello (ehl **peh**-loh/ehl kah-**beh**-yoh)
hairdresser: el barbero; el peluquero/la peluquera (ehl bahr-**beh**-roh; ehl peh-loo-**keh**-roh/lah peh-loo-**keh**-rah)
half: la mitad (lah mee-**tahd**)
half: medio (**meh**-dyoh)
hallway: el pasillo (ehl pah-**see**-yoh)
ham: el jamón (ehl hah-**mohn**)
hammer: el martillo (ehl mahr-**tee**-yoh)
hand: la mano (lah **mah**-noh)
handkerchief: el pañuelo (ehl pah-**nyweh**-loh)
hanger: la percha (lah **pehr**-chah)
happy: alegre/contento (ah-**leh**-greh/kohn-**tehn**-toh)
hard (tough): duro (**doo**-roh)
hard-working: trabajador (trah-bah-hah-**dohr**)
hat: el sombrero (ehl sohm-**breh**-roh)
have (to): tener (*irr.*) (teh-**nehr**)
have a good time (to): divertirse (ie) (dee-behr-**teer**-seh)
he: él (ehl)
head: la cabeza (lah kah-**beh**-sah)
headache: el dolor de cabeza (ehl doh-**lohr** deh kah-**beh**-sah)
health: la salud (lah sah-**lood**)
healthy: saludable/sano (sah-loo-**dah**-bleh/**sah**-noh)
hear (to): oír (*irr.*) (oh-**eer**)
heart: el corazón (ehl koh-rah-**sohn**)
heat: la calefacción (lah kah-leh-fahk-**syohn**)
heater: el calentador (ehl kah-lehn-tah-**dohr**)

heavy: pesado (peh-**sah**-doh)

heel: el tacón (ehl tah-**kohn**)

height: la altura (lah ahl-**too**-rah)

helmet: el casco (ehl **kahs**-koh)

help (to): ayudar (ah-yoo-**dahr**)

helper: el/la ayudante (ehl/lah ah-yoo-**dahn**-teh)

hem: el falso (ehl **fahl**-soh)

her: su (soo)

here: aquí (ah-**kee**)

hinge: la bisagra (lah bee-**sah**-grah)

hip: la cadera (lah kah-**deh**-rah)

his: su (soo)

hit (to): golpear (gohl-peh-**ahr**)

hole: el hoyo (ehl **oh**-yoh)

holiday: la fiesta nacional (lah **fyehs**-tah nah-syoh-**nahl**)

holy day: la fiesta religiosa (lah **fyehs**-tah rreh-lee-**hyoh**-sah)

homework: la tarea (lah tah-**reh**-ah)

honest (trustworthy): honrado (ohn-**rrah**-doh)

horn: la bocina (lah boh-**see**-nah)

horse: el caballo (ehl kah-**bah**-yoh)

horsepower: el caballo de fuerza (ehl kah-**bah**-yoh deh **fwehr**-sah)

hose (garden): la manguera (lah mahn-**geh**-rah)

hospital: el hospital (ehl ohs-pee-**tahl**)

hot: caliente (kah-**lyehn**-teh)

house: la casa (lah **kah**-sah)

how: cómo (**koh**-moh)

how many: cuántos/cuántas (**kwahn**-tohs/**kwahn**-tahs)

how much: cuánto/cuánta (**kwahn**-toh/**kwahn**-tah)

hungry (to be [feel]): tener hambre (teh-**nehr ahm**-breh)

hurry (to): apresurarse/darse prisa (ah-preh-soo-**rahr**-seh/**dahr**-seh **pree**-sah)

husband: el esposo (ehl ehs-**poh**-soh)

hurt (ache) (to): doler (ue) (doh-**lehr**)

I

I: yo (yoh)

ice: el hielo (ehl **yeh**-loh)

illness: la enfermedad (lah ehn-fehr-meh-**dahd**)
immediately: en seguida/inmediatamente (ehn seh-**gee**-dah/een-meh-**dyah**-tah-mehn-teh)
in: en (ehn)
inch: la pulgada (lah pool-**gah**-dah)
include (to): incluir (*irr.*) (een-kloo-**eer**)
independent: independiente (ehn-deh-pehn-**dyehn**-teh)
inexpensive: barato (bah-**rah**-toh)
infected: infectado (een-fehk-**tah**-doh)
ingredient: el ingrediente (ehl een-greh-**dyehn**-teh)
ink: la tinta (lah **teen**-tah)
insecticide: el insecticida (ehl een-sehk-tee-**see**-dah)
insert (to): meter (meh-**tehr**)
inside: adentro (ah-**dehn**-troh)
insurance: el seguro (ehl sch-**goo**-roh)
intelligent: inteligente/listo (een-teh-lee-**hehn**-teh/**lees**-toh)
interested: interesado (een-teh-reh-**sah**-doh)
interesting: interesante (een-teh-reh-**sahn**-teh)
intersection: la bocacalle (lah boh-kah-**kah**-yeh)
interview: la entrevista (lah ehn-treh-**bees**-tah)
iron (metal): el hierro (ehl **yeh**-rroh)
iron (to): planchar (plahn-**chahr**)
iron (clothes): la plancha (lah **plahn**-chah)

J

jacket: el saco/la chaqueta (ehl **sah**-koh/lah chah-**keh**-tah)
jail: la cárcel (lah **kahr**-sehl)
janitor: el conserje (ehl kohn-**sehr**-heh)
jar: el frasco/el pote/el jarro (ehl **frahs**-koh/ehl **poh**-teh/ehl **hah**-rroh)
jeans: los blue jeans/los vaqueros (lohs bloo yeens/lohs bah-**keh**-rohs)
jewelry: las joyas (lahs **hoh**-yahs)
job: el trabajo/el empleo (ehl trah-**bah**-hoh/ehl ehm-**pleh**-oh)
joint (pipe): la unión (lah oo-**nyohn**)
juice: el jugo (ehl **hoo**-goh)
just (fair): justo (**hoos**-toh)

K

key: la llave (lah **yah**-beh)
kilogram: el kilogramo (ehl kee-loh-**grah**-moh)
kind: amable (ah-**mah**-bleh)
kitchen: la cocina (lah koh-**see**-nah)
knee: la rodilla (lah rroh-**dee**-yah)
knife: el cuchillo (ehl koo-**chee**-yoh)
know (information or facts) (to): saber (*irr.*) (sah-**behr**)
know (be acquainted with) (to): conocer (*irr.*) (koh-noh-**sehr**)
kosher: autorizado por la ley judía (ah-oo-toh-ree-**sah**-doh pohr lah **leh**-ee hoo-**dee**-ah)

L

laborer: el obrero/la obrera (ehl oh-**breh**-roh/lah oh-**breh**-rah)
ladder: la escalera (lah ehs-kah-**leh**-rah)
lamb: el cordero (ehl kohr-**deh**-roh)
lamp: la lámpara (lah **lahm**-pah-rah)
large: grande (**grahn**-deh)
last: último (**ool**-tee-moh)
last name: el apellido (ehl ah-peh-**yee**-doh)
last night: anoche (ah-**noh**-cheh)
latch: el cerrojo (ehl seh-**rroh**-hoh)
late: tarde (**tahr**-deh)
later: luego/más tarde (**lweh**-goh/mahs **tahr**-deh)
laundromat: la lavandería (lah lah-bahn-deh-**ree**-ah)
laundry room: la lavandería (lah lah-bahn-deh-**ree**-ah)
lawnmower: el cortacésped (ehl kohr-tah-**sehs**-pehd)
leaf: la hoja (lah **oh**-hah)
learn (to): aprender (ah-prehn-**dehr**)
leash: la correa (lah koh-**rreh**-ah)
leather: el cuero (ehl **kweh**-roh)
leave (go out) (to): salir (*irr.*) (sah-**leer**)
leave (behind) (to): dejar (deh-**hahr**)
left: la izquierda (lah ees-**kyehr**-dah)
leftovers: las sobras (lahs **soh**-brahs)
leg: la pierna (lah **pyehr**-nah)

lemon: el limón (ehl lee-**mohn**)
length: el largo (ehl **lahr**-goh)
letter: la carta (lah **kahr**-tah)
lettuce: la lechuga (lah leh-**choo**-gah)
library: la biblioteca (lah bee-blyoh-**teh**-kah)
lid (of pot): la tapa (lah **tah**-pah)
lift (to): levantar (leh-bahn-**tahr**)
light (color): claro (**klah**-roh)
light: la luz (lah loos)
light switch: el interruptor (ehl een-teh-rroop-**tohr**)
like (to): gustar (goos-**tahr**)
lime: la lima (lah **lee**-mah)
lip: el labio (ehl **lah**-byoh)
liquid: el líquido (ehl **lee**-kee-doh)
listen (to): escuchar (ehs-koo-**chahr**)
liter: el litro (ehl **lee**-troh)
live (to): vivir (bee-**beer**)
living room: la sala (lah **sah**-lah)
load: la carga (lah **kahr**-gah)
lock: la cerradura (lah seh-rrah-**doo**-rah)
long: largo (**lahr**-goh)
look for (to): buscar (boos-**kahr**)
lose (to): perder (ie) (pehr-**dehr**)
lost: perdido (pehr-**dee**-doh)
lotion: la loción (lah loh-**syohn**)
lucky (to be): tener suerte (teh-**nehr swehr**-teh)
lukewarm: tibio (**tee**-byoh)
lunch: el almuerzo (ehl ahl-**mwehr**-soh)
lunch (to eat): almorzar (ue) (ahl-mohr-**sahr**)

M

machine: la máquina (lah **mah**-kee-nah)
magazine: la revista (lah rreh-**bees**-tah)
mail: la correspondencia (lah koh-rrehs-pohn-**dehn**-syah)
mailbox: el buzón (ehl boo-**sohn**)
make (to): hacer (*irr.*) (ah-**sehr**)
make the bed (to): hacer la cama (ah-**sehr** lah **kah**-mah)

mall: el centro comercial (ehl **sehn**-troh koh-mehr-**syahl**)

man: el hombre (ehl **ohm**-breh)

manager: el/la gerente (ehl/lah heh-**rehn**-teh)

marble: el mármol (ehl **mahr**-mohl)

market: el mercado (ehl mehr-**kah**-doh)

married: casado (kah-**sah**-doh)

matches: los fósforos (lohs **fohs**-foh-rohs)

material (cloth): la tela (lah **teh**-lah)

material: el material (ehl mah-teh-**ryahl**)

mattress: el colchón (ehl kohl-**chohn**)

meal: la comida (lah koh-**mee**-dah)

measurements: las medidas (lahs meh-**dee**-dahs)

meat: la carne (lah **kahr**-neh)

medicine chest: el botiquín (ehl boh-tee-**keen**)

medium: mediano (meh-**dyah**-noh)

message: el mensaje (ehl mehn-**sah**-heh)

meter (measurement): el metro (ehl **meh**-troh)

meter (utilities): el contador (ehl kohn-tah-**dohr**)

microwave oven: el horno a microondas (ehl **ohr**-noh ah mee-kroh-**ohn**-dahs)

middle: el medio (ehl **meh**-dyoh)

midnight: la medianoche (lah meh-dyah-**noh**-cheh)

milk: la leche (lah **leh**-cheh)

mine: mío (**mee**-oh)

mirror: el espejo (ehl ehs-**peh**-hoh)

miss: la señorita (lah seh-nyoh-**ree**-tah)

miss (to): echar de menos (eh-**chahr** deh **meh**-nohs)

mister: el señor (ehl seh-**nyohr**)

Monday: el lunes (ehl **loo**-nehs)

money: el dinero (ehl dee-**neh**-roh)

month: el mes (ehl mehs)

mop: el trapeador (ehl trah-peh-ah-**dohr**)

more: más (mahs)

morning: la mañana (lah mah-**nyah**-nah)

mosque: la mezquita (lah mehs-**kee**-tah)

mosquito: el mosquito (ehl mohs-**kee**-toh)

mother: la madre (lah **mah**-dreh)

mother-in-law: la suegra (lah **sweh**-grah)
motor: el motor (ehl moh-**tohr**)
motorcycle: la motocicleta/la moto (lah moh-toh-see-**kleh**-tah/lah **moh**-toh)
mouth: la boca (lah **boh**-kah)
move (to): mover (ue) (moh-**behr**)
movie: la película (lah peh-**lee**-koo-lah)
movie theater: el cine (ehl **see**-neh)
Mrs.: la señora (lah seh-**nyoh**-rah)
museum: el museo (ehl moo-**seh**-oh)
mushroom: la seta/el hongo (lah **seh**-tah/ehl **ohn**-goh)
music: la música (lah **moo**-see-kah)
mustard: la mostaza (lah mohs-**tah**-sah)
my: mi (mee)

N

nail (finger): la uña (lah **oo**-nyah)
nail (metal): el clavo (ehl **klah**-boh)
name: el nombre (ehl **nohm**-breh)
named (to be): llamarse (yah-**mahr**-seh)
nanny: la niñera (lah nee-**nyeh**-rah)
nap: la siesta (lah **syehs**-tah)
napkin: la servilleta (lah sehr-bee-**yeh**-tah)
near: cerca (**sehr**-kah)
neck: el cuello (ehl **kweh**-yoh)
need (to): necesitar (neh-seh-see-**tahr**)
needle: la aguja (lah ah-**goo**-hah)
neighborhood: el barrio (ehl **bah**-rryoh)
neither: tampoco (tahm-**poh**-koh)
nervous: nervioso (nehr-**byoh**-soh)
never: nunca (**noon**-kah)
newspaper: el periódico (ehl peh-**ryoh**-dee-koh)
next: próximo (**prohk**-see-moh)
nice: simpático (seem-**pah**-tee-koh)
night: la noche (lah **noh**-cheh)
nine: nueve (**nweh**-beh)
nobody (no one): nadie (**nah**-dyeh)

noise: el ruido (ehl **rrwee**-doh)

noon: el mediodía (ehl meh-dyoh-**dee**-ah)

north: el norte (ehl **nohr**-teh)

nose: la nariz (lah nah-**rees**)

not yet: todavía no (toh-dah-**bee**-ah noh)

nothing: nada (**nah**-dah)

now: ahora (ah-**oh**-rah)

number: el número (ehl **noo**-meh-roh)

nurse: el enfermero/la enfermera (ehl ehn-fehr-**meh**-roh/lah ehn-fehr-**meh**-rah)

nut (metal): la tuerca (lah **twehr**-kah)

nylon: el nilón (ehl nee-**lohn**)

O

obedient: obediente (oh-beh-**dyehn**-teh)

occupied: ocupado (oh-koo-**pah**-doh)

of: de (deh)

offer (to): ofrecer (*irr.*) (oh-freh-**sehr**)

office: la oficina (lah oh-fee-**see**-nah)

often: a menudo (ah meh-**noo**-doh)

oil: el aceite (ehl ah-**seh**-ee-teh)

olive: la aceituna (lah ah-seh-ee-**too**-nah)

on: en (ehn)

on time: a tiempo (ah **tyehm**-poh)

onion: la cebolla (lah seh-**boh**-yah)

only: sólo/solamente (**soh**-loh/soh-lah-**mehn**-teh)

open (to): abrir (ah-**breer**)

open: abierto (ah-**byehr**-toh)

orange (color): anaranjado (ah-nah-rahn-**hah**-doh)

orange (fruit): la naranja (lah nah-**rahn**-hah)

order: la orden/el pedido (lah **ohr**-dehn/ehl peh-**dee**-doh)

organized: organizado (ohr-gah-nee-**sah**-doh)

ounce: la onza (lah **ohn**-sah)

our: nuestro/nuestra (**nwehs**-troh/**nwehs**-trah)

outside: afuera (ah-**fweh**-rah)

oven: el horno (ehl **ohr**-noh)

over there: allí (ah-**yee**)

P

pacifier (baby's): el chupete (ehl choo-**peh**-teh)
package: el paquete (ehl pah-**keh**-teh)
padlock: el candado (ehl kahn-**dah**-doh)
paint: la pintura (lah peen-**too**-rah)
painter: el pintor/la pintora (ehl peen-**tohr**/lah peen-**toh**-rah)
pair: el par (ehl pahr)
pajamas: el piyama (ehl pee-**yah**-mah)
pan: la cazuela/la olla (lah kah-**sweh**-lah/lah **oh**-yah)
pantry: la despensa (lah dehs-**pehn**-sah)
pants: los pantalones (lohs pahn-tah-**loh**-nehs)
paper: el papel (ehl pah-**pehl**)
paper towel: la toalla de papel (lah toh-**ah**-yah deh pah-**pehl**)
park (to): estacionar (ehs-tah-syoh-**nahr**)
park: el parque (ehl **pahr**-keh)
parking lot: el estacionamiento (ehl ehs-tah-syoh-nah-**myehn**-toh)
pasta: la pasta (lah **pahs**-tah)
patient: el/la paciente (ehl/lah pah-**syehn**-teh)
patio: el patio (ehl **pah**-tyoh)
paw (animal): la pata (lah **pah**-tah)
pay (to): pagar (pah-**gahr**)
payment: el pago (ehl **pah**-goh)
peach: el melocotón (ehl meh-loh-koh-**tohn**)
peanut: el cacahuete/el maní (ehl kah-kah-**weh**-teh/ehl mah-**nee**)
pear: la pera (lah **peh**-rah)
pedestrian: el peatón (ehl peh-ah-**tohn**)
peel (to): pelar (peh-**lahr**)
pen (writing): la pluma (lah **ploo**-mah)
pencil: el lápiz (ehl **lah**-pees)
penny: el centavo (ehl sehn-**tah**-boh)
people: la gente (lah **hehn**-teh)
pepper: la pimienta (lah pee-**myehn**-tah)
person: la persona (lah pehr-**soh**-nah)
personality: la personalidad (lah pehr-soh-nah-lee-**dahd**)
pet: el animal doméstico (ehl ah-nee-**mahl** doh-**mehs**-tee-koh)
pharmacy: la farmacia (lah fahr-**mah**-syah)
pick up (to): recoger (*irr.*) (rreh-koh-**hehr**)

picture: el cuadro (ehl **kwah**-droh)

piece: el pedazo (ehl peh-**dah**-soh)

pig: el cerdo (ehl **sehr**-doh)

pill: la píldora (lah **peel**-doh-rah)

pillow: la almohada (lah ahl-moh-**ah**-dah)

pin (sewing): el alfiler (ehl ahl-fee-**lehr**)

pink: rosado (rroh-**sah**-doh)

pint: la pinta (lah **peen**-tah)

pipe: el tubo (ehl **too**-boh)

place: el lugar (ehl loo-**gahr**)

plan: el plano (ehl **plah**-noh)

plant: la planta (lah **plahn**-tah)

plaster: el yeso (ehl **yeh**-soh)

plastic: el plástico (ehl **plahs**-tee-koh)

plate: el plato (ehl **plah**-toh)

playroom: el cuarto de juego (ehl **kwahr**-toh deh **hweh**-goh)

pleasant: agradable (ah-grah-**dah**-bleh)

please: por favor (pohr fah-**bohr**)

pliers: los alicates (lohs ah-lee-**kah**-tehs)

plug (wallplate): el enchufe (ehl ehn-**choo**-feh)

plumber: el plomero/la plomera (ehl ploh-**meh**-roh/lah ploh-**meh**-rah)

plumbing: la plomería (lah ploh-meh-**ree**-ah)

pocket: el bolsillo (ehl bohl-**see**-yoh)

police station: el cuartel de policía (ehl kwahr-**tehl** deh poh-lee-**see**-ah)

polite: cortés (kohr-**tehs**)

polyester: el poliéster (ehl poh-**lyehs**-tehr)

porch: el portal (ehl pohr-**tahl**)

pork: la carne de cerdo (lah **kahr**-neh deh **sehr**-doh)

post office: la oficina de correos/el correo (lah oh-fee-**see**-nah deh koh-**rreh**-ohs/ehl koh-**rreh**-oh)

pot: la cacerola/la olla (lah kah-seh-**roh**-lah/lah **oh**-yah)

potato: la papa/la patata (lah **pah**-pah/lah pah-**tah**-tah)

pound (weight): la libra (lah **lee**-brah)

pour (to): echar (eh-**chahr**)

prepare (to): preparar (preh-pah-**rahr**)

prescription: la receta (lah rreh-**seh**-tah)

pretty: bonito/lindo (boh-**nee**-toh/**leen**-doh)

price: el precio (ehl **preh**-syoh)
pull out (to): arrancar (ah-rrahn-**kahr**)
purple: morado (moh-**rah**-doh)
put (to): poner (*irr.*) (poh-**nehr**)
put away (to): guardar (gwahr-**dahr**)
put in (to): meter (meh-**tehr**)
put on (to): ponerse (*irr.*) (poh-**nehr**-seh)

Q

quantity: la cantidad (lah kahn-tee-**dahd**)
quart: el cuarto de galón (ehl **kwahr**-toh deh gah-**lohn**)
question: la pregunta (lah preh-**goon**-tah)
quickly: de prisa/rápidamente (deh **pree**-sah/**rrah**-pee-dah-mehn-teh)
quiet: silencioso/callado (see-lehn-**syoh**-soh/kah-**yah**-doh)

R

radio: el radio (ehl **rrah**-dyoh)
rag: el trapo (ehl **trah**-poh)
railing: la baranda (lah bah-**rahn**-dah)
rain: la lluvia (lah **yoo**-byah)
rain (to): llover (ue) (yoh-**behr**)
raisin: la pasa (lah **pah**-sah)
rake (tool): el rastrillo (ehl rrahs-**tree**-yoh)
range (kitchen): el fogón (ehl foh-**gohn**)
rash: la erupción (lah eh-roop-**syohn**)
raw: crudo (**kroo**-doh)
rayon: el rayón (ehl rrah-**yohn**)
read (to): leer (leh-**ehr**)
recipe: la receta (lah rreh-**seh**-tah)
recommend (to): recomendar (ie) (rreh-koh-mehn-**dahr**)
red: rojo (**rroh**-hoh)
refrigerator: el refrigerador/la nevera (ehl rreh-free-heh-rah-**dohr**/lah neh-**beh**-rah)
relative: el pariente/la parienta (ehl pah-**ryehn**-teh/lah pah-**ryehn**-tah)
religion: la religión (lah rreh-lee-**hyohn**)
remedy: el remedio (ehl rreh-**meh**-dyoh)

remove (to): quitar/remover (ue) (kee-**tahr**/rreh-moh-**behr**)
rent: el alquiler (ehl ahl-kee-**lehr**)
rent (to): alquilar (ahl-kee-**lahr**)
repair (to): remendar (ie)/reparar (rreh-mehn-**dahr**/rreh-pah-**rahr**)
request (to): pedir (i) (peh-**deer**)
restaurant: el restaurante (ehl rrehs-tah-oo-**rahn**-teh)
return (to): regresar/volver (ue) (rreh-greh-**sahr**/bohl-**behr**)
return (to) (give back [to]): devolver (ue) (deh-bohl-**behr**)
rice: el arroz (ehl ah-**rrohs**)
right (to be): tener razón (teh-**nehr** rrah-**sohn**)
right (direction): la derecha (lah deh-**reh**-chah)
right now: ahora mismo (ah-**oh**-rah **mees**-moh)
ring: el anillo (ehl ah-**nee**-yoh)
rock: la roca (lah **rroh**-kah)
roll (bread): el panecillo (ehl pah-neh-**see**-yoh)
roof: el techo (ehl **teh**-choh)
root: la raíz (lah rrah-**ees**)
rose: la rosa (lah **rroh**-sah)
rotten (food): podrido (poh-**dree**-doh)
rubber: la goma (lah **goh**-mah)
rug: la alfombra (lah ahl-**fohm**-brah)
rule: la regla (lah **rreh**-glah)

S

sad: triste (**trees**-teh)
safe: seguro (seh-**goo**-roh)
salesperson: el vendedor/la vendedora (ehl behn-deh-**dohr**/lah behn-deh-**doh**-rah)
salt: la sal (lah sahl)
Saturday: el sábado (ehl **sah**-bah-doh)
sauce: la salsa (lah **sahl**-sah)
sausage: la salchicha (lah sahl-**chee**-chah)
save (up) (to): ahorrar (ah-oh-**rrahr**)
savor (to): saborear (sah-boh-reh-**ahr**)
saw (tool): el cerrucho (ehl seh-**rroo**-choh)
say (to): decir (*irr.*) (deh-**seer**)
scale: la pesa (lah **peh**-sah)

scarf: la bufanda (lah boo-**fahn**-dah)

school: la escuela (lah ehs-**kweh**-lah)

scissors: las tijeras (lahs tee-**heh**-rahs)

scouring pad: el estropajo (ehl ehs-troh-**pah**-hoh)

scraper: el raspador (ehl rrahs-pah-**dohr**)

scratch (to): rascar (rrahs-**kahr**)

screw: el tornillo (ehl tohr-**nee**-yoh)

screwdriver: el destornillador (ehl dehs-tohr-nee-yah-**dohr**)

seasoning: el condimento (ehl kohn-dee-**mehn**-toh)

seat: el asiento (ehl ah-**syehn**-toh)

seatbelt: el cinturón de seguridad (ehl seen-too-**rohn** deh seh-goo-ree-**dahd**)

see (to): ver (*irr.*) (behr)

sell (to): vender (behn-**dehr**)

service station: el taller de reparaciones (ehl tah-**yehr** deh rreh-pah-rah-**syoh**-nehs)

seven: siete (**syeh**-teh)

shade: la sombra (lah **sohm**-brah)

shampoo: el champú (ehl chahm-**poo**)

she: ella (**eh**-yah)

sheet: la sábana (lah **sah**-bah-nah)

shelf: el estante (ehl ehs-**tahn**-teh)

shellfish: los mariscos (lohs mah-**rees**-kohs)

shingle: la tablilla (lah tah-**blee**-yah)

shirt: la camisa (lah kah-**mee**-sah)

shoe: el zapato (ehl sah-**pah**-toh)

shopping list: la lista de compras (lah **lees**-tah deh **kohm**-prahs)

short (person): bajo (**bah**-hoh)

short (hair, etc.): corto (**kohr**-toh)

shoulder: el hombro (ehl **ohm**-broh)

shovel: la pala (lah **pah**-lah)

show (to): mostrar (ue) (mohs-**trahr**)

shower: la ducha (lah **doo**-chah)

shrimp: el camarón (ehl kah-mah-**rohn**)

shrub: el arbusto (ehl ahr-**boos**-toh)

sick: enfermo (ehn-**fehr**-moh)

sidewalk: la acera (lah ah-**seh**-rah)

sign (to) (one's name): firmar (feer-**mahr**)

sign: la señal (lah seh-**nyahl**)

silk: la seda (lah **seh**-dah)

silver: la plata (lah **plah**-tah)

silverware: la vajilla de plata (lah bah-**hee**-yah deh **plah**-tah)

single (not married): soltero (sohl-**teh**-roh)

sink (bathroom): el lavabo/el lavamanos (ehl lah-**bah**-boh/ehl lah-bah-**mah**-nohs)

sink (kitchen): el fregadero (ehl freh-gah-**deh**-roh)

sister: la hermana (lah ehr-**mah**-nah)

sister-in-law: la cuñada (lah koo-**nyah**-dah)

six: seis (**seh**-ees)

size: la talla/el tamaño (lah **tah**-yah/ehl tah-**mah**-nyoh)

skillet: la sartén (lah sahr-**tehn**)

skim milk: la leche desnatada (lah **leh**-cheh dehs-nah-**tah**-dah)

skin: la piel (lah pyehl)

skinny: flaco (**flah**-koh)

skirt: la falda (lah **fahl**-dah)

slab (flagstone): la losa (lah **loh**-sah)

sleep (to): dormir (ue) (dohr-**meer**)

sleepy (to be [feel]): tener sueño (teh-**nehr sweh**-nyoh)

sleeve: la manga (lah **mahn**-gah)

slice: la tajada/la rebanada (lah tah-**hah**-dah/lah rreh-bah-**nah**-dah)

slow: lento (**lehn**-toh)

slowly: despacio/lentamente (dehs-**pah**-syoh/lehn-tah-**mehn**-teh)

small: pequeño (peh-**keh**-nyoh)

smoke alarm: la alarma de humo (lah ah-**lahr**-mah deh **oo**-moh)

snack: la merienda (lah meh-**ryehn**-dah)

sneakers: los zapatos de tenis (lohs sah-**pah**-tohs deh **teh**-nees)

snow: la nieve (lah **nyeh**-beh)

snow (to): nevar (ie) (neh-**bahr**)

soap: el jabón (ehl hah-**bohn**)

socks: los calcetines (lohs kahl-seh-**tee**-nehs)

soda: el refresco (ehl rreh-**frehs**-koh)

sofa: el sofá (ehl soh-**fah**)

soft: blando (**blahn**-doh)

soft drink: el refresco (ehl rreh-**frehs**-koh)

soil: la tierra (lah **tyeh**-rrah)
some: unos/unas (**oo**-nohs/**oo**-nahs)
someone: alguien (**ahl**-gyehn)
something: algo (**ahl**-goh)
sometimes: a veces (ah **beh**-sehs)
son: el hijo (ehl **ee**-hoh)
son-in-law: el yerno (ehl **yehr**-noh)
sour: agrio (**ah**-gryoh)
south: el sur (ehl soor)
spice: la especia (lah ehs-**peh**-syah)
spicy: picante (pee-**kahn**-teh)
spill (to): derramar (deh-rrah-**mahr**)
spinach: la espinaca (lah ehs-pee-**nah**-kah)
spoiled (person): malcriado (mahl-**kryah**-doh)
sponge: la esponja (lah ehs-**pohn**-hah)
spoon: la cuchara (lah koo-**chah**-rah)
sport: el deporte (ehl deh-**pohr**-teh)
spring (season): la primavera (lah pree-mah-**beh**-rah)
square (city): la plaza (lah **plah**-sah)
stainless steel: el acero inoxidable (ehl ah-**seh**-roh ee-nohk-see-**dah**-bleh)
staircase: la escalera (lah ehs-kah-**leh**-rah)
start (to): empezar (ie)/comenzar (ie) (ehm-peh-**sahr**/koh-mehn-**sahr**)
steak: el bistec (ehl bees-**tehk**)
steering wheel: el volante (ehl boh-**lahn**-teh)
stir (to): revolver (ue) (rreh-bohl-**behr**)
stitch (sewing): el punto (ehl **poon**-toh)
stomach: el estómago (ehl ehs-**toh**-mah-goh)
stomachache: el dolor de estómago (ehl doh-**lohr** deh ehs-**toh**-mah-goh)
stone: la piedra (lah **pyeh**-drah)
stop (to): parar (pah-**rahr**)
stop (bus, etc.): la parada (lah pah-**rah**-dah)
story: el cuento (ehl **kwehn**-toh)
stove: la cocina (lah koh-**see**-nah)
strange: raro/extraño (**rrah**-roh/ehs-**trah**-nyoh)
strawberry: la fresa (lah **freh**-sah)
street: la calle (lah **kah**-yeh)

stroller: el cochecito (ehl koh-cheh-**see**-toh)
strong: fuerte (**fwehr**-teh)
student: el/la estudiante (ehl/lah ehs-too-**dyahn**-teh)
study (to): estudiar (ehs-too-**dyahr**)
subway: el metro (ehl **meh**-troh)
subway station: la estación de metro (lah ehs-tah-**syohn** deh **meh**-troh)
suddenly: de pronto (deh **prohn**-toh)
sugar: el azúcar (ehl ah-**soo**-kahr)
suit: el traje (ehl **trah**-heh)
summer: el verano (ehl beh-**rah**-noh)
Sunday: el domingo (ehl doh-**meen**-goh)
sunglasses: los anteojos de sol (lohs ahn-teh-**oh**-hohs deh sohl)
supermarket: el supermercado (ehl soo-pehr-mehr-**kah**-doh)
supervisor: el supervisor/la supervisora (ehl soo-pehr-bee-**sohr**/lah soo-pehr-bee-**soh**-rah)
surface: la superficie (lah soo-pehr-**fee**-syeh)
sweater: el suéter (ehl **sweh**-tehr)
sweatshirt: la sudadera (lah soo-dah-**deh**-rah)
sweep (to): barrer (bah-**rrehr**)
sweet: dulce (**dool**-seh)
swimming pool: la piscina (lah pee-**see**-nah)
swollen: hinchado (een-**chah**-doh)
symptom: el síntoma (ehl **seen**-toh-mah)

T

table: la mesa (lah **meh**-sah)
tablecloth: el mantel (ehl mahn-**tehl**)
tablespoon: la cuchara (lah koo-**chah**-rah)
tablet (lozenge): la pastilla (lah pahs-**tee**-yah)
take (to): tomar (toh-**mahr**)
take (carry) (to): llevar (yeh-**bahr**)
take care of (to): cuidar (kwee-**dahr**)
talcum powder: el talco (ehl **tahl**-koh)
talk (to): hablar (ah-**blahr**)
tall: alto (**ahl**-toh)
tank: el tanque (ehl **tahn**-keh)
tap (water): el grifo (ehl **gree**-foh)

tape (adhesive): la cinta adhesiva/la cinta de pegar (lah **seen**-tah ahd-eh-see-bah/lah **seen**-tah deh peh-**gahr**)

taste (to): probar (ue) (proh-**bahr**)

tax: el impuesto (ehl eem-**pwehs**-toh)

tea: el té (ehl teh)

teach (to): enseñar (ehn-seh-**nyahr**)

teacher: el maestro/la maestra (ehl mah-**ehs**-troh/lah mah-**ehs**-trah)

teaspoon: la cucharita (lah koo-chah-**ree**-tah)

tee shirt: la camiseta (lah kah-mee-**seh**-tah)

telephone: el teléfono (ehl teh-**leh**-foh-noh)

television set: el televisor (ehl teh-leh-bee-**sohr**)

tell (to): decir (*irr.*) (deh-**seer**)

ten: diez (dyehs)

thanks: gracias (**grah**-syahs)

that: ese/aquel (**eh**-seh/ah-**kehl**)

the: el/la/los/las (ehl/lah/lohs/lahs)

their: su (soo)

there is/there are: hay (**ah**-ee)

thermometer: el termómetro (ehl tehr-**moh**-meh-troh)

thermostat: el termostato (ehl tehr-mohs-**tah**-toh)

these: estos (**ehs**-tohs)

they: ellos/ellas (**eh**-yohs/**eh**-yahs)

thigh: el muslo (ehl **moos**-loh)

thin: delgado/flaco (dehl-**gah**-doh/**flah**-koh)

thirsty (to be [feel]): tener sed (teh-**nehr** sehd)

this: este (**ehs**-teh)

those: esos/aquellos (**eh**-sohs/ah-**keh**-yohs)

thread: el hilo (ehl **ee**-loh)

three: tres (trehs)

throat: la garganta (lah gahr-**gahn**-tah)

throw away (to): tirar (tee-**rahr**)

Thursday: el jueves (ehl **hweh**-behs)

tie: la corbata (lah kohr-**bah**-tah)

tile (floor): la baldosa (lah bahl-**doh**-sah)

tile (wall): el azulejo (ehl ah-soo-**leh**-hoh)

tip: la propina (lah proh-**pee**-nah)

tire (car): la llanta (lah **yahn**-tah)

tired: cansado (kahn-**sah**-doh)

toaster: la tostadora (lah tohs-tah-**doh**-rah)

today: hoy (**oh**-ee)

toe: el dedo del pie (ehl **deh**-doh dehl pyeh)

toilet: el retrete/el inodoro (ehl rreh-**treh**-teh/ehl ee-noh-**doh**-roh)

toilet paper: el papel higiénico (ehl pah-**pehl** ee-**hyeh**-nee-koh)

tomato: el tomate (ehl toh-**mah**-teh)

tomorrow: mañana (mah-**nyah**-nah)

tongue: la lengua (lah **lehn**-gwah)

tool: la herramienta (lah eh-rrah-**myehn**-tah)

tooth: el diente (ehl **dyehn**-teh)

top (toy): el trompo (ehl **trohm**-poh)

touch (to): tocar (toh-**kahr**)

tough: duro (**doo**-roh)

towel: la toalla (lah toh-**ah**-yah)

town: el pueblo (ehl **pweh**-bloh)

toy: el juguete (ehl hoo-**geh**-teh)

traffic light: el semáforo (ehl seh-**mah**-foh-roh)

train: el tren (ehl trehn)

trashcan: el basurero (ehl bah-soo-**reh**-roh)

tray: la bandeja (lah bahn-**deh**-hah)

tree: el árbol (ehl **ahr**-bohl)

trip: el viaje (ehl **byah**-heh)

truck: el camión (ehl kah-**myohn**)

truth: la verdad (lah behr-**dahd**)

Tuesday: el martes (ehl **mahr**-tehs)

tuna: el atún (ehl ah-**toon**)

turn off (to): apagar (ah-pah-**gahr**)

turn on (to): encender (ie) (ehn-sehn-**dehr**)

two: dos (dohs)

U

umbrella: el paraguas (ehl pah-**rah**-gwahs)

uncle: el tío (ehl **tee**-oh)

underneath: abajo (ah-**bah**-hoh)

understand (to): comprender (kohm-prehn-**dehr**)

uniform (clothing): el uniforme (ehl oo-nee-**fohr**-meh)

university: la universidad (lah oo-nee-behr-see-**dahd**)
until: hasta (**ahs**-tah)
upstairs: arriba (ah-**rree**-bah)
use (to): usar (oo-**sahr**)
utensil: el utensilio (ehl oo-tehn-**see**-lyoh)

V

vacuum cleaner: la aspiradora (lah ahs-pee-rah-**doh**-rah)
valve: la válvula (lah **bahl**-boo-lah)
van: la camioneta (lah kah-myoh-**neh**-tah)
vanilla: la vainilla (lah bah-ee-**nee**-yah)
vase: el florero (ehl floh-**reh**-roh)
VCR: la videocasetera/la videograbadora: (lah bee-deh-oh-kah-seh-**teh**-rah/lah bee-deh-oh-grah-bah-**doh**-rah)
vegetable: el vegetal (ehl beh-heh-**tahl**)
vegetarian: vegetariano (beh-heh-tah-**ryah**-noh)
very: muy (**moo**-ee)
video: el vídeo (ehl **bee**-deh-oh)
vinegar: el vinagre (ehl bee-**nah**-greh)
visa: la visa (lah **bee**-sah)
vitamin: la vitamina (lah bee-tah-**mee**-nah)

W

wake up (to): despertarse (ie) (dehs-pehr-**tahr**-seh)
walk (to): caminar (kah-mee-**nahr**)
wall: la pared (lah pah-**rehd**)
wallet: la billetera/la cartera (lah bee-yeh-**teh**-rah/lah kahr-**teh**-rah)
warm: tibio (**tee**-byoh)
wash (to): lavar (lah-**bahr**)
washing machine: la lavadora (lah lah-bah-**doh**-rah)
watch (to): mirar (mee-**rahr**)
watch (wrist): el reloj de pulsera (ehl rreh-**loh** deh pool-**seh**-rah)
water: el agua (ehl **ah**-gwah)
watermelon: la sandía (lah sahn-**dee**-ah)
wax: la cera (lah **seh**-rah)
we: nosotros/nosotras (noh-**soh**-trohs/noh-**soh**-trahs)

weak: débil (**deh**-beel)

wear (to): llevar (yeh-**bahr**)

weather: el tiempo (ehl **tyehm**-poh)

Wednesday: el miércoles (ehl **myehr**-koh-lehs)

weekend: el fin de semana (ehl feen deh seh-**mah**-nah)

weight: el peso (ehl **peh**-soh)

well: bien (byehn)

west: el oeste (ehl oh-**ehs**-teh)

wet: mojado (moh-**hah**-doh)

what: qué (keh)

wheel: la rueda (lah **rrweh**-dah)

wheelchair: la silla de ruedas (lah **see**-yah deh **rrweh**-dahs)

when: cuándo (**kwahn**-doh)

where: dónde (**dohn**-deh)

while: mientras (**myehn**-trahs)

white: blanco (**blahn**-koh)

who: quién (kyehn)

whose: de quién (deh kyehn)

why: por qué (pohr keh)

width: el ancho (ehl **ahn**-choh)

wife: la esposa/la mujer (lah ehs-**poh**-sah/lah moo-**hehr**)

wind: el viento (ehl **byehn**-toh)

window: la ventana (lah behn-**tah**-nah)

windshield: el parabrisas (ehl pah-rah-**bree**-sahs)

wine: el vino (ehl **bee**-noh)

winter: el invierno (ehl een-**byehr**-noh)

with: con (kohn)

without: sin (seen)

woman: la mujer (lah moo-**hehr**)

wood: la madera (lah mah-**deh**-rah)

wool: la lana (lah **lah**-nah)

wound: la herida (lah eh-**ree**-dah)

wrench (tool): la llave inglesa (lah **yah**-bch cen-**gleh**-sah)

wrist: la muñeca (lah moo-**nyeh**-kah)

Y

yard (garden): el patio (ehl **pah**-tyoh)
year: el año (ehl **ah**-nyoh)
yellow: amarillo (ah-mah-**ree**-yoh)
yesterday: ayer (ah-**yehr**)
you (*pl.*): ustedes (oos-**teh**-dehs)
you (*sing.*): tú (too) (*familiar*)/usted (oos-**tehd**) (*formal*)
your: tu (too) (*familiar*)/su (soo) (*formal*)

Z

zero: cero (**seh**-roh)

Spanish-English

A

a menudo: (ah meh-**noo**-doh) often
a tiempo: (ah **tyehm**-poh) on time
a veces: (ah **beh**-sehs) sometimes
abajo: (ah-**bah**-hoh) downstairs/underneath
abeja: (ah-**beh**-hah) bee
abierto: (ah-**byehr**-toh) open
abono: (ah-**boh**-noh) compost/fertilizer
abrazadera: (ah-brah-sah-**deh**-rah) brace/clamp
abrelatas: (ah-breh-**lah**-tahs) can opener
abrigo: (ah-**bree**-goh) coat/overcoat
abrir: (ah-**breer**) open (to)
abuela: (ah-**bweh**-lah) grandmother
abuelo: (ah-**bweh**-loh) grandfather
accidente: (ahk-see-**dehn**-teh) accident
aceite: (ah-**seh**-ee-teh) oil
aceituna: (ah-seh-ee-**too**-nah) olive
acera: (ah-**seh**-rah) sidewalk
acero inoxidable: (ah-**seh**-roh ee-nohk-see-**dah**-bleh) stainless steel
acostarse (ue): (ah-kohs-**tahr**-seh) go to bed (to)
adentro: (ah-**dehn**-troh) inside
adiós: (ah-**dyohs**) good-bye
afuera: (ah-**fweh**-rah) outside
agradable: (ah-grah-**dah**-bleh) pleasant
agrio: (**ah**-gryoh) sour/bitter
agua: (**ah**-gwah) water
aguja: (ah-**goo**-hah) needle
ahora: (ah-**oh**-rah) now
ahora mismo: (ah-**oh**-ra **mees**-moh) right now
ahorrar: (ah-oh-**rrahr**) save (up) (to)
aire acondicionado: (**ah**-ee-reh ah-kohn-dee-syoh-**nah**-doh) air conditioner
ajo: (**ah**-hoh) garlic
alacena: (ah-lah-**seh**-nah) cupboard

alarma: (ah-**lahr**-mah) alarm

alarma de humo: (ah-**lahr**-mah deh **oo**-moh) smoke alarm

alegre: (ah-**leh**-greh) happy

alergia: (ah-**lehr**-hyah) allergy

alfiler: (ahl-fee-**lehr**) pin

alfombra: (ahl-**fohm**-brah) carpet/rug

algo: (**ahl**-goh) something

algodón: (ahl-goh-**dohn**) cotton

alguien: (**ahl**-gyehn) someone/anybody

alicates: (ah-lee-**kah**-tehs) pliers

alimentar: (ah-lee-mehn-**tahr**) feed (to)

allí: (ah-**yee**) over there

almacén: (ahl-mah-**sehn**) department store

almohada: (ahl-moh-**ah**-dah) pillow

almorzar: (ahl-mohr-**sahr**) to eat lunch

almuerzo: (ahl-**mwehr**-soh) lunch

alquilar: (ahl-kee-**lahr**) rent (to)

alto: (**ahl**-toh) tall

altura: (ahl-**too**-rah) height

amable: (ah-**mah**-bleh) kind

amarillo: (ah-mah-**ree**-yoh) yellow

ambulancia: (ahm-boo-**lahn**-syah) ambulance

amistoso: (ah-mees-**toh**-soh) friendly

anaranjado: (ah-nah-rahn-**hah**-doh) orange (color)

ancho: (**ahn**-choh) wide/width

anillo: (ah-**nee**-yoh) ring

animal doméstico: (ah-nee-**mahl** doh-**mehs**-tee-koh) pet

anoche: (ah-**noh**-cheh) last night

anteojos: (ahn-teh-**oh**-hohs) eyeglasses

anteojos de sol: (ahn-teh-**oh**-hohs deh sohl) sunglasses

antes: (**ahn**-tehs) before

añadir: (ah-nyah-**deer**) add (to)

año: (**ah**-nyoh) year

apagar: (ah-pah-**gahr**) turn off (to)

aparato: (ah-pah-**rah**-toh) device/appliance

apartamento: (ah-pahr-tah-**mehn**-toh) apartment

apellido: (ah-peh-**yee**-doh) last name

apio: (**ah**-pyoh) celery
aprender: (ah-prehn-**dehr**) learn (to)
aquel/aquella: (ah-**kehl**/ah-**keh**-yah) that
aquí: (ah-**kee**) here
árbol: (**ahr**-bohl) tree
arbusto: (ahr-**boos**-toh) bush/shrub
armadura: (ahr-mah-**doo**-rah) frame
armario: (ahr-**mah**-ryoh) closet/cupboard
arrancar: (ah-rrahn-**kahr**) pull out (to)
arreglar: (ah-rreh-**glahr**) fix (to)
arriba: (ah-**rree**-bah) upstairs
arroz: (ah-**rrohs**) rice
ascensor: (ah-sehn-**sohr**) elevator
asiento: (ah-**syehn**-toh) seat
asistir a: (ah-sees-**teer** ah) attend (to)
aspiradora: (ahs-pee-rah-**doh**-rah) vacuum cleaner
aspirina: (ahs-pee-**ree**-nah) aspirin
atado: (ah-**tah**-doh) bunch
atascado: (ah-tahs-**kah**-doh) clogged
atún: (ah-**toon**) tuna
autobús: (ah-oo-toh-**boos**) bus
autorizado por la ley judía: (ah-oo-toh-ree-**sah**-doh pohr lah **leh**-ee hoo-**dee**-ah) kosher
avenida: (ah-beh-**nee**-dah) avenue
ayer: (ah-**yehr**) yesterday
ayudante: (ah-yoo-**dahn**-teh) helper
ayudar: (ah-yoo-**dahr**) help (to)
azúcar: (ah-**soo**-kahr) sugar
azul: (ah-**sool**) blue
azulejo: (ah-soo-**leh**-hoh) tile (wall)

B

babero: (bah-**beh**-roh) bib
bajar: (bah-**hahr**) go down (descend) (to)
bajarse de: (bah-**hahr**-seh deh) get off (to)

bajo: (**bah**-hoh) short (person)
balcón: (bahl-**kohn**) balcony
baldosa: (bahl-**doh**-sah) tile (floor)
balón: (bah-**lohn**) ball
banco: (**bahn**-koh) bank/bench
bandeja: (bahn-**deh**-hah) tray
bañar: (bah-**nyahr**) bathe (to)
bañera: (bah-**nyeh**-rah) bathtub
baño: (**bah**-nyoh) bathroom/bath
baranda: (bah-**rahn**-dah) railing
barato: (bah-**rah**-toh) inexpensive
barba: (**bahr**-bah) beard
barbería: (bahr-beh-**ree**-ah) barbershop
barbero: (bahr-**beh**-roh) barber/hairdresser
barbilla: (bahr-**bee**-yah) chin
barrer: (bah-**rrehr**) sweep (to)
barrio: (**bah**-rryoh) neighborhood
basura: (bah-**soo**-rah) garbage
basurero: (bah-soo-**reh**-roh) dump/trashcan
batería: (bah-teh-**ree**-ah) battery
beber: (beh-**behr**) drink (to)
bebida: (beh-**bee**-dah) drink
biberón: (bee-beh-**rohn**) baby bottle
biblioteca: (bee-blyoh-**teh**-kah) library
bicicleta: (bee-see-**kleh**-tah) bicycle
bien: (byehn) well
billete: (bee-**yeh**-teh) bill (banknote)
billetera: (bee-yeh-**teh**-rah) wallet
bisagra: (bee-**sah**-grah) hinge
bistec: (bees-**tehk**) steak
blanco: (**blahn**-koh) white
blando: (**blahn**-doh) soft
blanqueador: (blahn-keh-ah-**dohr**) bleach
bloque: (**bloh**-keh) block (toy)
blue jeans: (bloo yeens) jeans
blusa: (**bloo**-sah) blouse

boca: (**boh**-kah) mouth
bocacalle: (boh-kah-**kah-**yeh) intersection
bocina: (boh-**see**-nah) horn
bodega: (boh-**deh**-gah) grocery store
bolígrafo: (boh-**lee**-grah-foh) ballpoint pen
bolsa: (**bohl**-sah) bag/sack
bolsillo: (bohl-**see**-yoh) pocket
bombilla: (bohm-**bee**-yah) lightbulb
bonito: (boh-**nee**-toh) pretty
borde: (**bohr**-deh) edge
botella: (boh-**teh**-yah) bottle
botiquín: (boh-tee-**keen**) medicine chest
botón: (boh-**tohn**) button
brazo: (**brah**-soh) arm
brécol: (**breh**-kohl) broccoli
bueno: (**bweh**-noh) good
bufanda: (boo-**fahn**-dah) scarf
buscar: (boos-**kahr**) look for (to)
buzón: (boo-**sohn**) mailbox

C

caballo: (kah-**bah**-yoh) horse
caballo de fuerza: (kah-**bah**-yoh deh **fwehr**-sah) horsepower
cabello: (kah-**beh**-yoh) hair
cabeza: (kah-**beh**-sah) head
cacahuete: (kah-kah-**weh**-teh) peanut
cacerola: (kah-seh-**roh**-lah) pot
cada: (**kah**-dah) each
cadena: (kah-**deh**-nah) chain
cadera: (kah-**deh**-rah) hip
caerse (*irr.*): (kah-**ehr**-seh) fall (to)
café: (kah-**feh**) coffee/coffee shop
cafetera: (kah-feh-**teh**-rah) coffee pot
caja: (**kah**-hah) box/cash register
caja de fusibles: (**kah**-hah deh foo-**see**-blehs) fuse box
caja de primeros auxilios: (**kah**-hah deh pree-**meh**-rohs ah-oo-**see**-lyohs) first aid kit

cajero automático: (kah-**heh**-roh ah-oo-toh-**mah**-tee-koh) ATM

cajón: (kah-**hohn**) drawer

calcetines: (kahl-seh-**tee**-nehs) socks

caldo: (**kahl**-do) broth

calefacción: (kah-leh-fahk-**syohn**) heat

calentador: (kah-lehn-tah-**dohr**) heater

caliente: (kah-**lyehn**-teh) hot

callado: (kah-**yah**-doh) quiet

calle: (**kah**-yeh) street

calvo: (**kahl**-boh) bald

cama: (**kah**-mah) bed

camarón: (kah-mah-**rohn**) shrimp

cambiar: (kahm-**byahr**) change (to)

caminar: (kah-mee-**nahr**) walk (to)

camión: (kah-**myohn**) truck

camioneta: (kah-myoh-**neh**-tah) van

camisa: (kah-**mee**-sah) shirt

camiseta: (kah-mee-**seh**-tah) tee shirt

campo: (**kahm**-poh) field

canasta: (kah-**nahs**-tah) basket

candado: (kahn-**dah**-doh) padlock

canela: (kah-**neh**-lah) cinnamon

cansado: (kahn-**sah**-doh) tired

cantero: (kahn-**teh**-roh) flower bed

cantidad: (kahn-tee-**dahd**) quantity

cara: (**kah**-rah) face

cárcel: (**kahr**-sehl) jail

carga: (**kahr**-gah) load

carne: (**kahr**-neh) meat

carne molida: (**kahr**-neh moh-**lee**-dah) ground beef

carnicería: (kahr-nee-seh-**ree**-ah) butcher shop

caro: (**kah**-roh) expensive

carpintero/carpintera: (kahr-peen-**teh**-roh/kahr-peen-**teh**-rah) carpenter

carrito: (kah-**rree**-toh) cart

carro: (**kah**-rroh) car

carta: (**kahr**-tah) letter

cartera: (kahr-**teh**-rah) wallet
casa: (**kah**-sah) house
casado: (kah-**sah**-doh) married
casco: (**kahs**-koh) helmet
catarro: (kah-**tah**-rroh) cold (illness)
cazuela: (kah-**sweh**-lah) pan/pot
cebolla: (seh-**boh**-yah) onion
ceja: (**seh**-hah) eyebrow
celular: (seh-loo-**lahr**) cell phone
cemento: (seh-**mehn**-toh) cement
cena: (**seh**-nah) dinner
cenar: (seh-**nahr**) dine (to)/have dinner (to)
centavo: (sehn-**tah**-boh) cent
centro: (**sehn**-troh) downtown
centro comercial: (**sehn**-troh koh-mehr-**syahl**) shopping mall
cepillar: (seh-pee-**yahr**) brush (to)
cepillo: (seh-**pee**-yoh) brush
cera: (**seh**-rah) wax
cerca: (**sehr**-kah) fence/near
cerdo: (**sehr**-doh) pig
cereal: (seh-reh-**ahl**) cereal
cereza: (seh-**reh**-sah) cherry
cero: (**seh**-roh) zero
cerrado: (seh-**rrah**-doh) closed
cerradura: (seh-rrah-**doo**-rah) lock
cerrar (ie): (seh-**rrahr**) close (to)/lock (to)
cerrojo: (seh-**rroh**-hoh) latch
cerrucho: (seh-**rroo**-choh) saw (tool)
certificado: (sehr-tee-fee-**kah**-doh) certified
cerveza: (sehr-**beh**-sah) beer
cesta: (**sehs**-tah) basket
champú: (chahm-**poo**) shampoo
chaqueta: (chah-**keh**-tah) jacket
cheque: (**cheh**-keh) check
chimenea: (chee-meh-**neh**-ah) chimney/fireplace
chupete: (choo-**peh**-teh) (baby's) pacifier
cimiento: (see-**myehn**-toh) foundation/cement

cinco: (**seen**-koh) five

cine: (**see**-neh) movie theater

cinta adhesiva: (**seen**-tah ahd-eh-**see**-bah) (adhesive) tape

cinta de pegar: (**seen**-tah deh peh-**gahr**) (adhesive) tape

cinturón: (seen-too-**rohn**) belt

cinturón de seguridad: (seen-too-**rohn** deh seh-goo-ree-**dahd**) seatbelt

cita: (**see**-tah) date/appointment

clara: (**klah**-rah) egg white

claro: (**klah**-roh) light (color)

clavo: (**klah**-boh) nail (metal)

clínica: (**klee**-nee-kah) clinic

cloro: (**kloh**-roh) bleach

coche: (**koh**-cheh) car

cochecito: (koh-cheh-**see**-toh) baby carriage

cocina: (koh-**see**-nah) kitchen/stove

cocinar: (koh-see-**nahr**) cook (to)

codo: (**koh**-doh) elbow

cojín: (koh-**heen**) cushion

cola: (**koh**-lah) glue

colchón: (kohl-**chohn**) mattress

collar: (koh-**yahr**) collar/necklace

color: (koh-**lohr**) color

comedor: (koh-meh-**dohr**) dining room

comenzar (ie): (koh-mehn-**sahr**) start (to)

comer: (koh-**mehr**) eat (to)

comida: (koh-**mee**-dah) food/meal

comida para perros: (koh-**mee**-dah **pah**-rah **peh**-rrohs) dog food

cómo: (**koh**-moh) how

cómoda: (**koh**-moh-dah) chest of drawers/dresser

comportamiento: (kohm-pohr-tah-**myehn**-toh) behavior

comprar: (kohm-**prahr**) buy (to)

comprender: (kohm-prehn-**dehr**) understand (to)

computadora: (kohm-poo-tah-**doh**-rah) computer

con: (kohn) with

concreto: (kohn-**kreh**-toh) concrete

condimento: (kohn-dee-**mehn**-toh) seasoning

conducto: (kohn-**dook**-toh) duct

conductor: (kohn-dook-**tohr**) driver

confundido: (kohn-foon-**dee**-doh) confused

congelado: (kohn-heh-**lah**-doh) frozen

conocer (*irr.*): (koh-noh-**sehr**) know (be acquainted with) (to)

conseguir (*irr.*): (kohn-seh-**geer**) get (to)

consultorio del médico: (kohn-sool-**toh**-ryoh dehl **meh**-dee-koh) doctor's office

contador: (kohn-tah-**dohr**) meter (utilities)

contento: (kohn-**tehn**-toh) happy

contratista: (kohn-trah-**tees**-tah) contractor

contrato: (kohn-**trah**-toh) contract

corazón: (koh-rah-**sohn**) heart

corbata: (kohr-**bah**-tah) tie

cordero: (kohr-**deh**-roh) lamb

cordón eléctrico: (kohr-**dohn** eh-**lehk**-tree-koh) electrical cord

correa: (koh-**rreh**-ah) leash

corrector (de dientes): (koh-rrehk-**tohr** deh **dyehn**-tehs) braces (teeth)

correo: (koh-**rreh**-oh) post office

cortacésped: (kohr-tah-**sehs**-pehd) lawnmower

cortar: (kohr-**tahr**) cut (to)

cortés: (kohr-**tehs**) polite/courteous

cortina: (kohr-**tee**-nah) curtain

corto: (**kohr**-toh) short (hair, etc.)

costar (ue): (kohs-**tahr**) cost (to)

crema: (**kreh**-mah) cream

criticar: (kree-tee-**kahr**) criticize (to)

crudo: (**kroo**-doh) raw

cuadra: (**kwah**-drah) (city) block

cuándo: (**kwahn**-doh) when

cuánto/cuánta: (**kwahn**-toh/**kwahn**-tah) how much

cuántos/cuántas: (**kwahn**-tohs/**kwahn**-tahs) how many

cuartel de policía: (kwahr-**tehl** deh poh-lee-**see**-ah) police station

cuarto: (**kwahr**-toh) quart

cuarto: (**kwahr**-toh) room

cuarto de dormir: (**kwahr**-toh deh dohr-**meer**) bedroom

cuarto de juego: (**kwahr**-toh deh **hweh**-goh) playroom

cuatro: (**kwah**-troh) four

cubierta: (koo-**byehr**-tah) cover
cubiertos: (koo-**byehr**-tohs) cutlery
cubo: (**koo**-boh) bucket
cubo de basura: (**koo**-boh deh bah-**soo**-rah) garbage can
cuchara: (koo-**chah**-rah) spoon/tablespoon
cucharita: (koo-chah-**ree**-tah) teaspoon
cuchillo: (koo-**chee**-yoh) knife
cuello: (**kweh**-yoh) neck
cuenta: (**kwehn**-tah) bill (account)
cuenta corriente: (**kwehn**-tah koh-**rryehn**-teh) checking account
cuento: (**kwehn**-toh) story
cuero: (**kweh**-roh) leather
cuerpo: (**kwehr**-poh) body
cuidado: (kwee-**dah**-doh) care
cuidar: (kwee-**dahr**) take care of (to)
cuna: (**koo**-nah) crib
cuñada: (koo-**nyah**-dah) sister-in-law
cuñado: (koo-**nyah**-doh) brother-in-law
cupón: (koo-**pohn**) coupon
curita: (koo-**ree**-tah) band-aid

D

dar (*irr.*): (dahr) give (to)
darse prisa: (**dahr**-seh **pree**-sah) hurry (to)
de: (deh) of/from
de nuevo: (deh **nweh**-boh) again
de prisa: (deh **pree**-sah) quickly
de pronto: (deh **prohn**-toh) at once/suddenly
de quién: (deh kyehn) whose
débil: (**deh**-beel) weak
decir (*irr.*): (deh-**seer**) say (to)/tell (to)
dedo: (**deh**-doh) finger
dedo del pie: (**deh**-doh dehl pyeh) toe
dejar: (deh-**hahr**) leave (behind) (to)
delgado: (dehl-**gah**-doh) thin/slender
delicioso: (deh-lee-**syoh**-soh) delicious
dependiente: (deh-pehn-**dyehn**-teh) salesperson/clerk

deporte: (deh-**pohr**-teh) sport

derecha: (deh-**reh**-chah) right (direction)

derramar: (deh-rrah-**mahr**) spill (to)

desagüe: (deh-**sah**-gweh) drain (pipe)

desayuno: (deh-sah-**yoo**-noh) breakfast

describir: (dehs-kree-**beer**) describe (to)

descubrir: (dehs-koo-**breer**) discover (to)

descuento: (dehs-**kwehn**-toh) discount

desechable: (deh-seh-**chah**-bleh) disposable

desinfectante: (deh-seen-fehk-**tahn**-teh) disinfectant

desinfectar: (deh-seen-fehk-**tahr**) disinfect (to)

desodorante: (deh-soh-doh-**rahn**-teh) deodorant

desorganizado: (deh-sohr-gah-nee-**sah**-doh) disorganized

despacio: (dehs-**pah**-syoh) slowly

despensa: (dehs-**pehn**-sah) pantry

despertarse (ie): (dehs-pehr-**tahr**-seh) wake up (to)

después: (dehs-**pwehs**) after

destornillador: (dehs-tohr-nee-yah-**dohr**) screwdriver

desván: (dehs-**bahn**) attic

detergente: (deh-tehr-**gehn**-teh) detergent

detrás: (deh-**trahs**) behind

devolver (ue): (deh-bohl-**behr**) return (to) (give back [to])

día: (**dee**-ah) day

diente: (**dyehn**-teh) tooth

diente de león: (**dyehn**-teh deh leh-**ohn**) dandelion

diez: (dyehs) ten

dinero: (dee-**neh**-roh) money

dinero en efectivo: (dee-**neh**-roh ehn eh-fehk-**tee**-boh) cash

dirección: (dee-rehk-**syohn**) address

discutir: (dees-koo-**teer**) discuss (to)

disponible: (dees-poh-**nee**-bleh) available

divertido: (dee-behr-**tee**-doh) fun

divertirse (ie): (dee-behr-**teer**-seh) have a good time (to)

doblar: (doh-**blahr**) fold (to)

docena: (doh-**seh**-nah) dozen

dólar: (**doh**-lahr) dollar

doler (ue): (doh-**lehr**) hurt (ache) (to)

dolor de cabeza: (doh-**lohr** deh kah-**beh**-sah) headache
dolor de estómago: (doh-**lohr** deh ehs-**toh**-mah-goh) stomachache
dolor de oído: (doh-**lohr** deh oh-**ee**-doh) earache
domingo: (doh-**meen**-goh) Sunday
dónde: (**dohn**-deh) where
dormir (ue): (dohr-**meer**) sleep (to)
dormitorio: (dohr-mee-**toh**-ryoh) bedroom
dos: (dohs) two
ducha: (**doo**-chah) shower
dueño: (**dweh**-nyoh) owner
dulce: (**dool**-seh) sweet
duro: (**doo**-roh) hard/tough
DVD: (deh beh deh) DVD

E

echar: (eh-**chahr**) pour (to)
edificio: (eh-dee-**fee**-syoh) building
ejercicio: (eh-hehr-**see**-syoh) exercise
él: (ehl) he
eléctrico: (eh-**lehk**-tree-koh) electrical
ella: (**eh**-yah) she
ellos/ellas: (**eh**-yohs/**eh**-yahs) they
embrague: (ehm-**brah**-geh) clutch (car)
emergencia: (eh-mehr-**hehn**-syah) emergency
empezar (ie): (ehm-peh-**sahr**) start (to)
empleado: (ehm-pleh-**ah**-doh) employee
empleo: (ehm-**pleh**-oh) employment/job
en: (ehn) in/on
en seguida: (ehn seh-**gee**-dah) immediately
encender (ie): (ehn-sehn-**dehr**) turn on (to)
enchufe: (ehn-**choo**-feh) electrical outlet/plug
enfermedad: (ehn-fehr-meh-**dahd**) illness
enfermero/enfermera: (ehn-fehr-**meh**-roh/ehn-fehr-**meh**-rah) nurse
enfermo: (ehn-**fehr**-moh) sick/ill
engranaje: (ehn-grah-**nah**-heh) gear (car)
entrada: (ehn-**trah**-dah) entrance
entrada (para carros): (ehn-**trah**-dah **pah**-rah **kah**-rrohs) driveway

entre: (**ehn**-treh) between
entrevista: (ehn-treh-**bees**-tah) interview
envase: (ehn-**bah**-seh) container
erupción: (eh-roop-**syohn**) rash
escalera: (ehs-kah-**leh**-rah) stairs/ladder
escape: (ehs-**kah**-peh) exhaust (car)
escoba: (ehs-**koh**-bah) broom
escoger (*irr.*): (ehs-koh-**hehr**) choose (to)
escribir: (ehs-kree-**beer**) write (to)
escritorio: (ehs-kree-**toh**-ryoh) desk
escuchar: (ehs-koo-**chahr**) listen (to)
escuela: (ehs-**kweh**-lah) school
ese: (**eh**-seh) that
esos: (**eh**-sohs) those
espalda: (ehs-**pahl**-dah) back (body)
especia: (ehs-**peh**-syah) spice
espejo: (ehs-**peh**-hoh) mirror
espinaca: (ehs-pee-**nah**-kah) spinach
esponja: (ehs-**pohn**-hah) sponge
esposa: (ehs-**poh**-sah) wife
esposo: (ehs-**poh**-soh) husband
esquina: (ehs-**kee**-nah) corner (outside)
estación de metro: (ehs-tah-**syohn** deh **meh**-troh) subway station
estacionamiento: (ehs-tah-syoh-nah-**myehn**-toh) parking lot
estacionar: (ehs-tah-syoh-**nahr**) park (to)
estante: (ehs-**tahn**-teh) bookcase/shelf
estar (*irr.*): (ehs-**tahr**) be (to)
estar de acuerdo: (ehs-**tahr** deh ah-**kwehr**-doh) agree (to)
este: (**ehs**-teh) east
este: (**ehs**-teh) this
estómago: (ehs-**toh**-mah-goh) stomach
estos: (**ehs**-tohs) these
estropajo: (ehs-troh-**pah**-hoh) scouring pad
estudiante: (ehs-too-**dyahn**-teh) student
estudiar: (ehs-too-**dyahr**) study (to)
estupendo: (ehs-too-**pehn**-doh) great
excavar: (ehs-kah-**bahr**) dig (to)

experiencia: (ehs-peh-**ryehn**-syah) experience
extintor: (ehs-teen-**tohr**) fire extinguisher
extraño: (ehs-**trah**-nyoh) strange

F

falda: (**fahl**-dah) skirt
falso: (**fahl**-soh) hem
familia: (fah-**mee**-lyah) family
farmacia: (fahr-**mah**-syah) drugstore/pharmacy
fecha: (**feh**-chah) date (day)
fichero: (fee-**cheh**-roh) file cabinet
fiebre: (**fyeh**-breh) fever
fiesta nacional: (**fyehs**-tah nah-syoh-**nahl**) holiday
fiesta religiosa: (**fyehs**-tah rreh-lee-**hyoh**-sah) religious holiday
filtro de café: (**feel**-troh deh kah-**feh**) coffee filter
fin: (feen) end
fin de semana: (feen deh seh-**mah**-nah) weekend
finca: (**feen**-kah) farm
firmar: (feer-**mahr**) sign (to) (one's name)
flaco: (**flah**-koh) skinny/thin
flor: (flohr) flower
florero: (floh-**reh**-roh) vase
fogón: (foh-**gohn**) (kitchen) range
fondo: (**fohn**-doh) back/bottom
fósforos: (**fohs**-foh-rohs) matches
franela: (frah-**neh**-lah) flannel
frasco: (**frahs**-koh) jar
frazada: (frah-**sah**-dah) blanket
fregadero: (freh-gah-**deh**-roh) sink (kitchen)
freno: (**freh**-noh) brake (car)
frente: (**frehn**-teh) front
frente a: (**frehn**-teh ah) facing
fresa: (**freh**-sah) strawberry
fresco: (**frehs**-koh) cool/fresh
frijol: (free-**hohl**) bean
frío: (**free**-oh) cold (temperature)
frito: (**free**-toh) fried

fruta: (**froo**-tah) fruit
fuego: (**fweh**-goh) fire
fuente: (**fwehn**-teh) fountain
fuerte: (**fwehr**-teh) strong
fumigador: (foo-mee-gah-**dohr**) exterminator
función: (foon-**syohn**) show/performance
fundación: (foon-dah-**syohn**) foundation

G

galleta: (gah-**yeh**-tah) cookie
galleta salada: (gah-**yeh**-tah sah-**lah**-dah) cracker
galón: (gah-**lohn**) gallon
ganar: (gah-**nahr**) to win/earn (money)
ganga: (**gahn**-gah) bargain
garaje: (gah-**rah**-heh) garage
garganta: (gahr-**gahn**-tah) throat
gas: (gahs) gas (cooking)
gasolina: (gah-soh-**lee**-nah) gasoline
gasolinera: (gah-soh-lee-**neh**-rah) gas station
gato: (**gah**-toh) cat
generoso: (heh-neh-**roh**-soh) generous
gente: (**hehn**-teh) people
gerente: (heh-**rehn**-teh) manager
gimnasio: (heem-**nah**-syoh) gym
goma: (**goh**-mah) glue/rubber
gordo: (**gohr**-doh) fat
gorra: (**goh**-rrah) cap
gota: (**goh**-tah) drop (liquid)
gracias: (**grah**-syahs) thanks
gramo: (**grah**-moh) gram
grande: (**grahn**-deh) big/large
grano: (**grah**-noh) grain
grasa: (**grah**-sah) fat/grease
grava: (**grah**-bah) gravel
grieta: (**gryeh**-tah) crack
grifo: (**gree**-foh) faucet
gripe: (**gree**-peh) flu

gris: (grees) gray
grueso: (**grweh**-soh) fat
guante: (**gwahn**-teh) glove
guantera: (gwahn-**teh**-rah) glove compartment
guardar: (gwahr-**dahr**) put away (to)
gustar: (goos-**tahr**) like (to)

H

hablar: (ah-**blahr**) speak (to)/talk (to)
hacer (*irr.*): (ah-**sehr**) do (to)/make (to)
hacer cola: (ah-**sehr** koh-lah) stand in line (to)
hacer la cama: (ah-**sehr** lah **kah**-mah) make the bed (to)
harina: (ah-**ree**-nah) flour
hasta: (**ahs**-tah) until
hay: (**ah**-ee) there is/there are
herida: (eh-**ree**-dah) wound/injury
hermana: (ehr-**mah**-nah) sister
hermano: (ehr-**mah**-noh) brother
herramienta: (eh-rrah-**myehn**-tah) tool
hervir (ie): (ehr-**beer**) boil (to)
hielo: (**yeh**-loh) ice
hierba: (**yehr**-bah) grass
hierba mala: (**yehr**-bah **mah**-lah) weed
hierro: (**yeh**-rroh) iron (metal)
hija: (**ee**-hah) daughter
hijo: (**ee**-hoh) son
hilo: (**ee**-loh) thread
hinchado: (een-**chah**-doh) swollen
hoja: (**oh**-hah) leaf
hombre: (**ohm**-breh) man
hombro: (**ohm**-broh) shoulder
hongo: (**ohn**-goh) mushroom
honrado: (ohn-**rrah**-doh) honest/trustworthy
hormigón: (ohr-mee-**gohn**) concrete
horno: (**ohr**-noh) oven
horno a microondas: (**ohr**-noh ah mee-kroh-**ohn**-dahs) microwave oven

hospital: (ohs-pee-**tahl**) hospital
hoy: (**oh**-ee) today
hoyo: (**oh**-yoh) hole
huevo: (**weh**-boh) egg

I

iglesia: (ee-**gleh**-syah) church
impuesto: (eem-**pwehs**-toh) tax
incluir (*irr.*): (een-kloo-**eer**) include (to)
infectado: (een-fehk-**tah**-doh) infected
ingrediente: (een-greh-**dyehn**-teh) ingredient
inmediatamente: (een-meh-**dyah**-tah-mehn-teh) immediately
inodoro: (ee-noh-**doh**-roh) toilet
insecticida: (een-sehk-tee-**see**-dah) insecticide
inteligente: (een-teh-lee-**hehn**-teh) intelligent
interesado: (een-teh-reh-**sah**-doh) interested
interesante: (een-teh-reh-**sahn**-teh) interesting
interruptor: (een-teh-rroop-**tohr**) light switch
invierno: (een-**byehr**-noh) winter
invitado: (een-bee-**tah**-doh) guest
ir (*irr.*): (eer) go (to)
ir de compras: (eer deh **kohm**-prahs) go shopping (to)
izquierda: (ees-**kyehr**-dah) left (direction)

J

jabón: (hah-**bohn**) soap
jamón: (hah-**mohn**) ham
jardín: (hahr-**deen**) garden
jardinero/jardinera: (hahr-dee-**neh**-roh/hahr-dee-**neh**-rah) gardener
jaula: (**ha**-oo-lah) cage
jefe/jefa: (**heh**-feh/**heh**-fah) boss
joven: (**hoh**-behn) young
joyas: (**hoh**-yahs) jewelry
jueves: (**hweh**-behs) Thursday
jugar (ue): (hoo-**gahr**) play (to)
jugar (ue) golf: (hoo-**gahr** gohlf) golf (to)

jugo: (**hoo**-goh) juice
juguete: (hoo-**geh**-teh) toy
justo: (**hoos**-toh) just

K

kilogramo: (kee-loh-**grah**-moh) kilogram

L

labio: (**lah**-byoh) lip
ladrillo: (lah-**dree**-yoh) brick
lámpara: (**lahm**-pah-rah) lamp
lana: (**lah**-nah) wool
lápiz: (**lah**-pees) pencil
largo: (**lahr**-goh) long/length
lata: (**lah**-tah) can
latón: (lah-**tohn**) brass (metal)
lavabo: (lah-**bah**-boh) sink (bathroom)
lavadora: (lah-bah-**doh**-rah) washing machine
lavamanos: (lah-bah-**mah**-nohs) sink (bathroom)
lavandería: (lah-bahn-deh-**ree**-ah) laundromat/laundry room
lavaplatos: (lah-bah-**plah**-tohs) dishwasher
lavar: (lah-**bahr**) wash (to)
leche: (**leh**-cheh) milk
leche desnatada: (**leh**-cheh dehs-nah-**tah**-dah) skim milk
lechuga: (leh-**choo**-gah) lettuce
leer: (leh-**ehr**) read (to)
lejía: (leh-**hee**-ah) bleach
lejos: (**leh**-hohs) far
lengua: (**lehn**-gwah) tongue
lento: (**lehn**-toh) slow
levantar: (leh-bahn-**tahr**) lift (to)
levantarse: (leh-bahn-**tahr**-seh) get up (to)
libra: (**lee**-brah) pound (weight)
libre: (**lee**-breh) free
librería: (lee-breh-**ree**-ah) bookstore
libro: (**lee**-broh) book

lima: (**lee**-mah) lime
limón: (lee-**mohn**) lemon
limpiar: (leem-**pyahr**) clean (to)
limpio: (**leem**-pyoh) clean
lindo: (**leen**-doh) pretty
linterna: (leen-**tehr**-nah) flashlight/lantern
líquido: (**lee**-kee-doh) liquid
litro: (**lee**-troh) liter
llamada: (yah-**mah**-dah) call
llamar: (yah-**mahr**) call (to)
llamarse: (yah-**mahr**-seh) be called (to)/be named (to)
llanta: (**yahn**-tah) tire (car)
llanta pinchada: (**yahn**-tah peen-**chah**-dah) flat tire
llave: (**yah**-beh) key/faucet
llave inglesa: (**yah**-beh een-**gleh**-sah) wrench
llegar: (yeh-**gahr**) arrive (to)
lleno: (**yeh**-noh) full
llevar: (yeh-**bahr**) carry (to)/wear (to)
lluvia: (**yoo**-byah) rain
loción: (loh-**syohn**) lotion
loco: (**loh**-koh) crazy
losa: (**loh**-sah) slab/flagstone
luego: (**lweh**-goh) later
lugar: (loo-**gahr**) place
lunes: (**loo**-nehs) Monday
luz: (loos) light

M

maceta: (mah-**seh**-tah) flowerpot
madera: (mah-**deh**-rah) wood
madre: (**mah**-dreh) mother
madrina: (mah-**dree**-nah) godmother
maestro/maestra: (mah-**ehs**-troh/mah-**ehs**-trah) teacher
maíz: (mah-**ees**) corn
mal: (mahl) badly
malcriado: (mahl-**kryah**-doh) spoiled (person)
manga: (**mahn**-gah) sleeve

manguera: (mahn-**geh**-rah) hose (garden)

maní: (mah-**nee**) peanut

mano: (**mah**-noh) hand

manojo: (mah-**noh**-hoh) bunch

mantel: (mahn-**tehl**) tablecloth

mantequilla: (mahn-teh-**kee**-yah) butter

manzana: (mahn-**sah**-nah) apple

mañana: (mah-**nyah**-nah) morning/tomorrow

máquina: (**mah**-kee-nah) machine

marca: (**mahr**-kah) brand

mariscos: (mah-**rees**-kohs) shellfish

mármol: (**mahr**-mohl) marble

marrón: (mah-**rrohn**) brown

martes: (**mahr**-tehs) Tuesday

martillo: (mahr-**tee**-yoh) hammer

más: (mahs) more

más tarde: (mahs **tahr**-deh) later

masticar: (mahs-tee-**kahr**) chew (to)

material: (mah-teh-**ryahl**) material

mediano: (meh-**dyah**-noh) medium

medianoche: (meh-dyah-**noh**-cheh) midnight

médico/médica: (**meh**-dee-koh/**meh**-dee-kah) doctor

medidas: (meh-**dee**-dahs) measurements

medio: (**meh**-dyoh) middle/half

mediodía: (meh-dyoh-**dee**-ah) noon

medir (i): (meh-**deer**) measure (to)

mejilla: (meh-**hee**-yah) cheek

melocotón: (meh-loh-koh-**tohn**) peach

mensaje: (mehn-**sah**-heh) message

mercado: (mehr-**kah**-doh) market

merienda: (meh-**ryehn**-dah) snack

mes: (mehs) month

mesa: (**meh**-sah) table

mesita de centro: (meh-**see**-tah deh **sehn**-troh) coffee table

meter: (meh-**tehr**) put in (to)/insert (to)

metro: (**meh**-troh) meter (measurement)/subway

mezclilla: (mehs-**klee**-yah) denim

mezquita: (mehs-**kee**-tah) mosque
mi: (mee) my
mientras: (**myehn**-trahs) while
miércoles: (**myehr**-koh-lehs) Wednesday
mirar: (mee-**rahr**) watch (to)
mitad: (mee-**tahd**) half
mochila: (moh-**chee**-lah) backpack
mojado: (moh-**hah**-doh) wet
moneda: (moh-**neh**-dah) coin
mosca: (**mohs**-kah) fly
mostaza: (mohs-**tah**-sah) mustard
mostrador: (mohs-trah-**dohr**) counter (store)
mostrar (ue): (mohs-**trahr**) show (to)
motocicleta (moto): (moh-toh-see-**kleh**-tah [**moh**-toh]) motorcycle
motor: (moh-**tohr**) engine
mover (ue): (moh-**behr**) move (to)
mudarse: (moo-**dahr**-seh) move (residence) (to)
muebles: (**mweh**-blehs) furniture
muerto: (**mwehr**-toh) dead
mujer: (moo-**hehr**) woman/wife
muñeca: (moo-**nyeh**-kah) wrist/doll
museo: (moo-**seh**-oh) museum
música: (**moo**-see-kah) music
muslo: (**moos**-loh) thigh
muy: (**moo**-ee) very

N

nacimiento: (nah-see-**myehn**-toh) birth
nada: (**nah**-dah) nothing
nadie: (**nah**-dyeh) nobody/no one
naranja: (nah-**rahn**-hah) orange (fruit)
nariz: (nah-**rees**) nose
necesitar: (neh-seh-see-**tahr**) need (to)
negro: (**neh**-groh) black
nervioso: (nehr-**byoh**-soh) nervous
nevera: (neh-**beh**-rah) refrigerator
nieta: (**nyeh**-tah) granddaughter

nieto: (**nyeh**-toh) grandson
nieve: (**nyeh**-beh) snow
nilón: (nee-**lohn**) nylon
niñera: (nee-**nyeh**-rah) nanny
noche: (**noh**-cheh) evening/night
nombre: (**nohm**-breh) name
norte: (**nohr**-teh) north
nosotros/nosotras: (noh-**soh**-trohs/noh-**soh**-trahs) we
novia: (**noh**-byah) girlfriend/fiancée
novio: (**noh**-byoh) boyfriend/fiancé
nuera: (**nweh**-rah) daughter-in-law
nuestro/nuestra: (**nwehs**-troh/**nwehs**-trah) our
nueve: (**nweh**-beh) nine
nuevo: (**nweh**-boh) new
nunca: (**noon**-kah) never

O

obediente: (oh-beh-**dyehn**-teh) obedient
obrero/obrera: (oh-**breh**-roh/oh-**breh**-rah) laborer
ocho: (**oh**-choh) eight
ocupado: (oh-koo-**pah**-doh) busy/occupied
oeste: (oh-**ehs**-teh) west
oficina: (oh-fee-**see**-nah) office
oficina de correos: (oh-fee-**see**-nah deh koh-**rreh**-ohs) post office
ofrecer (*irr.*): (oh-freh-**sehr**) offer (to)
oído: (oh-**ee**-doh) inner ear
oír (*irr.*): (oh-**eer**) hear (to)
ojo: (**oh**-hoh) eye
olla: (**oh**-yah) pot/pan
onza: (**ohn**-sah) ounce
orden: (**ohr**-dehn) order
oreja: (oh-**reh**-hah) ear
organizado: (ohr-gah-nee-**sah**-doh) organized
oro: (**oh**-roh) gold
oscuro: (ohs-**koo**-roh) dark
oso: (**oh**-soh) bear
otoño: (oh-**toh**-nyoh) autumn

otra vez: (**oh**-trah behs) again
otro: (**oh**-troh) another

P

paciente: (pah-**syehn**-teh) patient
padre: (**pah**-dreh) father
padrino: (pah-**dree**-noh) godfather
pagar: (pah-**gahr**) pay (to)
pago: (**pah**-goh) payment
país: (pah-**ees**) country
pájaro: (**pah**-hah-roh) bird
pala: (**pah**-lah) shovel
palanca de cambio: (pah-**lahn**-kah deh **kahm**-byoh) gearshift
pan: (pahn) bread
panadería: (pah-nah-deh-**ree**-ah) bakery
panecillo: (pah-neh-**see**-yoh) roll (bread)
pantalones: (pahn-tah-**loh**-nehs) pants
pañal: (pah-**nyahl**) diaper
pañuelo: (pah-**nyweh**-loh) handkerchief
papá: (pah-**pah**) dad/daddy
papa: (**pah**-pah) potato
papel: (pah-**pehl**) paper
papel higiénico: (pah-**pehl** ee-**hyeh**-nee-koh) toilet paper
paquete: (pah-**keh**-teh) package
par: (pahr) pair
parabrisas: (pah-rah-**bree**-sahs) windshield
parachoques: (pah-rah-**choh**-kehs) bumper
parada: (pah-**rah**-dah) stop (bus, taxi, etc.)
paraguas: (pah-**rah**-gwahs) umbrella
parar: (pah-**rahr**) stop (to)
pared: (pah-**rehd**) wall
pariente/parienta: (pah-**ryehn**-teh/pah-**ryehn**-tah) relative
parque: (**pahr**-keh) park
parrilla: (pah-**rree**-yah) grill
parte: (**pahr**-teh) part
pasa: (**pah**-sah) raisin
paseo: (pah-**seh**-oh) boulevard

pasillo: (pah-**see**-yoh) hallway
pasta: (**pahs**-tah) pasta
pastilla: (pahs-**tee**-yah) tablet (lozenge)
pata: (**pah**-tah) (animal) paw
patata: (pah-**tah**-tah) potato
patio: (**pah**-tyoh) backyard/patio/yard
peatón: (peh-ah-**tohn**) pedestrian
pecho: (**peh**-choh) chest (body)
pedazo: (peh-**dah**-soh) piece
pedido: (peh-**dee**-doh) order
pedir (i): (peh-**deer**) ask for (to)/request (to)
pedir prestado: (peh-**deer** prehs-**tah**-doh) borrow (to)
peine: (**peh**-ee-neh) comb
pelar: (peh-**lahr**) peel (to)
película: (peh-**lee**-koo-lah) movie/film
peligroso: (peh-lee-**groh**-soh) dangerous
pelo: (**peh**-loh) hair
pelota: (peh-**loh**-tah) ball
peluquería: (peh-loo-keh-**ree**-ah) beauty salon
peluquero/peluquera: (peh-loo-**keh**-roh/peh-loo-**keh**-rah) hairdresser
pendiente: (pehn-**dyehn**-teh) earring
pepino: (peh-**pee**-noh) cucumber
pequeño: (peh-**keh**-nyoh) small
pera: (**peh**-rah) pear
percha: (**pehr**-chah) hanger (clothes)
perder (ie): (pehr-**dehr**) lose (to)
perdido: (pehr-**dee**-doh) lost
periódico: (peh-**ryoh**-dee-koh) newspaper
permiso de conducir: (pehr-**mee**-soh deh kohn-doo-**seer**) driver's license
permitir: (pehr-mee-**teer**) allow (to)
perro: (**peh**-rroh) dog
persona: (pehr-**soh**-nah) person
personalidad: (pehr-soh-nah-lee-**dahd**) personality
pesa: (**peh**-sah) scale
pesado: (peh-**sah**-doh) heavy
pescado: (pehs-**kah**-doh) fish (at a meal)

peso: (**peh**-soh) weight
pestillo: (pehs-**tee**-yoh) deadbolt (lock)
pez: (pehs) fish (live)
picante: (pee-**kahn**-teh) spicy
pie: (pyeh) foot
piedra: (**pyeh**-drah) stone
piel: (pyehl) skin/fur
pierna: (**pyehr**-nah) leg
pila: (**pee**-lah) battery
píldora: (**peel**-doh-rah) pill
pimienta: (pee-**myehn**-tah) pepper
pinta: (**peen**-tah) pint
pintor/pintora: (peen-**tohr**/peen-**toh**-rah) painter
piscina: (pee-**see**-nah) swimming pool
piso: (**pee**-soh) floor
piyama: (pee-**yah**-mah) pajamas
plancha: (**plahn**-chah) iron (clothes)
planchar: (plahn-**chahr**) iron (to)
plano: (**plah**-noh) plan
planta: (**plahn**-tah) plant
plástico: (**plahs**-tee-koh) plastic
plata: (**plah**-tah) silver
plátano: (**plah**-tah-noh) banana
plato: (**plah**-toh) plate
playa: (**plah**-yah) beach
plaza: (**plah**-sah) square
plomería: (ploh-meh-**ree**-ah) plumbing
plomero/plomera: (ploh-**meh**-roh/ploh-**meh**-rah) plumber
pluma: (**ploo**-mah) feather/pen
poder (ue): (poh-**dehr**) be able to (to)
podrido: (poh-**dree**-doh) rotten/spoiled (food)
policía: (poh-lee-**see**-ah) police
poliéster: (poh-**lyehs**-tehr) polyester
pollo: (**poh**-yoh) chicken
polvo: (**pohl**-boh) dust/powder
poner (irr.): (poh-**nehr**) put (to)/place (to)
ponerse: (poh-**nehr**-seh) put on (to)

por favor: (pohr fah-**bohr**) please
por fin: (pohr feen) finally
por lo menos: (por loh **meh**-nohs) at least
por qué: (pohr keh) why
porque: (**pohr**-keh) because
portal: (pohr-**tahl**) porch
portarse bien: (pohr-**tahr**-seh byehn) behave (to)
portarse mal: (pohr-**tahr**-seh mahl) misbehave (to)
portero: (pohr-**teh**-roh) doorman
postre: (**pohs**-treh) dessert
precio: (**preh**-syoh) price
pregunta: (preh-**goon**-tah) question
preparar: (preh-pah-**rahr**) prepare (to)
presupuesto: (preh-soo-**pwehs**-toh) estimate
primavera: (pree-mah-**beh**-rah) spring (season)
primer/primero: (pree-**mehr**/pree-**meh**-roh) first
primo/prima: (**pree**-moh/**pree**-mah) cousin
probar (ue): (proh-**bahr**) taste (to)/try (to)
propina: (proh-**pee**-nah) tip
próximo: (**prohk**-see-moh) next
pueblo: (**pweh**-bloh) town
puente: (**pwehn**-teh) bridge
puerta: (**pwehr**-tah) door
puerta del garaje: (**pwehr**-tah dehl gah-**rah**-heh) garage door
pulgada: (pool-**gah**-dah) inch
puño: (**poo**-nyoh) cuff (of shirt)

Q

qué: (keh) what
quehaceres: (keh-ah-**seh**-rehs) chores
quemado: (keh-**mah**-doh) burned
quemadura: (keh-mah-**doo**-rah) burn
queso: (**keh**-soh) cheese
quién: (kyehn) who
quieto: (**kyeh**-toh) calm/still/motionless
quitar: (kee-**tahr**) remove (to)

R

racimo: (rrah-**see**-moh) bunch
radio: (**rrah**-dyoh) radio
raíz: (rrah-**ees**) root
rama: (**rrah**-mah) branch
rápidamente: (**rrah**-pee-dah-mehn-teh) quickly
rápido: (**rrah**-pee-doh) fast
raro: (**rrah**-roh) strange
rascar: (rrahs-**kahr**) scratch (to)
raspador: (rrahs-pah-**dohr**) scraper
rastrillo: (rrahs-**tree**-yoh) rake (tool)
rayón: (rrah-**yohn**) rayon
rebanada: (rreh-bah-**nah**-dah) slice
receta: (rreh-**seh**-tah) recipe/prescription
recipiente: (rreh-see-**pyehn**-teh) container
recoger (*irr.*): (rreh-koh-**hehr**) pick up (to)
recomendar (ie): (rreh-koh-mehn-**dahr**) recommend (to)
refresco: (rreh-**frehs**-koh) soda/soft drink
refrigerador: (rreh-free-heh-rah-**dohr**) refrigerator
regla: (**rreh**-glah) rule
regresar: (rreh-greh-**sahr**) return (to)
religión: (rreh-lee-**hyohn**) religion
reloj: (rreh-**loh**) clock/watch
remedio: (rreh-**meh**-dyoh) remedy/cure
remendar (ie): (rreh-mehn-**dahr**) repair (to)
remover (ue): (rreh-moh-**behr**) remove (to)
reparar: (rreh-pah-**rahr**) repair (to)
repartir: (rreh-pahr-**teer**) deliver (to)
resfriado: (rrehs-**fryah**-doh) cold (illness)
respirar: (rrehs-pee-**rahr**) breathe (to)
restaurante: (rrehs-tah-oo-**rahn**-teh) restaurant
retrete: (rreh-**treh**-teh) toilet
revisar: (rreh-bee-**sahr**) check (to)
revista: (rreh-**bees**-tah) magazine
revolver (ue): (rreh-bohl-**behr**) stir (to)
rico: (**rree** koh) delicious/rich
rincón: (rreen-**kohn**) corner (inside)

roca: (**rroh**-kah) rock
rodilla: (rroh-**dee**-yah) knee
rojo: (**rroh**-hoh) red
romper: (rrohm-**pehr**) break (to)
ropa: (**rroh**-pah) clothes
rosa: (**rroh**-sah) rose
rosado: (rroh-**sah**-doh) pink
roto: (**rroh**-toh) broken
rubio: (**rroo**-byoh) blond
rueda: (**rrweh**-dah) wheel
ruido: (**rrwee**-doh) noise

S

sábado: (**sah**-bah-doh) Saturday
sábana: (**sah**-bah-nah) sheet
saber (*irr.*): (sah-**behr**) know (information or facts) (to)
saborear: (sah-boh-reh-**ahr**) taste (to)/savor (to)
sacacorchos: (sah-kah-**kohr**-chohs) corkscrew
saco: (**sah**-koh) jacket
sacudir el polvo: (sah-koo-**deer** ehl **pohl**-boh) dust (to)
sal: (sahl) salt
sala: (**sah**-lah) living room
salchicha: (sahl-**chee**-chah) sausage
salida: (sah-**lee**-dah) exit
salir (*irr.*): (sah-**leer**) leave (to)/go out (to)
salsa: (**sahl**-sah) sauce/dressing
salud: (sah-**lood**) health
saludable: (sah-loo-**dah**-bleh) healthy/healthful
saludar: (sah-loo-**dahr**) greet (to)
sandía: (sahn-**dee**-ah) watermelon
sangrando: (sahn-**grahn**-doh) bleeding
sangre: (**sahn**-greh) blood
sano: (**sah**-noh) healthy
sartén: (sahr-**tehn**) skillet/frying pan
secadora: (seh-kah-**doh**-rah) dryer
secar: (seh-**kahr**) dry (to)
seco: (**seh**-koh) dry

seda: (**seh**-dah) silk
seguro: (seh-**goo**-roh) insurance/safe (secure)
seis: (**seh**-ees) six
semáforo: (seh-**mah**-foh-roh) traffic light
semana: (seh-**mah**-nah) week
señal: (seh-**nyahl**) sign
señor: (seh-**nyohr**) Mr./mister/sir
señora: (seh-**nyoh**-rah) Mrs./madam
señorita: (seh-nyoh-**ree**-tah) miss
ser (*irr.*): (sehr) be (to)
serpiente: (sehr-**pyehn**-teh) serpent
servilleta: (sehr-bee-**yeh**-tah) napkin
seta: (**seh**-tah) mushroom
siempre: (**syehm**-preh) always
siesta: (**syehs**-tah) nap
siete: (**syeh**-teh) seven
silencioso: (see-lehn-**syoh**-soh) quiet
silla: (**see**-yah) chair
silla de ruedas: (**see**-yah deh **rrweh**-dahs) wheelchair
sillita de seguridad para niños: (see-**yee**-tah deh seh-goo-ree-**dahd**
pah-rah **nee**-nyohs) baby seat/car seat
simpático: (seem-**pah**-tee-koh) nice
sin: (seen) without
sin grasa: (seen **grah**-sah) fat-free
síntoma: (**seen**-toh-mah) symptom
sobras: (**soh**-brahs) leftovers
sobre: (**soh**-breh) envelope
sobretodo: (soh-breh-**toh**-doh) coat/overcoat
sobrino/sobrina: (soh-**bree**-noh/soh-**bree**-nah) nephew/niece
sofá: (soh-**fah**) sofa
solamente: (soh-lah-**mehn**-teh) only
solicitud: (soh-lee-see-**tood**) application
sólo: (**soh**-loh) only
soltero: (sohl-**teh**-roh) single (not married)
sombra: (**sohm**-brah) shade
sombrero: (sohm-**breh**-roh) hat
sopero: (soh-**peh**-roh) bowl

sótano: (**soh**-tah-noh) basement
su: (soo) her/his/their/your (*formal*)
subir a: (soo-**beer** ah) get on (to)
sucio: (**soo**-syoh) dirty
sudadera: (soo-dah-**deh**-rah) sweatshirt
suegra: (**sweh**-grah) mother-in-law
suegro: (**sweh**-groh) father-in-law
suéter: (**sweh**-tehr) sweater
superficie: (soo-pehr-**fee**-syeh) surface
supermercado: (soo-pehr-mehr-**kah**-doh) supermarket
supervisor/supervisora: (soo-pehr-bee-**sohr**/soo-pehr-bee-**soh**-rah)
supervisor
sur: (soor) south

T

tabla para cortar: (**tah**-blah **pah**-rah kohr-**tahr**) cutting board
tablilla: (tah-**blee**-yah) shingle (roof)
tacón: (tah-**kohn**) heel (shoe)
tajada: (tah-**hah**-dah) slice
taladro: (tah-**lah**-droh) drill
talco: (**tahl**-koh) talcum powder
talla: (**tah**-yah) size
taller de reparaciones: (tah-**yehr** deh rreh-pah-rah-**syoh**-nehs) service
station
tamaño: (tah-**mah**-nyoh) size
también: (tahm-**byehn**) also
tampoco: (tahm-**poh**-koh) neither/not . . . either
tanque: (**tahn**-keh) tank
tapa: (**tah**-pah) lid (of pot)
tarde: (**tahr**-deh) afternoon/late
tarea: (tah-**reh**-ah) homework
tarjeta de cobro automático: (tahr-**heh**-tah deh **koh**-broh ah-oo-toh-
mah-tee-koh) debit card
tarjeta de crédito: (tahr-**heh**-tah deh **kreh**-dee-toh) credit card
taxi: (**tahk**-see) cab
taza: (**tah**-sah) cup
tazón: (tah-**sohn**) bowl

té: (teh) tea

techo: (**teh**-choh) ceiling/roof

tela: (**teh**-lah) material (cloth)

teléfono: (teh-**leh**-foh-noh) telephone

teléfono celular: (teh-**leh**-foh-noh seh-loo-**lahr**) cell phone

televisor: (teh-leh-bee-**sohr**) television set

temprano: (tehm-**prah**-noh) early

tenedor: (teh-neh-**dohr**) fork

tener (*irr.*): (teh-**nehr**) have (to)

tener hambre: (teh-**nehr ahm**-breh) be (feel) hungry (to)

tener miedo: (teh-**nehr myeh**-doh) be (feel) afraid (to)

tener razón: (teh-**nehr** rrah-**sohn**) be right (to)

tener sed: (teh-**nehr** sehd) be (feel) thirsty (to)

tener suerte: (teh-**nehr** swehr-teh) be lucky (to)

terminar: (tehr-mee-**nahr**) finish (to)

termómetro: (tehr-**moh**-meh-troh) thermometer

termostato: (tehr-mohs-**tah**-toh) thermostat

tía: (**tee**-ah) aunt

tibio: (**tee**-byoh) warm/lukewarm

tiempo: (**tyehm**-poh) weather

tienda de comestibles: (**tyehn**-dah deh koh-mehs-**tee**-blehs) food store

tierra: (**tyeh**-rrah) soil

tiesto: (**tyehs**-toh) flowerpot

tijeras: (tee-**heh**-rahs) scissors

timbre: (**teem**-breh) doorbell

tinta: (**teen**-tah) ink

tintorería: (teen-toh-reh-**ree**-ah) dry cleaners

tío: (**tee**-oh) uncle

tirador: (tee-rah-**dohr**) doorknob

tirar: (tee-**rahr**) throw away (to)

toalla: (toh-**ah**-yah) towel

toalla de papel: (toh-**ah**-yah deh pah-**pehl**) paper towel

tobillo: (toh-**bee**-yoh) ankle

tocar: (toh-**kahr**) touch (to)

tocino: (toh-**see**-noh) bacon

todavía no: (toh-dah-**bee**-ah noh) not yet

tomar: (toh-**mahr**) take (drink) (to)

tomate: (toh-**mah**-teh) tomato
tono de marcar: (**toh**-noh deh mahr-**kahr**) dial tone
tonto: (**tohn**-toh) dumb
tornillo: (tohr-**nee**-yoh) screw
toronja: (toh-**rohn**-hah) grapefruit
tos: (tohs) cough
tostadora: (tohs-tah-**doh**-rah) toaster
trabajador/trabajadora: (trah-bah-hah-**dohr**/trah-bah-hah-**doh**-rah) hard-working
trabajar: (trah-bah-**hahr**) work (to)
trabajo: (trah-**bah**-hoh) job
traer (_irr._): (trah-**ehr**) bring (to)
traje: (**trah**-heh) suit
traje de baño: (**trah**-heh deh **bah**-nyoh) bathing suit
tranquilo: (trahn-**kee**-loh) calm
trapeador: (trah-peh-ah-**dohr**) mop
trapo: (**trah**-poh) rag
tren: (trehn) train
tres: (trehs) three
triste: (**trees**-teh) sad
trompo: (**trohm**-poh) top (toy)
tú: (too) you (_familiar_)
tu: (too) your (_familiar_)
tubo: (**too**-boh) pipe
tuerca: (**twehr**-kah) nut (metal)

U

último: (**ool**-tee-moh) last
un/una: (oon/**oo**-nah) one
uniforme: (oo-nee-**fohr**-meh) uniform (clothing)
unión: (oo-**nyohn**) joint (pipe)
universidad: (oo-nee-behr-see-**dahd**) college/university
uña: (**oo**-nyah) nail (finger)
usar: (oo-**sahr**) use (to)
usted: (oos-**tehd**) you (_formal_) (_sing._)
ustedes: (oos-**teh**-dehs) you (_formal_) (_pl._)
utensilio: (oo-tehn-**see**-lyoh) utensil

V

vaca: (**bah**-kah) cow
vaciar: (bah-**syahr**) empty (to)
vacío: (bah-**see**-oh) empty
vainilla: (bah-ee-**nee**-yah) vanilla
vajilla de plata: (bah-**hee**-yah deh **plah**-tah) silverware
valiente: (bah-**lyehn**-teh) brave
válvula: (**bahl**-boo-lah) valve
vaqueros: (bah-**keh**-rohs) jeans/blue jeans
vaso: (**bah**-soh) glass (drinking)
vegetal: (beh-heh-**tahl**) vegetable
vegetariano: (beh-heh-tah-**ryah**-noh) vegetarian
vela: (**beh**-lah) candle
vendar: (behn-**dahr**) bandage (to)
vendedor/vendedora: (behn-deh-**dohr**/behn-deh-**doh**-rah) salesperson
vender: (behn-**dehr**) sell (to)
venir (irr.): (beh-**neer**) come (to)
ventana: (behn-**tah**-nah) window
ventilador: (behn-tee-lah-**dohr**) fan (appliance)
ver (irr.): (behr) see (to)
verano: (beh-**rah**-noh) summer
verdad: (behr-**dahd**) truth
verde: (**behr**-deh) green
verja: (**behr**-hah) gate (garden)
vestido: (behs-**tee**-doh) dress
vestirse (i): (behs-**teer**-seh) dress (to)
viaje: (**byah**-heh) trip/voyage
vídeo: (**bee**-deh-oh) video
videocasetera: (bee-deh-oh-kah-seh-**teh**-rah) VCR
vidrio: (**bee**-dryoh) glass (material)
viejo: (**byeh**-hoh) old
viento: (**byehn**-toh) wind
viernes: (**byehr**-nehs) Friday
vinagre: (bee-**nah**-greh) vinegar
vino: (**bee**-noh) wine
visa: (**bee**-sah) visa
vitamina: (bee-tah-**mee**-nah) vitamin

vitrina: (bee-**tree**-nah) cabinet
vivir: (bee-**beer**) live (to)
vivo: (**bee**-boh) alive
volante: (boh-**lahn**-teh) steering wheel
volver (ue): (bohl-**behr**) return (to)

Y

y: (ee) and
yarda: (**yahr**-dah) yard (measure)
yema: (**yeh**-mah) egg yolk
yerno: (**yehr**-noh) son-in-law
yeso: (**yeh**-soh) plaster
yo: (yoh) I

Z

zanahoria: (sah-nah-**oh**-ryah) carrot
zapato: (sah-**pah**-toh) shoe
zapatos de tenis: (sah-**pah**-tohs deh **teh**-nees) sneakers

Index